I0138915

TO PREACH DELIVERANCE TO THE CAPTIVES

ANTISLAVERY, ABOLITION, AND THE ATLANTIC WORLD

R. J. M. Blackett and Edward Rugemer, Series Editors

James Brewer Stewart, Editor Emeritus

Collection of the Massachusetts Historical Society

To Preach Deliverance to the Captives

Freedom and Slavery in the Protestant Mind of George Bourne 1780–1845

Ryan C. McIlhenny

LOUISIANA STATE UNIVERSITY PRESS
BATON ROUGE

Published by Louisiana State University Press

Manufactured in the United States of America
First printing

DESIGNER: Michelle A. Neustrom
TYPEFACE: Adobe Caslon Pro
PRINTER AND BINDER: LSI

Portions of chapter 2 were first published in "'Remember, Church-Officers, Your Awful Responsibility': Presbyterians, Immediate Abolition, and George Bourne's *The Book and Slavery Irreconcilable*," *Southern Studies* 16, no. 1 (Spring/Summer 2009).

Portions of chapter 4 were first published in "'I am not my own director': Catholic Slavery and Protestant Freedom in George Bourne's *Lorette*," *Nineteenth-Century Prose* 39, no. 1 (Spring 2012): 377–410.

LIBRARY OF CONGRESS CATALOGING-IN-PUBLICATION DATA

Names: McIlhenny, Ryan C., 1975– author.
Title: To preach deliverance to the captives : freedom and slavery in the Protestant mind of George Bourne, 1780–1845 / Ryan C. McIlhenny.
Description: Baton Rouge : Louisiana State University Press, 2020. | Series: Antislavery, abolition, and the Atlantic world | Includes bibliographical references and index.
Identifiers: LCCN 2019045764 (print) | LCCN 2019045765 (ebook) | ISBN 978-0-8071-7266-7 (cloth) | ISBN 978-0-8071-7392-3 (pdf) | ISBN 978-0-8071-7393-0 (epub)
Subjects: LCSH: Bourne, George, 1780–1845. | Antislavery movements—United States—History—19th century. | Presbyterian Church—United States—History—19th century. | United States—Church history—19th century.
Classification: LCC BX9225.B68 M35 2020 (print) | LCC BX9225.B68 (ebook) | DDC 241/.675092—dc23
LC record available at https://lccn.loc.gov/2019045764
LC ebook record available at https://lccn.loc.gov/2019045765

The paper in this book meets the guidelines for permanence and durability of the Committee on Production Guidelines for Book Longevity of the Council on Library Resources. ♾

CONTENTS

ACKNOWLEDGMENTS

The history program at the University of California, Irvine, a highly engaging and collegial environment, has helped produce some of the most capable contemporary historians. I especially want to thank the late Dickson Bruce Jr. (1946–2014), a master scholar and kind mentor, for guiding me through the earliest drafts of this project. It is truly sad that he is not here to read this book, but I am confident he would be proud.

I also want to thank the Munger Research Center staff at the Huntington Library for providing me access to the Bourne family papers. When I learned that these sources had reached the Huntington, I contacted the center immediately. Staff members quickly cataloged the materials (within a couple of weeks, if I remember correctly). Much of what I gained from the Bourne papers appears in the introduction and conclusion.

A note of appreciation should also be given to the editors and reviewers of LSU's Antislavery, Abolition, and the Atlantic World series. Acquisitions editor Rand Dotson was patient as I interrupted his busy schedule with my frequent and admittedly not-so-urgent questions about the manuscript. A warm thanks also for the constructive observations offered by the initial reviewers of the project, including series editors Edward Rugemer and Richard Blackett.

But I must extend a special note of gratitude to James Brewer Stewart. A good part of the success of a work such as this comes by way of the support offered by wiser intellectuals in the field. Jim contacted me after he read my *Journal of the Early Republic* review of *Wendell Phillips, Social Justice, and the Power of the Past,* edited by A. J. Aiséirithe and Donald Yacovone. I took the opportunity of that initial contact to ask him if he would be interested in reading a version of this study. Spending nearly ten years at an intellectually hollow institution in Southern California, I was, given my heavy teaching load and administrative responsibilities, unable to make any substantial revision to the work, with the exception of two peer-reviewed publications. But with Jim's prompting and the time I had here in Shanghai, with a considerably lighter teaching load and more supportive environment, I had the opportunity to initiate a structural revision of the project, which included significant additions to a number of sections, resulting in more critical reflections on the impact of slavery and anti-Catholicism in contemporary culture. I am thrilled to offer this formal introduction of the work and mind of George Bourne to the historical community. It is a great privilege to refer to Jim as a friend and mentor. I hope he and I will have the opportunity to work together again soon.

This book is dedicated to my wife Becky, a faithful, loving, confident, self-reliant, godly, independent woman. She has never complained about living a life with an academic, though she has had plenty of opportunities to do so. Though the book is dedicated to my dear partner, I would be remiss if I failed to mention my children: Fish, Canon, Josiah, and Selah. They too have been with me through this project and this often penurious academic life.

TO PREACH DELIVERANCE TO THE CAPTIVES

INTRODUCTION

THE PROTESTANT MIND OF GEORGE BOURNE

> The only effectual and Christian method to destroy the natural effects of slavery upon the slaveholders . . . from our country; instantly, universally, and altogether, [is] to "proclaim liberty to the captives, to loose the bands of wickedness, to undo the heavy burdens, to break every yoke, and to let the oppressed go free."
>
> —GEORGE BOURNE, *Picture of Slavery in the United States of America*

In a private letter written a couple years before the outbreak of the Civil War, William Lloyd Garrison, New England's premier voice of radical abolitionism, confessed his "early and large indebtedness" to the Reverend George Bourne (1780–1845) for enabling him "to apprehend with irresistible clearness the inherent sinfulness of slavery under all circumstances, and its utter incompatibility with the spirit and precepts of Christianity."[1] Garrison was not the only one influenced by this vanguard opponent of the "Negro-hating religion." Bourne played a vital role in convincing a number of reformers of the moral and religious obligation to support immediacy: English scientist and philanthropist William Allen, Methodist abolitionist Orange Scott, Quaker author Benjamin Lundy, "come-outer" William Goodell, Lane Seminary rebel Amos Dresser, who had been publicly whipped in Nashville for simply carrying a copy of one of Bourne's books, Finneyite antislavery architect Theodore Dwight Weld, and slave husband and wife William and Ellen Craft, who collaborated to exploit the pliable nature of racial complexion in their courageous (and creative) scheme to escape bondage.[2] Joshua Leavitt, a zealous evangelical abolitionist and editor of the *Emancipator*, once said that the early abolitionist movement had the great "benefit of George Bourne's instruction."[3] Writing around the time of the Civil War, Lewis Tappan, who along with his brother Arthur became a close companion of Bourne, concurred: "[A]ll the important doctrines of abolitionists of the present day were clearly announced and published by Mr. Bourne as far back as 1816, long before Lundy, Garrison, and other champions of freedom had written or lectured upon the subject."[4] Garrison assured Bourne's son and fellow reformer, Theodore, "that the early and indomitable labors of your revered father will be duly remembered and honored by me, to the fullest extent," according to Bourne "the historical credit which he is due."[5]

Born in the summer of 1780, George Bourne was raised in a staunchly Protestant home in Westbury, Wiltshire, England. Uninterested in following his father Samuel, a cloth manufacturer and a deacon in a local Congregationalist church, into the world of business, Bourne studied Latin, Greek, Hebrew, church history, and logic at Homerton College outside of London with the intent of pursuing a career as a writer and minister.[6] Bourne set his sights on the American republic after receiving a generous endowment from his father. When he and his wife Mary relocated to Baltimore in 1805, Bourne immediately began a promising career as a journalist and newspaper editor.[7] He assumed editorship of the *Baltimore Evening Post,* a paper that lasted only a couple years for lack of subscribers. Bourne sold the paper to Hezekiah Niles, editor of "America's first national magazine," *Niles' National Register.*[8] Before the closing of the *Post,* Bourne published his first work, *The Spirit of the Public Journals,* an assortment of essays from leading journals in the United States and Great Britain, followed by a biography of Napoleon Bonaparte in 1806, and the first American biography of John Wesley in 1807. Not always wise in how he handled his finances, Bourne frequently moved with his family in pursuit of more economically stable opportunities to preach and write on issues related to theology and social reform.

Recognizing the difficulties in keeping an editorial position in the diverse and fast-paced urban environment of Baltimore and anxious to utilize his training as a minister, Bourne was offered an opportunity to become a pastor in a more bucolic area of Virginia in 1811. He immediately joined the Presbyterian Church, then under the leadership of Old School Presbyterians, and served as teaching elder at Port Republic. His first sermon, "The Majesty and Condescension of God," delivered December 25, 1812, exhibited a harsh disdain for the Anglican episcopacy. A few years earlier, he had defended the legitimacy of the Methodist establishment against the criticisms of an Anglican clergyman.[9] While in Virginia, Bourne contributed to the formation of the Virginia Bible Society, founded in 1813. He preached regularly around the area of Port Republic, traveling from church to church, but soon had to reduce his preaching load after contracting a severe cold while on circuit, which significantly damaged his hearing for the remainder of his life.[10]

It was during his time in Virginia that his hostility toward slavery manifested itself most acutely. Bourne was one among a handful of early reformers who experienced firsthand and became appalled by the proslavery antiabolitionist South. Although it is difficult to determine precisely when he turned to radical antislavery, his hostility to the institution nonetheless manifested itself while there. He publicly spoke out against human bondage, generating a controversy within the Presbyterian denomination that eventually compelled him to move to Philadelphia in 1817 to take a limited pastorate in Germantown. After a series of cases and appeals (discussed in chapter 2), Bourne was finally defrocked from the Virginia Presbytery at the 1818 General Assembly meeting of the Presbyterian Church for his radical opinions.

By 1818, he had moved to New York, "the early nineteenth-century nation's leading city," writes historian Kyle Roberts, a city that not only played a considerable role in giving shape to American evangelicalism but also directed the economic future of the country. The rise of such a city, especially around the time of the Market Revolution, and the changes occurring within Protestantism were, Roberts continues, "intricately intertwined."[11] Notwithstanding his brief stay in Canada, Bourne spent much of the remainder of his life in this economic and religiously bustling city. He became a schoolteacher at Mount Pleasant but later became a minister in the Dutch Reformed Church. Little is known about what Bourne was doing in regard to slavery during those years. Writing a series on the origins of the antislavery movement for the *Boston Commonwealth* in 1885, author Oliver Johnson states that around the time of the "Missouri Struggle," when Bourne had moved to New York, Bourne had "no connection with the subject of slavery." His son, William Oland Bourne (1819–1901), wrote a response in the same paper admitting that his father had less time to devote to antislavery after leaving Virginia due to his "increasing family and pastoral labors." "Soon after" the trial in the Presbyterian Church, his son Theodore wrote, Bourne "paid his *chief attention* to the Pope and his emissaries." Bourne, in other words, had not suspended his antislavery activism; he simply focused a bit more of his energy on battling popery during these years. Historians may not have clear evidence available to know what Bourne thought about slavery during these years, but his interest in battling slavery was renewed when Garrison, William Oland writes, "sounded the appeal that has made our country free."[12] Bourne intensified his antislavery activism after meeting Garrison in the late 1820s, incorporating anti-Catholicism in his views on emancipation.[13]

What we do know, however, is that by the end of the 1820s Bourne turned increasingly toward anti-Catholicism. In 1823, he published *Lectures on the Progress and Perfection of the Church,* an interpretation of sacred and secular history through the lens of the biblical book of Revelation. This work, though mildly anti-Catholic at the time, seemed to stay with him—or the basic historical theological lens, at least—for much of his life, especially the emphasis on the leading Protestant figures who fought for the advancement of biblical truth. *Progress and Perfection* was revised and republished as *The American Text-book of Popery,* published a year after his death, which focused more acutely on the developments of what he and many others called the anti-Christ, the papacy. Both his antislavery and anti-Catholicism, eventually becoming one piece by the late 1820s, were part of a larger millennial perspective related to the advancement of Christ and his church. By 1829–30, after a brief stay in Canada, writing what would become a widely read anti-Catholic novel, *Lorette* (1833), Bourne returned to New York. He also returned with earnest to the cause of immediate antislavery, now accompanied by an intensified anti-Catholicism. By this time and because of his influence, both antislavery and anti-Catholic agitation reached a high point. Bourne worked closely in both movements. He remained in New York until on the "20th day of Nov., 1845," Theodore wrote, he died of a sudden stroke "at his post in the very office of the *Christian Intelligencer.* . . . His last editorial was on *Christianity Unity,* entitled *'Be ye all of one mind.'*"[14]

Contemporary historians have correctly identified Bourne as the pioneer of immediate and universal abolition in the early American republic. Matthew Mason has most recently shown that while antislavery activism among whites was "isolated and disorganized in the early nineteenth century," it was far from absent, challenging Don E. Fehrenbacher's claim that "national discord over slavery was muted during the years" before and after the War of 1812.[15] To support his argument against Fehrenbacher, Mason specifically identifies Bourne as one who "carried the evangelical antislavery legacy to a new generation."[16] Historians like Mason and Manisha Sinha have helped to remind students of the history of antislavery activism in this earlier period, especially among

African Americans.[17] This has provided an opportunity to situate Bourne's influential activism into a longer history of abolitionism.

Up to this point, however, much of the contemporary discussions related to Bourne comes by way of a passing nod for his pre-1830s immediatism, centering particularly on his ecclesiastical trial (chapter 2) as a kind of preface to what may seem to have been the more important work of radicalism in the antebellum period. Part of the reason for such a deficiency may stem from the habit of scholars to cement American antislavery, in the words of James Stewart, "to the revivals of the 1820s," a period which had little impact on Bourne's own radicalism.[18] Indeed, nineteenth-century revival and benevolence, for the most part, had been built by faith groups that were galvanized by a democratic impulse and more in line with the revolutionary spirit that worked against traditional aspects of the Christian faith. Although influenced by early reformist movements and greatly appreciative of revivals, Bourne, in terms of the origins of immediacy, does not fit exactly the revivalist-reformist paradigm, the consequences of which have led to a passing glance at Bourne's ideology as well as his own mission. This is not an indictment of the historical community, for piecing together the life of Bourne has indeed been quite a challenge (often a maddening one at that). This project in no way attempts to overturn such interpretations, but it does try to give an account of an influential reformer whose activism may complicate a more familiar paradigm, which will further the discussion regarding the complexities of religion and radicalism in early America.

Bourne's approach to reform did not originate from the democratizing, anticlerical, or anti-institutional tendencies that have come to shape a uniquely American evangelicalism. He instead harked back to the doctrinal and ecclesiastical revolution of the sixteenth-century Protestant Reformation, second in historical significance in his mind only to the commissioning of the disciples by Christ to preach the gospel in the first century. This may explain why he joined the Presbyterian Church, a denomination that, according to Nathan Hatch, "faced the new century far more stable institutionally" despite the exodus of a number of revivalists—including Barton Stone, Alexander Campbell, and Charles Finney—who left largely because of the church's inflexible, nondemocratic confessional Calvinism.[19] Although the activism endemic to evangelicalism, including the use of print, certainly aided the advancement of religion, according to Bourne social and religious benevolence did not require the innovations of revivalism or the renovations of historical Protestant orthodoxy. As a key moment in history, the Reformation, Bourne wrote, was "a theme equally delightful in retrospect" as the Great Commission, but "as exhilarating in anticipation; and a view of the diversified means organized to extend universally the knowledge of Christ and him crucified with particular reference to the advancement of 'pure and undefiled religion.'"[20]

Next to the Protestant Reformation, the discovery of America was the most important event in history. America was the place where Protestantism would advance most rapidly and where citizens would witness a "powerful instance," Bourne wrote, of the "success of the gospel": "The Congregationalists, Presbyterians and Baptists, are all striving to spread the savor of the Redeemer's religion, and the Lord adds to the church daily such as 'shall be saved.'"[21] Seventeenth-century Protestants, Separatists and Puritans in particular, effectively broke the "iron yoke of Antichrist," he continued, in Europe by migrating to North America, a move that allowed them and their religion to flourish.[22] Likewise, Bourne believed that America was the best place for the spread of a virtuous republic, because it commenced its "social compact with pure and undefiled religion."[23] The health and progress of the United States rested on its heritage in the Protestant Reformation.

Bourne was a reformer whose activism was shaped by an older religious conservatism, accommodating the more radical issues of his own day by appropriating the past.[24] One way that may help contemporary readers understand better the connection between his hostility toward chattel slavery and Catholicism is to theoretically suspend for a moment the reified political spectrum that dominates the contemporary mind, to acknowledge, in other words, how an individual could be progressive on one issue and conservative—not to mention prejudicially so—on another. And herein lies a hidden and problematic assumption. In the contemporary context, radicalism and conservatism often seem diametrically opposed to one another. Yet Bourne was not working in political categories familiar to those in the twenty-first century. Nonetheless, I think we can still use the terms *radical* and *conservative* without becoming anachronistic. The former is often associated with the Left, originating in the French Revolution and later including the various anticapitalist, antistatist, and anti-imperialist schools of thought. We should not associate Bourne with the Left as it is understood today, since in large part he was conspicuously silent on the exploitive aspects of early industrial capitalism. *Conservative* traces its origins to the French Revolution itself. Many turned to "tradition" out of a concern about social and political devastation caused by revolution. Bourne does not align with this category either. His conservatism was associated not with tradition but with classical liberalism. Yet Bourne could be considered a conservative and a radical because of his desire to get back to the "roots" (*radical = radix,* meaning "roots") of Christianity for the purposes of completely dismantling slavery, an integral and vital component that defined nineteenth-century America. Craig Calhoun suggests in *Roots of Radicalism* that "early modern thinkers described analyses as radical when they went to foundations, first principles, or what was essential."[25] This type of radicalism was not one that sought the complete uprooting of society, a branch of modern radicalism. Historical tradition "offers sources of mobilizations that radically challenged both the existing social order and liberal agendas for 'progressive' change."[26] Such radicalism impacted not only religion but also modern philosophy. Thinkers like Rene Descartes or John Locke, for instance, pursued the central and unmovable starting point of being, thinking, and living. Religious thinkers like Martin Luther or John Calvin "claimed to grasp what was essential to Christianity and sought to restore the faith to its fundamentals."[27] This radicalism, in both faith and philosophy, had a shared method that privileged the unaided perspective of the individual, proclaiming absolute hostility over all forms of tyranny, to paraphrase Thomas Jefferson, over the mind, body, and spirit of humanity. Early modern radicalism encouraged individuals to rely on "their own reason, consciences, and interpretations," whether of the observable world or "sacred texts in judging what is right to believe and to do."[28] Radicalism was antitraditional in the way it challenged the accumulation of tradition (or "traditions"), which tended toward the corruption of both heart and mind, the initial step of enslavement.

Calhoun deals largely with European-style radicalism, a form absent in the American context, as many writers like Werner Sombert have noted. Bourne borrowed from European religious radicalism, adapting and applying it to the national developments of the Early Republic. Bourne came from a line of Scottish Protestant "martyrs and confessors," his son Theodore wrote, "who loved truth more than honor, or rewards, or life itself."[29] Theodore's father was not one to be manipulated by the crowd; he was not one to conform to the powerful intimidating notion that fighting for the immediate end of slavery would undermine the stability and growth of the nation. He was drawn, however, to and shaped by a host of historical figures who held fast to their virtuous principles in the face of great opposition from those in power. Such figures moved history. It may be helpful to say here—I will explore this later—that such a commitment to traditional Protestant orthodoxy hints at Bourne's reasons for connecting antislavery with a hostility to Catholicism. Catholic doctrine and government were inherently slavish; Protestants who stood up to the abusive authoritarianism of the church were, in Bourne's eyes, heroes to be celebrated and emulated across the ages. Protestantism represented the light of truth that set people free; Catholicism, on the other hand, enslaved and impeded the development of a free people. America's own Reformation would be accomplished by individuals courageous enough to fight against slavery and Catholicism.

In the mid-1960s, David Brion Davis wrote that "Bourne's main concern was not with the plight of Negroes but with the corruption of the Christian Church."[30] While correct in identifying Bourne as one who was centrally concerned with the purity of the church, Davis, I believe, misses Bourne's real concern for racial equality, developed in the 1830s. Said differently, the emphasis Davis places on Bourne's central goal (i.e., reforming the church) might be read in such a way as to take away Bourne's importance in the fight against slavery. What is more, Davis tends to create a false dichotomy between fighting slavery and reforming the church, driving a wedge between secular and sacred concerns, perhaps elevating the former over the latter. I say this not to reject Davis's observation; indeed, I agree with him. But we cannot leave it at that, especially if we want to delve deeper into the mind of such an important figure. The emphasis on "moral suasion" and the importance of racial equality were, in the more mature mind of Bourne, connected to issues related to doctrine and ecclesiology. The purity of the church, especially in regard to doctrine and governance, was foundational to Bourne's radicalism. The elimination of slavery, the defense of the constitutional rights of African Americans, and the eradication of false enslaving religion—all of which would be beneficial to society at large—would only be accomplished through a radical reformation of the institutional church and its leadership.

His opposition to slavery and later to Catholicism was, first and foremost, rooted in the Protestant doctrine of *sola scriptura* (the Bible "alone"). He came close to what I would call—anachronistically—a kind of "proto-fundamentalist" Biblicism, wherein the Bible, having sole authority over matters of the heart, trumped all other sources of authority, including church governance, confessional creeds, and the rational speculations of theologians. The democratization of American evangelicalism undoubtedly contributed to encouraging this type of Biblicism, but, given his detachment from populist evangelical theology, such a distinction, we must keep in mind, may be too strong when applied to Bourne. He used the creeds and confessions of Christendom in his case against physical and spiritual bondage. What is certain, however, is that he did not, as many fellow radicals did, elevate individual conscience—or, more appropriately, "inner light," given the influence of Quaker and Methodist theologies—or the pragmatic methods of Finney's evangelicalism over that of confessional Biblicism. Stated more directly, the message of the scriptures, the moral sense within humanity, the importance of theological activity, and radical reform were not at odds with one another. Bourne's goal was to maintain hermeneutical consistency in grappling with political and ecclesiastical issues.

A second aspect of Bourne's time-honored Protestantism was his allegiance to ecclesiastical order, which included a respect for ministerial officers, church discipline, and the sacraments as the means of communicating God's sanctifying grace. Abolitionists had always confronted the established church for its failures in the battle against slavery. By the 1850s, intensified by the splits in the major denominations—Methodists, Baptists, and Presbyterians between 1844 and 1856—a number of abolitionists heeded the call of Revelation 18:4 to "come out" of the false church so that the morally upright would "receive none of her plagues" or the judgment of God. A handful of "come-outer sects" appeared in the late antebellum period: "Wesleyan Methodist Connection, the American Baptist Free Mission Society, the Free Presbyterian Church, the Evangelical Luther Synod, the Indiana Yearly Meeting of Anti-Slavery Friends, and the Progressive Friends."[31] Many immediatists remained in the church, including Lewis Tappan, Amos Phelps, and George Cheever. Although forced out of the Presbyterian denomination, anticipating the actions of reformers to remove themselves from established churches, Bourne should not be considered a "come-outer" abolitionist. He never rejected institutional religion or moved in the direction of organizing groups for the central purpose of fighting slavery.[32] Nor did he break ties with those who left their churches. In opposition to slave-supporting organized religion, many reformers made the cause of antislavery their religion, an act of piety, and, in a sense, a kind of proof of their reverence toward God, which tended to reduce religious orthodoxy to practical morality.[33] But abolition for Bourne did not act "as a kind of surrogate religion," as Davis suggested years ago when discussing "come-outer" immediatism.[34] Rather, the exercise of true faith came with the proper reading and teaching of the scriptures and through the watchful care of ministerial shepherds. If ministers failed in that area, then both irreligion and, necessarily, immorality would flourish and thereby destroy a nation. Guarding the sanctity of the Bible through proper exegesis by church leaders, then, would necessarily keep sin from gaining a foothold in the minds and hearts of American citizens. At the same time, however, Bourne seemed to tolerate the disagreements over strategy among fellow leaders, maintaining a focus on the ultimate goal: setting captives free.

As Calhoun reminds us, radicals often considered tradition as something vital to the creation of a new social order. The notion that a progressive present would remain dependent on a traditional past best describes Bourne. Bourne's historical Protestantism through a firm Biblicism and ecclesiasticism opens another crucial and largely neglected aspect of Bourne's radicalism: namely, his militant anti-Catholicism. By the 1830s, George Bourne incorporated into his immediatism a virulent hostility to the "soul-enslaving" religion of Roman Catholicism. Bourne's commitment to liberty was total in the sense that it had to be both spiritual and physical. He vehemently opposed the idea used by slaveowners that one's spiritual state had no bearing on one's social status. In other words, conversion to Christianity did not change a slave's status. Conversely, an individual's material and physical freedom did not necessarily reflect the liberation of the soul. This was precisely the problem with Catholicism. Catholicism enslaved the soul, which, for Bourne, would eventually enslave the body. True liberation incorporated both body and soul. But this kind of holistic liberation was threatened by Catholicism.

The Catholic Church was one of the fastest growing denominations in the United States. Sixty percent of all Catholics in America lived in the city of Baltimore when Bourne settled there in the early nineteenth century. By 1830, the Catholic population in Maryland increased to 300,000 and to three million thirty years later, becoming the largest single denomination in the nation by the time of the Civil War.[35] After his trial in the southern branch of the Presbyterian Church for his radical views, Bourne traveled mainly between New York and Canada (eventually settling in New York) and joined the Dutch Reformed Church, a denomination influenced by the evangelical pietism of Theodore Frelinghuysen but one that was hotly anti-Catholic. A year before

Garrison published the first edition of the *Liberator* and three years before the formation of the American Anti-Slavery Society, Bourne and fellow Dutch Reformed minister and accomplished writer William C. Brownlee published the *Protestant,* one of the first anti-Catholic newspapers in America. Both men helped establish the New York Protestant Association, which later became the Protestant Reformation Society, and the American Society to Promote the Principles of the Protestant Reformation. Along with producing many "no-popery" publications, which began to appear in earnest in the late 1820s, including a widely read novel and a nationalistic history textbook, Bourne was one of a handful of Protestants who edited and profited from Maria Monk's *Awful Disclosure of the Hotel Dieu,* a controversial bestselling exposé of the Hotel Dieu nunnery in Montreal.[36]

Popular anti-Catholic polemicists in the United States often separated Catholic doctrine from the politics of Catholicism. Samuel Morse's *Foreign Conspiracy* (1835) placed less emphasis on the "*purely religious* character of the tenets of the Roman Catholic sect."[37] A similar sentiment was intimated in Lyman Beecher's *A Plea for the West* (1835) and newspapers like the *Fall of Babylon.* For Bourne, however, the politics and doctrines of Rome could not be disentangled. More directly, it was the latter that fed the former: a corrupted political perspective rested on corrupt doctrine. Protestantism allowed Bourne to imagine Roman Catholicism and southern chattel bondage as analogous, defining the very concept of "slavery" against the backdrop of the two institutions: Both presupposed a spiritual condition nurtured by a perversion of true doctrine by church leaders, whose censorship of the Bible was the master key of bondage. This is why Bourne concentrated on guarding the scriptures and reforming church leaders. "Man-stealing" ministers and Roman priests (not truly saved according to Bourne) imprisoned bodies and souls, extinguished the moral duties of men and women, obstructed spiritual progress, and severed all communal (i.e., family) relationships. The twin evils of slavery and Catholicism acted as the double helix that shaped Bourne's concept of true freedom, a freedom ultimately driven by the spiritual but not disconnected from the physical.[38] And he interpreted his struggle against the agents of darkness within a historical drama that recalled the Protestant Reformation, wherein spiritual enslavement would be defeated primarily through the faithful proclamation of the Bible's teaching by godly heroic preachers.

Within the past decade there have been a number of publications focusing on slavery and abolition. Since around the 1970s, historians have demonstrated increasing favorability to antislavery agitators. No longer portrayed as irrational fanatics (Bourne welcomed the moniker "fanatic"), immediatists, despite their many differences, are now part of the cast of heroic characters who sought to extend the rhetoric of liberty embedded in America's founding document, the Declaration of Independence.[39] In relation to this great body of literature, however, fewer studies have been done on anti-Catholicism in the years prior to the rise of the Know-Nothings.[40] This lack of attention is odd given not only the growth of the Catholic Church (mentioned above) and the contributions of its members in the Early Republic and antebellum periods, but also how anti-Catholicism shaped the culture of the Early Republic, including the activism of moral reformers. The failure to intellectually appreciate American Catholicism is an indication of where historians have fallen short and have presented an unbalanced picture of the cultural, social, and political ethos of the Early Republic. More recently, however, scholars have tried to correct this myopia. Jay Dolan, Chester Gillis, and Joseph Varacalli, for instance, have offered general surveys of the American Catholic experience.[41] Dale Light, William H. Warner, and Jason Duncan have provided local studies of Catholic social and political activities in places like Philadelphia, Washington DC, and New York.[42] Each work considers the contributions of Catholicism in America, especially the efforts of Catholics to reconcile their faith with the social, economic, and political developments of the American nation.

An even smaller number of publications exist that deal with the shared rhetoric of anti-Catholicism and antislavery. The scant work in anti-Catholicism has had a direct impact on studies relating to slavery and antislavery—and thus ideas related to freedom and liberty—in America. The integration of anti-Catholicism in the structure of antislavery is a subject that historians need to investigate further. In a 1993 article in the *American Quarterly,* Leslie Tentler lamented the fact that the academy has "still in some important ways essentially ghettoized" the American Catholic experience.[43] The contemporary sexual controversies within the Roman Catholic hierarchy "have kept alive," Tentler posits, "the anti-Catholic bias that has long been part of academic life."[44] But anti-Catholicism is not limited to academia. Contemporary no-popery rhetoric shares a family resemblance with that of the early nineteenth century, unwittingly projecting Catholic leaders as sexually deviant and subversive "others" who corrupt and psychologically enslave America's youth. Catholics have an uneasy place in America's historical imagination, and in a way the church continues to be the nation's peculiar "religious" institution, a reference point for the construction of American—a word that is often interchangeable with "Protestant"—freedom.

Catholicism has been used at times as a political category, appropriated as an aspersion against individuals and institutions that were thought to be "un-free," "tyrannical," and hence "un-American." Elizabeth Fenton's 2011 *Religious Liberties* is perhaps most pertinent here. Notions of American liberty (broadly defined to include pluralism, democracy, and representation), particularly "religious pluralism and its corresponding 'right of conscience,'" Fenton claims, "drew their force from anti-Catholicism."[45] From the Quebec Act of 1774 to Reconstruction, with a brief afterword on the role of anti-Catholicism in the politics of the 1960s, Fenton shows how popular American writers from Thomas Paine to Mark Twain exploited the ideology of a tyrannical—and thus inherently antidemocratic—Catholicism that functioned to construct an American political consensus, positioning, Fenton argues, "Protestantism as the guarantor of religious liberty."[46] Hostility to Catholicism, as Fenton and other writers on anti-Catholicism acknowledge, predates Bourne, but Bourne contributed much of his time to articulating a notion of American freedom shaped by traditional Protestant doctrine. "Any understanding of anti-Catholicism," Maura Jane Farrelly has recently argued, "requires us to interrogate the meaning of American freedom and, by extension, the promise of American identity."[47]

Because of these deficiencies in scholarship, students today are less aware of the numerous evangelicals who viewed slavery and Catholicism in the same light. This may be the result of how modern academia has inadvertently limited the religious for what may seem to be the more important political and cultural origins and consequences of antislavery. In an attempt to deal with an issue like religious prejudice, which seems to contradict the very notion of freedom and tolerance, historians for the most part have either ignored anti-Catholicism or have continued to consider the ultra-Protestant nativism of leading reformers as a symptom of social-psychological irrationality. Biographer Hugh Davis wrote that the Protestant "paranoid ramblings" of Bourne's friend Joshua Leavitt "warped his powers of reason," sidestepping an opportunity to make sense of such beliefs.[48] Likewise, in his study of the life of Lewis Tappan, Bertram Wyatt-Brown conspicuously avoided contextualizing this wealthy philanthropist's association with no-popery abolitionism, dismissing such bigotry, although it was not as acerbic as that of Lewis's brother Arthur Tappan, as entirely "without excuse" and apparently, on the part of Wyatt-Brown, without explanation.[49] A 2003 study that attempted to rationalize the association between Catholicism and slavery comes from John McGreevy's *Catholicism and American Freedom,* a history of "the interplay between Catholic and American ideas of freedom."[50] McGreevy's survey, as helpful as it is, paints a broad picture of how American Catholics attempted to reconcile their more conservative faith with the demands of an expanding democratic society; that is, how Catholics tried to maintain a specifically American identity that did not sever its ties with papal Rome. His chapter on slavery is indeed informative but it tends to focus more on Catholics' overwhelmingly negative view of the antislavery movement and less on how Protestants rationalized the unity between popery and chattel bondage and linked the fight to end slavery with the battle against Catholicism.

Historians should not ignore this sensitive issue any longer. The difficulties in accounting for such religious prejudice—at least from the standpoint of the contemporary mind—may be the result of the conceptual limitations of the historian's craft, narrowly seeing religious worldviews as ideologically functional, pragmatic, or symptomatic of a neurological disorder. Robert Abzug stated the problem well in the preface to *Cosmos Crumbling,* a study of a variety of religious "virtuousos" in antebellum America: "All too often scholars have been guided by the assumption that 'religion' exists largely as a conscious or unconscious cover for something else: status anxiety, the quest for control of one class by another, personal or collective neuroses, a reaction to the shocks and realities of new social and economic environments, or some other psychological or material concern." Abzug does not "deny the importance" of the psychological or the material (nor do I), but historians must, he contends, "concentrate on the religious imaginations of reformers in order to grasp the essential nature of reform." He thus argues for "the crucial importance of cosmological thinking," examining how such otherworldly perspectives reordered the sacred and secular "details of everyday life."[51] The intent of this project, then, is to take seriously the religious and theological logic of an influential reformer, to understand Bourne's Protestant mind—as no one else has to this point—in order to better understand how he linked slavery and Catholicism in the construction of freedom.

Yet despite the best efforts to understand that which appears strange to those of us in the present (i.e., a notion of freedom shaped by prejudice), there seems to remain a tension not so much between slavery and Catholicism but between an articulated faith and a developing notion of tolerance. Bourne intensified what he saw as the affinity between traditional Protestant doctrines and the consequential social and political philosophy emerging in a modern revolutionary context. And, at first, he seemed to defend religious liberty while at the same time restricting others from exercising a similar liberty. But perhaps we need to accept the problematic reality between faith and an ideologically consistent pluralism. To preserve what Fenton refers to as "deliberative democracy," defined as "a political mode that promotes a public sphere in which citizens engage in rational debate with one another," religious freedom had to be restricted if not fully denied, "sacrificing democracy in the name of deliberation."[52] Anti-Catholicism was used as a negative contrast to the freedoms supposedly endemic to a Protestant political establishment. Regardless of Catholicism's efforts to participate in "representative governance," a politically driven Protestantism could never recognize the possibility that non-Protestants could participate in a religiously plural society. In his attempt to examine the nature of religion in a purportedly pluralistic society, Dickson Bruce suggests that the "fundamental incompatibility between faith and tolerance" is something that contemporary scholars must confront rather than evade "in our own volatile religious world."[53] Bruce reiterates his bold position toward the end of his book: "Religion, *by its very nature,* may be said to make powerful demands on its adherents, its key functions directing thought, language, and action in ways that clearly work against a universalistic acceptance of differing perspectives—perspectives offering contradictory assessments of God, for example, teaching contradictory views of a proper order, or contradictory understandings of ultimate human ends."[54] Nowhere, according to Bruce, is this dilemma more clearly seen than in the Protestant confrontation with Catholicism: "No religious conflict in antebellum America was to do more to reveal both the reality of a Protestant hegemony and the countervailing tendencies to any broad conception of toleration than that between American Protestants and the Roman Catholic Church."[55] It seems that humans, regardless of faith commitments, will always draw a line somewhere. But I suspect, following Bruce's direction, that the challenge of tolerance becomes most acute when religion is at the center of public debate. To consider this in relation to Bourne, we must clarify that Bourne was a defender of religious liberty but also an opponent of any effort, religious or not, to suppress liberty. By its very nature, according to Bourne, Catholicism was a religion of suppression.

Historians continue to examine the myriad personalities, ideologies, and religious loyalties that made up the antislavery movement. As should be clear up to this point, the current study adds to the list. Only three biographies dedicated to George Bourne exist: a one-column essay written in *The Independent* by Lewis Tappan in 1861; a lengthier essay in the *Methodist Quarterly* by George's younger son, Theodore, in 1882 titled "George Bourne, Pioneer of American Antislavery"; and John Christie and Dwight Dumond's *George Bourne and "The Book and Slavery Irreconcilable,"* a 1969 joint publication of the Presbyterian Historical Society and the Historical Society of Delaware. Theodore's essay relies on Tappan's and is particularly helpful in emphasizing his father's dual aim: fighting slavery and fighting Catholicism. But Theodore, regardless of at least one biographical error, does not offer an overall critical evaluation of his father's religious presuppositions. Christie and Dumond's book is also enlightening; it fits within the emerging new social history of the late 1960s and early 1970s that began to take seriously the origins of abolition. Commendably, their book is one of the first attempts to highlight the genesis of Garrisonian reform. Yet Dumond and Christie, whose shared attitude of radical antislavery is similar to that of Gilbert Barnes, were intent on denouncing Garrisonian fanaticism.[56] Toward the end of the book, the authors ostensibly identify Garrison, who relied strongly on Bourne's writings, as a plagiarizer. The book seems to be driven by a particular scheme in which Bourne is used to critique the rise and importance of Garrisonian reform.[57] Moreover, the authors offer only an insignificant mention of his anti-Catholicism in the opening chapters and avoid an in-depth analysis of his Protestantism. This is unfortunate given that by the 1830s "slavery" for Bourne came to mean both the peculiar institution and papal Catholicism. Consequently, Christie and Dumond present an incomplete picture. The content and coherence as well as the development of Bourne's religious perspective have been largely overlooked.

Despite their deficiencies, Christie and Dumond have indeed offered the best biography of Bourne to date. This current research, however, is neither a simple reiteration of the earlier works, nor is it an attempt to add details to Bourne's life. Instead, as a kind of intellectual biography, it does what no other study has done before: it closely inspects and historically contextualizes Bourne's major works in an attempt to understand more comprehensively the development of his religious mind. Originally, the monograph was divided into two parts. The first dealt with Bourne's major antislavery works; the second part was devoted to his no-popery writings. But due to a bit of constructive criticism from a leading nineteenth-century historian, I became convinced that such a thematic scheme not only ignores the chronological development of Bourne's ideology, especially how Catholicism and slavery were sealed by the 1830s, but it may also instill the notion that Bourne, in his efforts to articulate complete and absolute freedom, was able to separate the two from one another. Before the 1830s, Bourne's anti-Catholicism was not only significantly muted, it had not been hermetically sealed to slavery. After 1830, however, slavery and Catholicism became one piece in Bourne's millennial perspective, representing the supreme enemies of pure religion and a liberal republic. The intent is for the reader to be mindful of the integrative overlap and equal consequences of both slavery and Catholicism in Bourne's religious perspective—Bourne's "many careers reconciled," as Ronald Walters has written.[58]

Given (or because of) the challenges in sources and details of Bourne's life (e.g., the gap between Bourne's 1818 immediacy and his return in 1833), this project is not, strictly speaking, a biography, but an intellectual one. I have organized each chapter around one or in some cases two of Bourne's major works. For the most part, readers should be able to trace the development of his mind in this way. Chapter 1 revolves around two major works: *History of Napoleon Bonaparte: Emperor of the French and King of Italy* (1806) and *The Life of the Rev. John Wesley* (1807). *History of Napoleon Bonaparte: Emperor of the French and King of Italy* revealed the author's interest in classical narratives that celebrated the religious and political achievements of one of the famous revolutionary leaders of the late eighteenth and early nineteenth centuries. The biography includes a brief essay on the origins of the French Revolution, linking it to the greater revolutionary spirit transforming the Atlantic world. But Bourne's intent was to present the virtuous character of a leader willing to preserve the ideals of a revolutionary republic. Bourne's enthusiasm for revolutionary politics extended into the religious realm, which led him to write the first American biography of John Wesley in 1807, "a volume," Bourne claimed, of the "most powerful recommendation, NOVELTY."[59] As he did in *Napoleon,* Bourne celebrated the laudable accomplishments of this religious figure and extolled the virtues of following his example. An important work in its own right, Bourne's *Life of the Rev. John Wesley,* which included a detailed outline of early Methodist theology and a brief sketch of the origins of Methodism in North America, came at a defining moment in the Early Republic, a time when post-Revolutionary Christianity experienced the great influence of the democratizing impact of Methodism. These early works also show Bourne's appreciation for the literary genre of biography. For Bourne, biography functioned to cultivate stability in an unstable era. The two biographies emphasized not only the compatibility of liberal republicanism and religious freedom, but also the importance of exceptional leaders who would both initiate change and stand as models for the development of moral character. The American nation could only survive by the principled character of those willing to protect the basic rights of its citizens. Bourne showed an enduring enthusiasm for political and religious figures, historical figures who courageously shaped history. And perhaps he saw himself as one who would inaugurate an ecclesiastical and political reformation in the United States.

Chapter 2 considers one of the most important moments not only in Bourne's life but also in that of the antislavery movement. Bourne's *The Book and Slavery Irreconcilable,* first published in 1816, and the additions made in its republication in 1834 under the title *Picture of Slavery in the United States of America,* introduced the twofold nature of the author's immediacy: to show the incompatibility of the Bible with slavery and to battle those who were primarily responsible for its continuance, namely, proslavery ministers. Included in this chapter is a consideration of (1) how Bourne used the Presbyterian church's confession, the Westminster Confession of Faith, to shape his antislavery position; (2) his ecclesiastical trial for his unflinching position against slavery; (3) the impact of the 1818 declaration against slavery by the Presbyterian General Assembly, the first of its kind by any church; and (4) the denomination's role in supporting African colonization. Bourne's prosecution in the church came at a crucial moment in the history of antislavery. In fact, as this chapter proposes, the hostility toward Bourne helped strengthen the church's commitment to colonization. Historians today agree that colonization was a turning point in the history of abolition, for it created a groundswell interracial cohort that opposed the moral failings of gradualism. His denomination's push toward colonization inadvertently projected Bourne as an extraordinary character, a foremost figure in the antislavery movement.

The central argument of *Book and Slavery,* as the full title makes clear, was that the Bible and slavery were diametrically opposed to one another, that not a single word in the Bible could justify slavery. But as a popular polemical work that mixed the Bible's teachings with republican thought, *Book and Slavery* avoided a thorough exegetical inspection of what the Bible said concerning slavery. One of the main goals of this early immediatist book was to confront proslavery ministers. Chapter 3 explores in greater detail Bourne's biblical arguments against proslavery religion as they appeared in his *Condensed Antislavery Bible Argument.* As a theological work, *Bible Argument,* an exegetical exploration as well as a careful systematic refutation of many of the popular proslavery theological arguments, was one among a handful of similar works published between 1830 and 1850, a period in which the arguments in defense of slavery exhibited greater sophistication. Inspired by Theodore Dwight Weld's *The Bible against Slavery,* Bourne was motivated to defend the integrity of scripture. And although published in the year of his death, Bourne's biblical argument against slavery was merely an elaboration of what he had presented thirty years earlier.

For most abolitionists, a proper interpretation of the Bible would attack the foundations of slavery in America. Yet the tension between the Bible and slavery in the antebellum period contributed to what Mark Noll has referred to as a theological crisis, a crisis that would only be settled by the movement of armies and the decisions of military commanders.[60] Anyone engaged in the debates entered a wider hermeneutical imbroglio. Northerners and southerners read the same Bible but did not read it the same way, which not only intensified regional tensions but portended a rising secularism that would reshape American society after the war. In the minds of some before the Civil War, the Bible seemed to be losing a place of central authority as a result of slavery. William Lloyd Garrison, for example, ultimately rejected traditional Protestant views of the Bible because of its inability to solve the dilemma of slavery.

Historians are correct in affirming that the existence of slavery created a significant challenge to hermeneutics, but it is not easy to conclude, as Molly Oshatz intimates in *Slavery as Sin,* that slavery complicated the plain meaning of the Bible's message, shifting hermeneutics away from a stricter literalism.[61] To address it in a different way, we must ask where these so-called complications came from. Many, both past and present, assume that the existence of slavery necessarily contradicts the plain teachings of the Bible. Because of the efforts of proslavery exegetes to use the Bible in support of their unjust institution, abolitionist leaders honed their approach to biblical interpretation. Bourne's *Bible Argument* brought to light the author's philosophy of biblical interpretation, especially his commitment to what came to be known in the nineteenth century as the historical-grammatical method. Writing to convince both northerners and southerners, the latter of whom could hardly engage in "a temperate discussion of the subject," Bourne wanted to avoid those who thought he was blinded by his radicalism, and so, like Angelina Grimké, he appealed to his former southern identity to lend credence to his position. Contrary to the accusations of antiabolitionists, Bourne was not an intrusive northerner, but someone who had eyewitness testimony of the proslavery South. Nor had he become, because of his hostility toward slavery, a heretic who undermined the authority of scripture. At its core, the message of the Bible, Bourne argued, was that of liberation.[62] This ex-southerner was both an unflagging opponent of slavery and a staunch defender of traditional orthodoxy, a merger that many abolitionists and defenders of slavery often severed. In this sense, he defies a simplistic division between, on the one hand, abolitionists as unorthodox or secular and, on the other, antiabolitionists as orthodox. He fought a two-front war against the theological distortions of southern fundamentalists and the religious doubts of a few abolitionist crusaders, but his high opinions regarding doctrine, in this case biblical inerrancy, did not pit him against the conclusions of those who did not hold to traditional religious theology. His argument seemed to comport with other Bible arguments from authors who did not share his traditionalist interpretive framework. Chapter 3 then attempts to reconceptualize a fundamental issue in nineteenth-century religion. If there was a breakdown of a consensus regarding the Bible's message that contributed to the outbreak of the Civil War, did it really come from those who advanced antislavery Bible arguments?

Chapter 4 moves the reader into Bourne's turn to anti-Catholicism, examining as its central text his first and only novel, *Lorette: A History of Louise, Daughter of a Canadian Nun.* Here readers get a brief glimpse into Bourne's involvement in anti-Catholicism in the 1820s. This widely read story clearly reflects the dominant features that ordered the author's religious perspective: true religion, false teachers, and the establishment of a spiritually pure identity. Although related to Catholicism, *Lorette* introduces the important gender themes that helped arrange his later work, *Slavery Illustrated* (hence the reason why I have placed them close together). The former was published four years before the latter. Like slavery, the false doctrine of Romanism corrupted women (primarily mothers and daughters), separated family members, and undermined individual self-knowledge. And consistent with his other works, the novel also reflects the author's allegiance to Protestant evangelical theology. Integrated into the plotline, which tells the harrowing tale of a girl who escapes from her enslaving priest after converting to the true faith of Protestantism, is an apology for the doctrines of the Christian faith that directly projects a notion of individual identity. The young girl's spiritual and physical redemption reconnects her with family members. In this way, Bourne skillfully connects true faith with the ideal family—one that reflects a middle-class form—and the ideal self. Bourne's hostility to Catholicism intensified when he returned to the cause of immediacy in the 1830s. For the remainder of his publishing career, he hardly ever severed slavery from Catholicism.

In his involvement in the battle to end chattel bondage, Bourne also witnessed the internal struggles that divided antislavery leaders. Chapter 5 addresses another disruptive issue engendered by antislavery: the status of women in the movement.[63] The key writings in this section include Bourne's *Slavery Illustrated in its Effects on Woman and Domestic Society* (1837) and his much earlier *Marriage Indissoluble and Divorce Unscriptural* (1813). Borrowing from the domestic allusions in *Lorette,* Bourne shows in *Slavery Illustrated* how slavery corrupts not only the character of women but also what women were to become. As both *Lorette* and *Slavery Illustrated* demonstrated, Bourne was an advocate of the nineteenth-century middle-class concept of true womanhood (i.e., domesticity), yet he was a leading supporter of public women in the antislavery crusade, going so far as to encourage women to publicly rebuke slaveholding ministers. While he believed that women were well within their "appropriate sphere" when they joined men in fighting the peculiar institution, he made no effort to reconcile his views regarding domesticity or the ways in which leading antislavery women were challenging those ideas.

Bourne's view on the involvement of women illustrates the instability of domesticity not only in his blueprint for reform, but also in the structure of nineteenth-century American culture. In recent years, historians have, according to Mary Kelley, "dismantled the boundaries that enclosed" Barbara Welter's groundbreaking opinion concerning the cult of true womanhood.[64] Rather than a "seamless ideology," domesticity and the separation of spheres were "shot through with ambivalence, tensions, and contradiction."[65] And the paradoxical quality of such an ideology was clearly seen in the abolitionist movement. Many women "blurred the distinction between private and public," "expanded the parameters of 'woman's sphere,' and suggested alternative meanings for gender norms."[66] Appeals to "true womanhood" could be used for both conservative and more liberating purposes.[67] According to Anna Speicher, commenting on the work of Nancy Hewitt and Lori Ginzberg, such ideas for contemporary historians should be understood more "as a perspective guideline than as an absolute statement of reality."[68] Recent studies make the case that nineteenth-century women were "everywhere": "in parades, in charitable associations, in literary circles, and even political parties." Carol Lasser and Stacey Robertson seek to "move beyond 'separate spheres'" in the way they show the "different forms of women's engagement in civic and political activities." In *Antebellum Women,* Lasser and Robertson focus on the dynamics of women's "publicness," positing "the evolution of different forms of women's engagement in civic and political activities."[69]

Women's "publicness," they argue, went through three distinct phases. The public activities of women in the first two phases, incorporating the period from the Revolution to the Jacksonian era, remained connected to the home. The authors use the term "deferential domesticity" to describe the public activity of women in the first phase.[70] The pious activism among women influenced by the Second Great Awakening and in the dynamic context of Jacksonian democracy, which raised the stakes in regard to the democratization of American life, inaugurated the second phase. Here women were afforded greater involvement "in public action within reform movements." Toward the end of this stage of "publicness," where women were "companionate co-laborers," to use Lasser and Robertson's categories, "a few particularly outspoken women slowly began to construct an argument for 'co-equality.'"[71] While their activism remained tied to the home for the most part, reforming women laid the groundwork for the third stage, transforming themselves into "passionate partisans," entering the "political fray claiming their rights as citizens to stake positions in electoral contests and in party matters." This stage, as it began to focus attention on the individual rights of women, furthered the distance from the home: "While women were pushed from participation in some types of public identity they had enjoyed, they continued to engage in activities beyond their households."[72] As Lydia Maria Child once wrote about the momentum of women's rights activism: "[Evangelical leaders] have changed the household utensil into a living, energetic being; and they have no spell to turn it into a broom again."[73] By the 1840s and 1850s, men feared that the increasing involvement of women would lead to the loss of their "selfless, calming influence, their salutary ability to soothe and tamp down the combustible party battles of the antebellum years."[74] There was no rolling back women's rights.

If Lasser and Robertson have provided a cogent layout of the dynamics of women's publicness, which I believe they have, then where does Bourne fit? To reconcile Bourne's position on women as fit for both the home but also activism in highly public reform campaigns, he should be situated within the second phase: the phase in which women "found new roles as partners in moral suasion, articulating their moral missions first within, and then on behalf of, the churches."[75] Bourne's *Slavery in Effects* was written during the time of what Lasser and Robertson identify as the second phase in the development of women's "publicness," which offers a way to understand how Bourne could, on the one hand, hold that the home was the proper place for women while, on the other hand, support the public presence and activism of women in the cause of antislavery, both of which harmonized with his overall concern for the role of the church in antislavery. Bourne wrote about such revolutionary activism within a more traditional conceptual framework. This is not to say that he simply used conservative rhetoric as a means to more radical ends, but that traditional conservative ideas did not necessarily contradict and could even complement radically new ones. Bourne had died around the time of the third stage, when the woman question reached the political point of no return. Bourne's silence on the place of women leadership in the movement suggests that he saw no inherent tension between traditional theology and the social changes brought by radical liberalism.

It would be difficult—and outside the scope of this project—to accurately determine the rigidity of Bourne's views on women and domesticity. Yet entertaining the question of how he would have reconciled his traditional beliefs with radical social change has indeed enlightening consequences, for it takes us back to his biblical cosmological thinking. Domestic life and the exemplary piety of the true woman seemed to be a kind of launching point to a more important spiritual battle. Earthly relationships, however arranged, were only temporary, especially when viewed in the context of Bourne's metaphysical framework. Men and women were part of a divine drama, mimicking heavenly realities (e.g., the relationship between Christ and the Father). The perfected ideal family and the individuals whose identities were shaped in such an economy would be fully realized at the dawn of the millennium. Chapter 3 posits that the reason Bourne did not directly engage the independent rights of women was because his "otherworldly" mindset kept him from doing so: earthly relationships, platonic reflections of heavenly ones, would ultimately pass away. His allegiance to Protestantism trumped social, cultural, and political change.

Moving from a discussion of how the false doctrines Bourne saw at the root of Catholicism and slavery undermined the relationship between faith and family, the final chapter looks at how Bourne's hatred of Catholicism helped structure his political nationalism. The ideals of the new American republic, especially in the way they uniquely synchronized enlightened political thought with orthodox Christianity, seemed to resonate with Bourne's own political and religious leanings.[76] He moved to the United States around the time when, according to Michael Durey, a "small portion" of liberty-loving "reformers, radicals, revolutionaries, rebels, and organic intellectuals" immigrated to the United States "from Britain and Ireland between 1783 and 1819."[77] These "transatlantic radicals" as Durey calls them, represented a diversity of political and religious (often unorthodox) beliefs. What they had in common—and Bourne is included in this—was an admiration for the accomplishments of the American Revolution, especially in the way the nation sought to ingrain the sacrosanct ideals of revolutionary republicanism into its founding documents.[78] This nascent republic—"a country where personal talents could be freely exercised, and where privilege and prescriptive status would not hinder individual advancement"—presented a host of social, economic, political, and religious possibilities.[79] Bourne found the United States to be the most fertile place for him to plant his religious seeds and help nurture the soul of an American society.

The supreme enemy of American liberty was spiritual and physical slavery; to combat it, Bourne turned to sacred history by laying out the origins of spiritual slavery as it began in the Roman Church, the premier chattel-making institution. Bourne viewed the relationship between religious history and national politics in his *Lectures on the Progress and Perfection of the Church of Christ* (1823) and *The American Text-book of Popery* (1836). The waves of Irish immigration in the late antebellum period, the distribution of public funds and the use of the Protestant Bible in the common school controversy, and the rise of European conservatism in the wake of Napoleon's demise fueled American anti-Catholicism. Bourne wrote on each of these issues and became an early proponent of anti-Catholicism. Such heightened anxiety and the violence it produced helped Bourne to define an exclusionary political ideology that forcefully associated "Protestantism" with "American." In her study of anti-Catholicism and American literature, Elizabeth Fenton has argued that "Catholicism has long operated as a test case" for the efficacy of liberal democracy in America.[80] Catholicism was a relic of the Old World, out of step with the revolutionary advance of American liberalism. Bourne traced the origins of Catholicism and positioned the United States as the true heir of the Protestant Reformation, using the New Testament book of Revelation as his interpretive guide. This apocalyptic letter detailed the rise of the antichristian pope, who initiated the practice of enslaving the souls and bodies of men and fashioning the historical model of modern slavery. Knowledge of history provided the tools necessary for the nation to adequately battle the expansion of plantation slavery and the Roman faith. The fight against Romanism, for Bourne, was not only essential in the creation of a free republic but also in illustrating the advancement of the millennium.

In 1832, an anonymous writer for the *Liberator* represented fellow abolitionists when saying, "Mr. Bourne, we consider one of the most extraordinary men of the age."[81] But such an extraordinary (and extraordinarily religious) reformer defies easy categorization. As an antislavery advocate, he seemed to fit each of the descriptive groups laid out by Lawrence Friedman in his book *Gregarious Saints.* Yet it was his strict religious beliefs that set him apart from fellow abolitionist leaders. As an anti-Catholic, concerned primarily with the reformation of the American church and the preservation of biblical theology, he was in a class separate from the more politically minded nativists of the middle to late nineteenth century. What the modern mind would consider contradictory and grossly intolerant in equating the tyranny of slavery with that of Catholicism, Bourne understood as not only logically consistent, but also the only way to understand the fullest extent of physical and spiritual freedom. This was the fundamental essence of Bourne's reform. His closest associates admired his focused "cosmological" confidence. "His disposition was cheerful," wrote Lewis Tappan, "and he soared above the provocations of his enemies, trusting in God to deduce good out of seeming evil, and taking even the wrath of man to praise him." The Reverend George Bourne knew that America's spiritual battles would be hard fought, but what made him "completely tranquil" in the eyes of his fellow reformers was "an abiding faith that God would set things right."[82]

Bourne addressed anyone willing to challenge abuses of power. But he spoke especially to church leaders, those who had a responsibility to break the "bands of wickedness, undo the heavy burdens, let the oppressed go free, [and] take away the yoke [of bondage]."[83] He followed the example of Christ and the many courageous figures in the history of the church who sought "to heal the broken-hearted, to preach deliverance to the captives, to set at liberty them that are bruised."[84] In a very real sense, Bourne's message was not only for the oppressed but also for their oppressors, the worst of whom were the leaders, false teachers, and hypocrites of the Christian faith. The title of this monograph, *To Preach Deliverance to the Captives,* is a variation of the prophetic announcement of the coming of Jesus Christ, the redeemer of both body and spirit, in Isaiah 61 and later by Jesus in Luke 4:18. The phrase was familiar among abolitionists. Joshua Leavitt used it as his motto for the *Emancipator.* It also appeared in the founding document of the American Anti-Slavery Society. After helping to organize the American Anti-Slavery Society in 1833, Bourne published a sermon, a recap of the position of the Presbyterian Church on the issue of slavery and a reminder to "expel" unrepentant slave owners from the church: "The most melancholy portion of all this wickedness and misery, is, that [slavery] has been clothed with a mask and honored by a Christian name. It is indubitable, that the present existence of slavery, in the United States, may chiefly be imputed to the professed disciples of Jesus, the Prince of philanthropists, one part of whose divine mission it was, to 'preach deliverance to the captives.'"[85]

CHAPTER 1

BOURNE, BIOGRAPHY, AND AMERICAN IDENTITY

Great events always produce extraordinary characters.
—GEORGE BOURNE, *The History of Napoleon Bonaparte*

In 1804, Bourne, according to a late nineteenth-century writer, "left England for America full of zeal and love for liberty—civil and religious."[1] Recognizing the political and economic conditions transforming England at the turn of the nineteenth century—though distant himself from the cohort of political dissenters and radicals, including those sympathetic to the concerns of an emerging laboring class whose lives were being fundamentally altered by industrialization—Bourne became convinced that in America "greater freedom of conscience and liberty could be enjoyed than in England."[2] Nonetheless, he left the challenges of one country for those roiling another. The young American republic faced challenges that included the ongoing partisanship between Federalists and Democrat-Republicans over the future direction of the nation; the conflicts between Native Americans and Euro-Americans in the Northwest and South; the geographical expansion of the United States with the still-fresh purchase of Louisiana and the political and economic consequences of such an acquisition; the success of the Haitians in establishing an independent nation and the specter of revolution-inspired slave uprisings throughout the Americas; the fear that the radicalism of revolution was a threat to traditional faith; and that the United States was caught in the middle of a war between Britain and France, made worse by America's failed embargoes. The Bourne family relocated to America during a time when there was an "absence of any clear consensus holding Americans together," Nicole Eustace and Frederika Teute write in *Warring for America*.[3] The social dislocation, political fragility, and economic uncertainties "that split American society from the outset" were considered by Bourne, as for many other Americans, as opportunities for creative nation building. Many American leaders, however, feared that the young republic would be undone by democratic chaos. Bourne never expressed concern over the radical implications of revolutionary democracy, made quite real by the Whiskey Rebellion ten years before his arrival, the slave revolution in Haiti, the Gabriel Prosser conspiracy, or the Haiti-inspired German Coast Uprising, the largest slave uprising in the history of the United States.[4]

A major concern among American leaders at the time was how to create a socially stable republic. One means of controlling the masses came through the creation of the Constitution in 1787, which gave a modicum of democracy to a few. Yet not even a revolution in government or a limited franchise could assuage the anxiety over the reality of a fuller democratic radicalism, especially among those inspired by revolutionary language but relegated to the margins of society. Events across the Atlantic served to intensify such anxieties. The French Revolution, including its legacy in Haiti and South America, "did the most to touch off," argues historian Seth Cotlar, "potentially radical conversations about democracy in America."[5] By the time King Louis VXI was executed, transitioning the French Revolution into its period of terror, both England and America became significantly concerned with the populist implications of what was happening in France, fearing that the violent turn of events was, according to Gordon Wood, "capable of dragging the United States into the same kind of popular anarchy."[6] Bourne was not yet a teenager when Edmund Burke's *Reflections on the Revolution in France* (1791), inspired by a host of transatlantic discussions over the ramifications of revolution, helped to set the markers along the modern political spectrum that have remained to this day. With the violent phase of the French Revolution that included a war between Britain and France, Americans, incessantly harassed by both countries, turned "away in disgust from the European conflagration," writes Philipp Ziesche, "to appreciate their nation's exceptional destiny."[7] They realized the "danger that their new and fragile nation would be dragged into a global conflict even as, closer to home, the slave regime on which half of the country's economy depended threatened collapse."[8] American leaders came to understand that the nation's immediate future could not be severed from the international conflict between France, England, and the rest of Europe. Factions in England, France, and America, however, were too intense to silence, in an ultimate sense, opposition within each country. Many dissidents sought refuge in the new American republic, where Republicans welcomed them, including the French (much to the disapproval of Federalists). It was not as easy to target those dissenters who escaped their own country: "the French and American governments became convinced either that their opponents would use recent immigrants to seize power or, more ominously, that their opponents were themselves 'foreigners,' out to subvert the nation from within."[9]

Bourne recognized the popular impulses of the young republic and offered his own contribution to what he thought would lead to national stability.[10] At the center of a healthy revolutionary republic was a citizenry radically changed by a "revolution in principles, opinions, and manners," to borrow from Benjamin Rush. Early in his professional career as a writer, Bourne believed strongly that the strength of a nation rested not so much on structures but on an educated citizenry, a citizenry dedicated not only to the Bible but more importantly to the lives of key historical figures who stood as examples for citizens to emulate. The means of preserving the "unfinished business of the Revolution" had to be established first by modeling the principled character of great individuals. In order to become a morally principled society, in other words, American citizens needed to study and emulate historical figures who exhibited not only principled lives—in both public and private—but also lives that seemed to transcend national, creedal, and geographic boundaries. The era of revolutions demanded universal citizens of the world. For Bourne, biography was a crucial instructional source for establishing a strong citizenry. He focused on those committed to principles beyond the traditions of their respective communities, whether nation or denomination, republican citizens willing to provide order and meaning by courageously applying their virtuous principles to a yet-to-be formed world.

Yet he did not find a worthy enough example from among Americans themselves. Bourne provided examples from outside the republic. The two figures worthy of imitation for the purposes of instilling the principles necessary to create a strong republican nation were John Wesley (1703–1791) and Napoleon Bonaparte (1769–1821). Bourne's *History of Napoleon Bonaparte* was one of the earliest of such works in both America and Europe.[11] His subsequently published *The Life of the Rev. John Wesley* is one of the first American biographies of the founder of Methodism.[12] As mentioned in the introduction, putting these two works together in a single chapter, I believe, teases out what Bourne believed was of central importance in the longevity of a nascent republic. The new country had to depend on the "fixed principles," according to

Bourne, and "moral tenour" of such figures, individuals who embodied a universal enlightened republicanism and simple primitive religion, both of which served as foundational to a virtuous republic.[13] Biography was also important to Bourne because the principles and structure of a republican government, true religion, and moral philosophy, which often fell into decay when neglected by a population, could not remain without the agency of people willing to embody and apply them. Republican principles and true faith, in other words, would not create a nation without the commitments of confident individuals. Bourne believed that biography would offer instruction in public virtue and private faith, assuaging fears related to what many believed to be the reasons behind the insecurities of the Early Republic.

Hundreds of biographies, mostly military, had been written between 1790 and 1900, as Scott Casper shows in *Constructing American Lives.* In a period where members of society looked anywhere for social and political grounding, Americans believed that biography had the power "to shape individuals' lives and character and to help define America's national character."[14] The creation of civic virtue "was essential to individual character," and biography was the means to cultivate it. The survival of the American republic "depended on its citizens' civic virtue, their commitment to participate in public life and place the public good before private interest."[15] This literary genre, Bourne argued in the early 1820s, represented the most "copious source of self knowledge of all the departments of historical record."[16] It "exhibits man in all his variegated hues, and of course enables the beholder accurately to estimate his diversified qualities."[17] Biography allowed people to appropriate the character attributes of others and to participate in the process of their own self-becoming, securing the ethics of republicanism.

Bourne does not provide a rationale for why he chose to write about either Napoleon or Wesley, although we would not be off the mark to say that he was certainly attracted to important issues related to the creation of the republic, and no one would deny that the French Revolution and the explosive growth of Methodism stood as two of the most important issues shaping the Early Republic. We can say with greater certainty after considering the two biographies that Bourne expressed a fascination with historical individuals who, to say it somewhat loftily, bore the weight of a new world on their shoulders, individuals willing to live in accordance with their own principles for the purposes of having a transformative influence on society. Both biographies reveal what Bourne believed to be the key pillars of a free republic: the freedom of conscience and the protection of true religion. In Bourne's mind, John Wesley exhibited a faith undefiled by the heaviness of tradition. Indeed, the disparagements against Wesley from an Old World denomination (Anglicanism) for his—and his brother's—efforts to return to a simple faith provided a strong impetus for establishing a denomination that had little to hold on to from the Old World. And Napoleon was the prime example of an individual "animated," Bourne writes, by the "revolutionary spirit."[18] He lived during a period of significant national uncertainty and political opposition but had the courage to apply the principles of revolution for the well-being of the French people. According to Matthew Rainbow Hale, Americans forged a new kind of democratic hero, a military hero of pomp and almost exaggerated performance forged from the intensity of war itself, a figure of inspiration for America's aspiring heroes of the Early Republic.[19] Both Wesley and Napoleon provided Americans a way to look back but also forward, a consideration of the life of two figures who appealed to the religious past and another who represented a revolutionary republican future.

Allow me to consider each biography in accordance with the year they appeared, beginning with *History of Napoleon Bonaparte: Emperor of the French, and King of Italy,* published in 1806, a couple of years after William Burdon's *Life and Character of Napoleon* and twenty years before Sir Walter Scott's popular—as well as more thorough—*Life of Napoleon.*[20] Indeed, by the 1820s, at least a dozen biographies were written about Bonaparte. Napoleon was becoming a figure that few could ignore. For many Europeans, he was first in a class of new modern heroes. In the same year that Bourne published his biography, for instance, German philosopher Georg Wilhelm Friedrich Hegel recast the image of Napoleon for the European continent with great rhetorical pomp, referring to him as the "*Weltgeist* [world-soul] riding out of the city on reconnaissance . . . astride a horse, reaches out over the world and masters it."[21] Yet not everyone in Europe was as hyperbolic as the German idealist. And like many Europeans, Americans held conflicting opinions on the famous Corsican. America's "admiration of Napoleon," Howard M. Jones wrote in the early twentieth century, "began early, wavered only as he took on a more despotic character, and, after his death, his faults forgot, wove around him their own version of the Napoleonic legend."[22] Robert Livingston, minister to France from 1801 to 1804, questioned more generally Napoleon's ability to lead. Washington Irving too seemed skeptical that Napoleon had preserved the democratic promises of the French Revolution. William Crawford, minister to France from 1813 to 1815, came to believe that the rights of the people were increasingly ignored under Napoleon's rule. Rembrandt Peale had used stronger words in articulating the social, economic, and political failings of the first consul and later emperor. The harshest of Napoleon's critics came not only from the Federalists but from New England Protestant leaders. The Reverend Samuel Austin described Napoleon as "the most cruel oppressor and murderer of his fellow beings, the vilest of men, who tramples upon all truth and justice."[23] William Ellery Channing, a leading Unitarian theologian, considered Napoleon as "dark, vindictive, [and] unrelenting."[24] A handful of influential New England ministers began to refer to Napoleon as the "anti-Christ."

Many Americans admired Napoleon, however. William MacLure, for one, rejected the word "tyrant" when referencing Napoleon, whose civil codes, McClure believed, restored justice and protected private property, ushering France out of a feudal era. The more favorable opinion of Napoleon came from among the Jeffersonians. George Douglass of Baltimore considered Napoleon as the "secular marvelous of the Enlightenment."[25] Virginian author Henry Banks praised Bonaparte for his early accomplishments in battle: "Never did any man before perform so many great actions, or acquire so much glory in so short a time."[26] The radical nineteenth-century reformer Henry Clarke Wright reminisced about Napoleon's exploits, which as a child, Wright confessed, had "kindled up my young heart."[27] And then, of course, there are those who detached themselves from taking sides for or against Napoleon to appreciate the ironies of such a figure. What is often lost among the opinions of either admiration or aversion is the complicated and polarizing character of Napoleon, which has baffled biographers and historians since the turn of the nineteenth century. Writers in Napoleon's day to those in the twenty-first century have presented Bonaparte as a complicated and polarizing figure, which may contribute to the enduring fascination of the man himself.

Perhaps it was Napoleon's failures in the years following Bourne's biography that tilted opinion toward a dislike of him. If this is accurate, then Bourne would not be among that number, for he admired the French emperor and ended the biography at a high point of Napoleon's career, a few years before his final exile. Bourne had been invited by a "group of publishers," according to Christie and Dumond, to write a biography of Napoleon. Although there is no confirmation of "the extent of its sales or of the financial return to the author," Christie and Dumond continue, the biography "launched his career as a writer."[28] One of the first to add his contribution to the Napoleonic legacy in America, Bourne wrote that modern history "affords no parallel to Napoleon Bonaparte."[29] For him, Napoleon represented a figure not only possessed by a love for republican liberty but also one willing to apply the principles of the revolution to the citizens among a new nation.

Bourne prioritized the American Revolution as that which first, in his words, "operated like an electric shock upon the French people" and also on Napoleon.[30] He highlighted the shared causes that produced both revolutions: the "excessive load of taxes, which fell almost exclusively upon the lower class of people"; the "abuses of the clergy"; the introduction to the public of "an education more republican"; the "great freedom" for members of society to converse on the "subjects of government"; the corrupt administration of justice, the "arbitrary exactions of the nobles," and the incessant demands an improvident government made upon them to maintain its extravagances. As the French Revolution continued, Bourne and others used it as a lens to cast light on an emerging American culture. The American and French Revolutions created a "world in motion," according to Janet Polasky, author of *Revolutions without Borders,* and citizens in both countries employed "a variety of visions in an era of possibility."[31] From the eighteenth century, revolutionary ideas and actions cascading "through all of the continents bordering the Atlantic" inspired the building of national republics.[32] Revolutionary possibilities do not always lead to social stability, however. The French Revolution intensified what Wood identifies as "the quarrel that Americans were having among themselves over the direction of their own revolution."[33] Ziesche argues that both America and France "were linked by the idea that nations were not facts of nature but could and needed to be actively built": "In the last two decades of the eighteenth century, the newly empowered political elites on both sides of the Atlantic self-consciously set out to build nations through declarations, constitutions, laws, education, festivals, and other forms of political culture."[34] Nation building forced Americans "resolutely outward," writes François Furstenberg in *When the United States Spoke French,* "toward Europe, toward the Caribbean, and toward the outer edges of its continental frontiers."[35] And with the early developments of the French Revolution, many Americans were inspired by "abstract ideals such as liberty, equality, and the rights of man."[36]

Late eighteenth-century transatlantic thinkers, whom Ziesche refers to as "cosmopolitan patriots," appealed to "universal principle and an inclusive definition of citizenship" to assimilate the various factions in the United States. While France and the United States began to adopt "more exclusive concepts of national citizenship," by the 1790s, cosmopolitans highlighted the notion that "all human beings shared essential moral characteristics that transcended the boundaries of nationality, language, religion, and custom."[37]

Bourne believed that Napoleon was possessed and motivated by the French Revolution and was thus the most suited to lead a new France. "Great events," Bourne wrote at the beginning of his Napoleon biography, "always produce extraordinary characters."[38] *Napoleon* was primarily offered as a way for readers to make a "due estimate of the character of Bonaparte."[39] Preserving the legacy of a revolution demands more than a system of government; it demands a vigilant citizenry, which itself, like a nation, is created by mimicking key historical figures. The French Revolution created Napoleon, a self-made and determined Corsican whose love of republican liberty instilled within him "an active and irresistibly powerful principle," operating "with an electric power" that "inflames the whole mass of society."[40] Napoleon's charisma, shaped by his enthusiasm for revolution and the republic, was infectious. By 1799, becoming first consul at a young age, Napoleon created a dictatorship that utilized populist rhetoric and hence galvanized the French people. In the image of Napoleon, Bourne recognized a balance as well as an embodiment of one who believed strongly in the ideals of the French Revolution but one who was able to maintain order, an order that rested largely on his character. Bourne identified Napoleon as the one who would not only protect the ideals of the French Revolution but also act as a rallying point for a new France.

After introducing the importance of Napoleon's character and place in history, including his birth in 1769 and his advancement in learning, Bourne spends much of the remainder of the book detailing Napoleon's life up to 1806, the year in which Napoleon reached the pinnacle of his power on the continent. The young Napoleon, according to Bourne, showed himself to be an astute learner, who early on acquired a love for philosophy, mathematics, and science. Indeed, throughout "his public life," Bourne writes, Napoleon demonstrated his commitment to "those improvements which expand the mind and dignify the intellect of man; and to his endeavours and example must be attributed all the increase of knowledge which we have derived from his expeditions." Along with the training of his intellect, Napoleon also exhibited skill in the "government of his passions"; he was contemplative, calculating, never drunk, and always ate with moderation. He was neither self-interested nor was he given to "plunder and devastation" on the field of battle (an opinion that not a few subsequent biographers dispute). From the time he received his first military appointment as a young officer, Napoleon set his eyes on fixing "peace on the continent" through the advancement of revolutionary liberty.[41]

In his early military career, which Bourne ends at the Battle of Trafalgar and Austerlitz in 1805, Napoleon provided "proof of the prudence and judgment of the directory in appointing to the most difficult service of the republic, a man, to whom as a general, the renowned heroes of Greece and Rome must relinquish their laurels, and acknowledge that our times have produced their superior."[42] Napoleon had started his military career as an artillery officer when the French Revolution began. The Directory gave him command of the army of Italy when he was in his mid-twenties, and he won the campaigns against Italy and Austria. Each European campaign drew out aspects of Napoleon's unique character. He "displayed his scientifick [*sic*] knowledge," Bourne wrote, in his campaigns across Europe and North Africa. All the qualities of a great military hero came together in Napoloeon in his operations in Egypt, which, Bourne writes, "required profound genius, a penetrating mind, a legislating spirit, vast local knowledge, much coolness and intrepidity, vigor of plan, energy in execution, and boldness nearly allied to temerity."[43] By the end of 1805, in the famous Ulm Campaign, he defeated the Third Coalition (Russia, Britain, and Austria), crushing the Russians and Austrians at Austerlitz. The Austerlitz campaign softened the continent for further conquest; it also helped to create the Confederation of the Rhine, which effectively brought an end to the Holy Roman Empire, creating a buffer between France and the rest of Europe. His activities on the battlefield demonstrated two central qualities instilled in him by the French Revolution. He was creative in terms of military strategy and was other-directed, humane, and benevolent in his social interaction, but he was always committed to his country. The detailing of Napoleon's early campaigns, however, ends on a low point: namely, his defeat at Trafalgar, a battle that "deprived the French emperor of a considerable portion of his maritime force."[44]

Napoleon's campaign in Egypt strengthened his position in French politics. By the end of the eighteenth century, the republic was struggling financially and was unpopular among the citizenry. Despite the significant loss in the number of men as a result of the Egyptian campaign and its aftermath, Napoleon returned home to take power in France. He overthrew the Directory by late 1799, creating a new kind of dictatorship all with the trappings of a people's republic. In 1804, France implemented the famous Code Napoleon, a legal document that influenced much of the European and Latin American continents. The Treaty of Amiens brought Europe to a temporary peace, which then allowed Napoleon to strengthen his power in France. He also had time to deal with the Louisiana Territory in North America. (Bourne says nothing about Haiti or Napoleon's dealings with it.) Napoleon's devotion to the French Revolution was likewise demonstrated by his commitment to the French people. The citizens of France, Bourne noted, saw him as a hero:

> Bonaparte's presence kindled a spirit of enthusiasm inexpressible; all parties looked to him as the cause of some unknown good to the republic; they trusted unreservedly in him for peace and every other blessing: . . . his courage, military art, affability of manners; his acuteness, penetration, coolness, vigour and presence of mind; his boldness in design, and intrepidity in execution; his firmness, activity and perseverance; his unparalleled sublime genius, which distinguished difficulties from impossibilities, and improved every event to his own advantage . . . his former letters, speeches and actions, and his almost miraculous return from Egypt . . . all proclaimed him to be the man who was appointed to redress the grievances of the nation, and excited the unbounded confidence of the people.[45]

Napoleon in turn dedicated himself to the citizens of France: "The French people demand, that I shall devote myself to their service; I obey their will."[46] Immediately after his coronation and in obedience to the will of the people, Napoleon set out "to give stability to the new form of government."[47] In carrying out the ideals of the French Revolution but also restoring the nation to order, Napoleon created the "myth of the savior," in the words of Jean Tulard.[48] Bourne compelled Americans to "examine the character of any public individual" in light of Napoleon's own. His character shown forth most acutely in how he cared for those under his authority, especially to his soldiers, "sympathizing with them in all their concerns." This proved in Bourne's mind that Bonaparte's civic virtue was possessed by "a considerable share of the 'milk of human kindness.'"[49]

Although politicians were wary of him, Napoleon never expressed a desire to suppress his critics, even when some accused him of being overly ambitious in his rise to power. French writer Stendhal (Marie-Henri Beyle) wrote of Napoleon as exhibiting "a dangerous ambition."[50] Bourne denied that France's emperor was "an ignorant upstart, without genius or learning, without science or courage, and dependent altogether upon the advice, prudence, and management of others in his civil government." Such a view, according to Bourne, was "so preposterous as to require no refutation."[51] Ambition, especially in the actions of a military hero, was something that many citizens of the Early Republic craved. Matthew Rainbow Hale recently made an exceptional argument related to Early Republican citizens' admiration for Napoleon. Challenging the negative views coming especially from New England Federalists, who believed that Napoleon was clearing a path for his own dictatorship, Hale argues that "self-interested, go-getting soldiering, entrepreneurialism, and politicking seemed to many less a path to military dictatorship, corrosive luxury, and anarchic factionalism."[52] Instead, images of Napoleon became a popular "means of engineering inspirational heroes and a brilliant international reputation."[53] Napoleon represented a new kind of heroic figure, a determined figure willing to take daring (even lawless) risks to shine gloriously and be admired by citizens of a revolutionary nation. Napoleon, according to Hale, recast an entire culture around the military hero, which in turn offered a paradoxical "neo-monarchical-democratic sovereignty."[54] American military leaders, including Oliver Hazard Perry, Stephen Decatur, and David Porter, were "motivated," Hale says, "by a brazen desire to garner accolades," doing so by mimicking Napoleon's flamboyant style, bravery, risky endeavors, and even his speech and clothing. The examples of military heroes were key to national victory and longevity, according to Hale: "when led by a charismatic democratic leader [a nation] would perform unprecedentedly glorious deeds."[55]

In the final portions of the biography, Bourne spends time examining Napoleon's attitude toward religion, especially as it related to the new French republic. One of the greatest accomplishments of the French Revolution—however "awful and bitter were the miseries which flowed" from it, Bourne wrote in his 1823 publication *Lectures on the Progress and Perfection of the Church*—was that it "produced a new era in the moral and religious history of mankind."[56] Bourne's opinion, however, runs contrary to the beliefs among many Protestants across the continents who became increasingly concerned over the coming demise of morality and religion caused by the radical supporters of the French Revolution. "The orthodox Christian clergy," writes Wood, "suddenly lost their earlier enthusiasm for the French Revolution and in 1794–1796 turned on Paris, the Revolution, and the Republican party with a vengeance."[57]

Napoleon, according to Bourne, believed strongly that religion was crucial for the establishment of a revolutionary republic. At the time of his conquest of Egypt, for instance, Napoleon forbade his men from disrespecting the "Mohammadans" and the Catholics and their sacred places of worship, which revealed his commitment to religious liberty. When interacting with Muslims in Egypt, Napoleon commanded his soldiers to "cherish the same spirit of toleration for the Mosques that you have entertained for the religion of Moses and Jesus Christ."[58] Before his ascension to the emperorship, Napoleon sought to restore the "national religion" of the French people while also granting religious tolerance to the oppressed Protestants of France, who had been unable to worship freely in the days of the Old Regime. Indeed, Napoleon conciliated the clergy in order to "gain the affections of the people."[59] As emperor, Bourne writes, Napoleon expressed his "pleasure" for the "pastors of the reformed churches of France," which compelled him to take the opportunity to articulate his "satisfaction with the fidelity and good conduct of the pastors and citizens of the several protestant communions." In the final lines of *History of Napoleon,* Bourne quotes France's emperor saying in regard to religion, "I wish it to be published, that my firm resolve and desire are to maintain the liberty of worship. The empire of the law ends where the empire of conscience begins. Neither the law nor the sovereign dare to diminish that liberty. Such are my principles and those of the nation, and if any of my race, who may succeed me, shall forget my coronation oath, and, misled by a false confidence, shall violate it, I devote him to publick [*sic*] animadversion, and authorize you to denominate him Nero."[60] The freedom of conscience was the key to religious freedom; without such liberty a nation was doomed.

Republics had to be built by virtuous citizens; a virtuous citizenry, in turn, never a static entity, had to be created and maintained. The establishment of religious colleges, moral reform societies, and the expansion of the religious press aided in the creation of an educated, morally upright, and principled American society, "the source," Wood writes, "of republican freedom and security."[61] For Bourne especially, a vigilant republic rested on protecting the free expression of religion in its various modes (e.g., education, print, moral societies), but it also meant protecting "true" religion: Christianity shaped by the ancient creeds and that of historic Protestantism. Historical Protestantism, for Bourne, was born from a principled resistance against any force that sought to suppress "private interpretations" of the scriptures. Any threat to the faith of another, whether from church or state, should itself be removed. It was not that Bourne opposed the practice of certain non-Christian religions, though he was vocal about what constituted true from false religion; rather, he was hostile to religions that sought to restrict the beliefs and practices of other faiths or ones that by their very nature conflicted with the ideals of a free republic, as in the case of Romanism. As his anti-Catholic polemics demonstrated beginning in the late 1820s, Bourne believed that Catholicism would destroy a revolutionary republic, since Romanism was primarily a dictatorial faith that did not allow adherents to think for themselves nor allow them to freely participate in a democratic republic. According to historian Dickson Bruce, Bourne's hostility to Catholicism was not seen as an "intolerance of religious differences but, rather, as a defense of American religious freedom against an authoritarian onslaught."[62]

Although it could be suppressed or lost either by aggressive opposition, the accumulation of tradition, or simply by ignoring it over time, a pure and undefiled faith could never be snuffed out. Someone would always arise to remind society of the truth. Additionally, some in North America and Europe feared that the French Revolution would dismantle established religion and thus true faith. Uninhibited democracy, which could, in the minds of many, spill over into lawless anarchy, was a fear that the revolution, especially in France, could contribute to increasing godlessness. Such worries became acute after the publication of Paine's *Age of Reason.* Americans felt betrayed by their adopted patriot. They also must have feared that the decline of faith was part of a logical progression of Paine's radicalism and France's revolutionary ethos. Bourne never affirmed an inherent tension between the radicalism of either the American or French Revolutions that would lead to an imminent decline of Christianity; he nonetheless understood the anxiety among Americans as they sought to protect the true faith. For Bourne, however, the decline of pure and undefiled religion was not the result of a single event like a revolution or of secular ideas propagated by an individual (as in the case of Paine), but the neglect of religion itself. Just like God's people in the Old Testament, Bourne reminded his readers that the faithful had a penchant for forgetting the redemptive acts of God. Bourne instructed his readers to be vigilant against the deception of sin and the devil.

The freedom of conscience was the prerequisite for an authentic encounter with God. Pure faith came by way of an individual's unmediated meeting of God through the reading of the Bible. Such a notion has become a central tenet of evangelicalism, an "ism" that is considerably averse to anyone or anything, including a Christian sect or denomination, that would keep the individual from freely searching the scriptures.[63] Interfering with an individual's reading of scripture was the beginning of tyranny, the fount of enslavement. True faith included an emotional response to God that was at the same time (or by the degree of the emotional experience itself) a verification of true conversion. It was not merely an engagement with the Bible in a disinterested manner, but rather an emotional response of the individual reader, a kind of ineffable heartfelt moment of spiritual enlightenment generated by the Holy Spirit. Thus, reading the scriptures, an enrapturing by the Holy Spirit from without, and an emotional response from the subject within produced a pure evangelical experience. The British, American, and Continental strands of modern evangelicalism share a common emphasis on the heart over the head. This does not mean that evangelicalism rejected learning, tradition, or the cerebral rigors of systematic theology, though many evangelicals have derided these elements of organized religion. Yet the content of head knowledge meant nothing without the final assent of the heart.

The democratizing tendencies created by the American Revolution led many to take Christianity in the direction of either reacting against the Revolution to maintain traditional authority or by accommodating some of the changes caused by it. Up until Nathan Hatch's *Democratization of American Christianity,* modern historians viewed religion in early America as a cohesive force that provided order in an unsettling period, a means of "social control." A sense of grounding and an interpretive grid to develop as a human were both fundamental for moral virtue. Indeed, religion does provide a sense of solace and an instrument that shapes our worldview. Hatch, however, emphasizes the centrifugal expansion of Christianity "that drove churches apart and gave new significance to local and grass-roots endeavors; and the stark emotionalism, disorder, extremism, and crudeness that accompanied expression of the faith fed by the passions of ordinary people."[64] American Christianity was shaped not by way of consensus but by the creation of numerous versions of

Christianity that competed for the attention of American citizens, although hostility toward Catholicism seemed to be a shared commitment among Protestants. Bourne, like many other transatlantic evangelicals, considered this post-Revolutionary democratization of Christianity as an opportunity to recover an unadulterated faith, which in turn would contribute to the legitimization of the American republic. The American Revolution—and that of the French—wiped the social and cultural slate clean, so to speak. This process of creating a new religiously stable society required going back not only to first principles but to a historic faith, a faith Bourne believed would flourish in a revolutionary context.

The growth of faith in the Early Republic was aided not only by the Revolution but also by a thriving print culture.[65] Bourne connected the importance of expression in relation to the propagation of truth to the power of the press. "The press," he later wrote in *Lectures,* "aided the cause" of Luther's Reformation. Indeed, were it not for the "invention of printing [and] without a miraculous intervention of God," the Reformation would have been "totally demolished."[66] Print was an insurmountable weapon against the abuse of religious authority. What is more, in an age of revolution, the press was a dangerous instrument that some believed unleashed unrestricted popular expression; in America the more radically "Jacobin" newspapers during and after the Revolution were widely feared by the political and religious elite. Yet such newspapers sought to create an "engaged, radicalized, and cosmopolitan citizenry."[67] Both England and the American republic feared the political opinions, polemics, and invectives of a "free" press and sought to punish, exclude, or expel the growing number of dissenters. But for Bourne, the press was not only the direct means to preserve and advance the truth, but it was also a means to speak truth to power. He lauded the press in America particularly for its advancing true religion: "A delightful feature of the present era is the accelerating increase of regular issues of religious publications devoted exclusively to the theological discussions and missionary intelligence."[68] The expansion of religious publications "transformed the reading character of the Christian world": "God speed the *Press.*"[69]

True religion and the social institutions put in place to protect the faith of the republic meant nothing, however, without the agency of those committed to guarding the faith. And once again, Americans, especially in a religious democratizing context, needed direction. They needed exemplary figures to follow and learn from. Bourne searched for the embodiment of a pure and democratically appealing faith, a faith both conservative and progressive. He found it among the Methodists, a religious group that exhibited a more ecumenical piety, though eventually congealing into a distinct denomination. The Methodists, along with the Baptists, were the fastest growing religious sect in post-Revolutionary America. The Baptists went from more than ninety congregations in 1760 to close to a thousand by 1790, becoming the largest denomination in the fledgling republic at the time. The Methodists, however, with no adherents in 1760, grew to about seven hundred congregations by 1790. By 1805, "the Methodists soon overtook the Baptists to become the largest denomination in America," experiencing intense growth, "from forty-six thousand in 1801 to 80,000 by 1807," the year Bourne published the first American biography of Wesley.[70] Methodism became the fastest growing religious group in the nineteenth century, constituting a third of church membership in America by the time of the Civil War. "No part of the Ecclesiastical History of the New World is more interesting," Bourne wrote in his biography of Wesley, "than that which details the rise, progress, and present state of the Methodist Episcopal Church. From a grain of mustard seed, it is become in a few years a spreading tree."[71]

The growth of Methodism stemmed from its popular appeal in a revolutionary context, even though few Methodists could be counted among those who supported the American Revolution. The post-Revolutionary organization of American Methodism fell on the shoulders of Francis Asbury. "Bishop Asbury alone," Bourne writes, "remained" in America during the conflict with England "to fulfill the duties of the mission to which the Providence of God had called him."[72] And "amidst all the hurry, confusion and distress" caused by the Revolution, including a significant absence of Methodists themselves, "the gospel was propagated."[73] Asbury contributed to the growth of Methodism not only by his intense managerial regulations among leaders and laity—which later prompted Bourne to refer to Methodism as the "popery" of Protestantism—but also by appropriating Revolutionary-charged rhetoric that helped to lay the groundwork for a populist strand within American Methodism. By utilizing words like *liberty*, *freedom*, and *power*, "Asbury described a new order of reality, a new dominion, a new society." Methodist preachers, as did leaders in other denominations, crafted their message to appeal to the ordinary masses, offering the "humble a marvelous sense of individual potential and of collective aspiration."[74]

The Revolution compelled "common people to put their religious world back together on new democratic terms."[75] Even the more conservative denominations like the Presbyterians, an organization for which Bourne would later become a minister, had to "concede greater and greater lay control" over the administration of the church.[76] The war against Britain created, according to Hatch, "a cultural ferment over the meaning of freedom. Turmoil swirled around crucial issues of authority, organization, and leadership."[77] As a branch of evangelical Protestantism that was able to transcend geographic, nationalistic, and even denominational boundaries, Methodism certainly benefited from the impact of the Revolution like few other religious sects, though democratization had a profound influence on all religious groups. The Methodists grew not by exploiting directly the collapse of traditional authority but because of it, speaking in particular to those on the margins of society, "whose voices had not been heard before—the illiterate, the lowly, and the dependent."[78] This new popular faith appealed to women, "the movement's primary community builders," according to Methodist historian John Wigger, and African Americans.[79] Methodism helped give shape to a democratic mood that has often created a significant amount of anxiety among an established elite. Much of Methodism's "astounding success," Wigger writes, "could be traced to the way in which American Methodists took advantage of the revolutionary religious freedoms of the early republic, and in a sense institutionalized, elements of popular religious enthusiasm long latent in American and European Protestantism."[80] Indeed, the Methodists became the primary drivers in creating an American religious culture "dominated by the interests and aspirations of ordinary people."[81] Republicans found that the pure or simple faith of the Methodists aligned nicely with the spirit of revolutionary republicanism. Even Thomas Jefferson himself admitted this: "the Christian religion when divested of the rags in which they [traditional clergy] have enveloped it, and brought to the original purity and simplicity of its benevolent institor, is a religion of all others most friendly to liberty, science, and the freest expression of the human mind."[82]

Part of the success of creating a democratized evangelicalism embodied in Methodism was its appeal to a primitive Christianity, a faith untainted by tradition. The religious slate had been wiped clean, so to speak, by the Revolution. The emerging republican mood united with continental pietism, a "transatlantic and transconfessional" strand of faith that sought "to recover the authentic (and personal) witness of the faith": "The resources that Pietism offered—new identity, community voluntarily created, a competitive missionary spirit, courage to persist despite society's disdain, outreach to the poor and marginalized, willingness to forge new alliances—proved highly functional in community-formation in the new American environment."[83] Methodism became a faith for the spiritually neglected (but now empowered in a new age), organized by preachers not ultimately bound by cultural convention or social deference but by their own voluntary commitments to the simple truths of the gospel. This was potentially empowering for some but threatening to others, especially among the established religious elite. Methodism created a unique American evangelicalism—individual, intensely emotional, and experiential—a radical faith that was much more "enthusiastic, individualistic, egalitarian, entrepreneurial, and lay oriented."[84] American Methodism aligned with the social, economic, and political consequences of the Revolution, helping in the profound transition from—as Edmund Morgan argued, reflecting on Wood's *Radicalism of the American Revolution*—"a world where people knew their place, to a world where they made their place."[85] Methodism, writes Wigger, appealed to "people on the make."[86] The legitimacy of American Methodism depended on the voluntary commitments of the faithful who courageously accepted their new social and political context to create something new. Something new, of course, was created by appealing to the old, by exploiting the "sense of boundless possibility," in the words of Robert Darlton, created by the revolutionary era that "ordinary people can make history instead of suffering it."[87] Created from the bottom up by family communities but also "families without established 'heads,' without formal structure, with little literature other than the Bible, with little purpose beyond themselves, connected to no larger ecclesial authorities, lacking clarity about norms, ritual, beliefs, and practices," Methodism was a radical faith; it fit a revolutionary context and appealed to people without Old World status, a people with only a future.

But the challenge came in how exactly to create that future people, a virtuous, moral, and religiously stable yet vigilant citizenry. Bourne's *Life of the Rev. John Wesley,* published a year after his biography of Napoleon's young life and early military career (1807), focused not so much on the conditions that would allow for the freedom of religion, but rather on the importance of protecting true faith. Bourne articulates at the outset of the biography his fascination with John Wesley and a considerable optimism that America and American Methodism were part of a larger divine story. Bourne reconciled Methodist beliefs with the young nation's dynamic political culture. For instance, the success of society rested on the separation of church and state.[88] In his mind, no other religious sect, other than the Baptists, demonstrated this better than the Methodists. At the time of the publication of Bourne's Wesley biography, the Congregationalists were the last tax-based established denomination in the country. The American Revolution, Bourne argued, allowed Americans to be "totally disentangled both from the state, and from the English hierarchy," which, in turn, allowed Protestantism, Methodism in particular, "full liberty simply to follow the scriptures and the primitive church." This is a view of Methodism that has continued to be held by contemporary scholars. Methodist historian Dee Andrews notes that Wesleyan Methodism "arose in a period of substantial change in British and American religion, beginning with the redefinition of the relationship between church and state at the end of the seventeenth century."[89] The church became an institution of free voluntary association, separate from the civil realm, providing "theoretical justification for toleration and the moral foundations of denominationalism."[90] This does not mean that Bourne separated religion completely from politics; rather, he was speaking in terms of institutional freedom, freedom from the encroachments of the state. Some time before his death, Bourne wrote that politics should not "be placed beyond the control of our piety." Rather than making religion political, he said, "one should make his politics religious."[91]

The central means for creating a virtuous public was for individuals to emulate the lives and work of those who were the protectors of pure religious and republican principles. A religious biography, which according to Casper had "no static or unanimously shared definition" in early America, was a prime "vehicle for encouraging conversion or offering examples of active Christian engagement in the world."[92] If biography was the most important course for self-knowledge, then the biographies that included "the government of Jehovah in connection with the disciples of the Prince of Peace," Bourne later wrote, "must be the most instructive and important."[93] The "variegated hues" of human character, he continued, are "more advantageously and precisely ascertained in the records of the Christian Church."[94] Bourne wanted to focus the attention of his readers on what he called the "stars of the first magnitude who have successively shone in the Christian constellations."[95] The intent was to present to his readers those extraordinary lights to guide those in a new age. Bourne believed that his biography on Wesley would "expand the hearts of all those who may study it," and reading about the "brilliancy" of Wesley's character would "stimulate" the reader to follow Wesley "as he followed Christ."[96] Bourne felt, in his words, "a peculiar interest" in the portrait of Wesley, "whose piety 'like a city set upon a hill,' could not be hid." Wesley was "so luminous" in his example for others to live by and to glorify "the Father who is in heaven." Wesley's "perseverance and efforts" in surmounting "every difficulty to propagate that heavenly doctrine" led to the conversion of "numberless sinners . . . from darkness to light."[97] Bourne wanted his readers to appreciate "the general tenour [*sic*] of [Wesley's] conduct; that fixed principle which uniformly operates upon him, that forms his character."[98] Bourne writes that Wesley had a "strong and capacious mind," and he writes about Wesley's reputation of being "an acute and sensible collegian" while studying at Oxford. He was pious, placable (i.e., the "facility in forgiving injuries"), industrious, a good thinker and writer, and ambitious. "[If] the greatest benefactors to mankind be the most estimable," Bourne concluded, "Mr. Wesley will long be remembered as one of the best, most diligent and most indefatigable [of] men."[99]

Bourne offers a detailed chronology of the events in Wesley's life: his birth in 1703, the fire that nearly took his life as a young child, his early religious training by his pious parents, his studies at Oxford, his participation in and the controversies surrounding the "Holy Club" he helped create, the challenges he faced on his mission to the British colony of Georgia in North America, and his interaction with the Moravians. What Bourne emphasizes in particular throughout the biography are the significant moments in Wesley's spiritual development. (Remember, Bourne wanted his readers to model their own lives after this great figure. Doing so would bring readers closer to the realities of their own sanctification.)

The first critical experience came by way of Wesley's faithfully religious parents, Samuel and Susannah, both of whom trained and supported him in his spiritual growth and offered the "first rudiments of knowledge." His tutelage in doctrines of the faith continued during his time at Oxford, particularly when he read Martin Luther's exposition of Galatians 2, where Wesley came to an understanding of the power of "faith alone—not an idle dead faith, but a faith which works by love, and is incessantly productive of all good works and all holiness."[100] The doctrine of justification by "faith alone," a topic Bourne returned to throughout the biography, remained with Wesley throughout his ministry. The doctrine of justification was the second most important aspect of Wesley's spiritual journey emphasized in Bourne's biography. After Wesley's conversion, which came late in his ministry, according to Bourne Wesley "hungered and thirsted more and more after the righteousness that is of God by faith. He saw the promise of justification and life as the free gift of God through Jesus Christ."[101] The knowledge of salvation by faith became Wesley's "assurance." When he went out to preach, Wesley "boldly declared, *by grace ye are saved through faith.*"[102] Wesleyan theology, Bourne and his more Reformed companions believed, leaned more toward the active agency of individual sinners not only to come to the faith but also to maintain it, a position that moved Methodism further away from a stricter Calvinistic view. Wesley defined faith as something a "supernatural evidence of things not seen; of past, future, or spiritual things: it is a spiritual sight of God and the things of God. A sinner is first convinced by the Holy Ghost, that Christ loved me and gave himself for me—This is that faith by which he is justified or pardoned, the moment he received it. Immediately the same spirit bears witness, thou are pardoned: thou hast redemption in his blood."[103] Yet at the same time, true faith is "cast away" when a "believer willfully sin[s]."[104]

The third critical point in Wesley's spiritual life was his study of piety. A gifted "collegiate" who "excelled at every branch of literature," Wesley had been moved by reading the works of Thomas à Kempis and Jeremy Taylor's *Rule for Holy Living and Dying;* both books revealed to Wesley, according to Bourne, the basic notion that religion "operates on the heart."[105] After such a revelation, Wesley began keeping a journal, which allowed him to remain, Geordan Hammond writes, "accountable in disciplined living and as a means to measure his spiritual growth."[106] This led him to intensify his piety and help with the maintenance of a piety club at Oxford, created in part to "consult on the most advantageous methods" of employing true Christian piety.

Finally, what is arguably the most important experience that, as even Wesley admits, led to his full conversion was his observations and interactions with the simple piety of the German Moravians. Wesley had been invited to the colony of Georgia to minister to those literally outside the British Empire. In observing the "great simplicity" and "solemnity of the whole," Wesley writes that the Moravians demonstrated "the spirit of truth and power." They "walked worthy of the vocation wherewith they were called, and adorned the Gospel of our Lord in all things."[107] On one of his journeys home from Georgia, Wesley observed the fixed moral character of this pietist sect, and not too long after engaged in "a close and severe examination of himself."[108] Wesley was able to distinguish between his advanced book learning, the conventions of liturgy, and the hierarchy of the clergy to engage in a deeply inward look at his own heart.

For Bourne, great events—like the Reformation, the European discovery of America, and the French Revolution—created extraordinary individuals. The events that produce such figures included persecution. Conflict is what shapes the principled, courageous, and confident individual. Trials of whatever kind were precisely what the individual needed to shape his or her character. And the character of those who observed the lives of these figures would also be transformed; hence the critical importance of biography. Persecution, individual sanctification, and the growth of the church, for instance, were two sides of the same coin, mutually constituting one another. The death of the martyrs, for Bourne and many other Protestants, was the "seed bed" of the church. What protected pure and undefiled religion was the numerous historical figures who illuminated the truth and faced all forms and degrees of persecutions. Indeed, the church would not remain strong or faithful to the truth of the gospel without trials. Bourne wrote in his 1823 *Lectures on the Progress and Perfection of the Church* that "when persecution ceased, the spirituality of the Christian was lost in a worldly temper."[109] Trials play an important role in advancing divine truth, but they helped to shape character.

Wesley, Bourne noted, was emboldened by persecution, to one degree or another. His method of open-air preaching was condemned by authorities in places like Epworth, Birmingham, Oxford, London, and St. Ives, to name a few. He likewise faced hostility, Bourne writes, from the "dissenters" in Georgia, those who "possessed unbounded liberality of sentiment."[110] Despite the considerable social, ethnic, and environmental challenges, as Hammond argues in *John Wesley in America,* Wesley's mission to Georgia, viewed by the majority of Wesley's biographers as a failure, was a "laboratory for implementing his views of primitive Christianity."[111] Wesley had also been disparaged for his participation in the holy club at Oxford. Despite the many leaders and students who scoffed at such a "*Godly Club,*" each member "observed the fasts of the ancient church, communicated weekly, and became more strictly attentive to the duties of religion, until their conduct was censured in the university."[112] Efforts by the religious elites, including the Bishop of Oxford, were employed to sanction their pious proceedings. Both John and Charles Wesley, however, were encouraged by their father to "Stand thou fast" in the midst of such opposition. Those who opposed him, whether the established theologians in Oxford, governing authorities in the towns at which he preached, or his hearers, "stimulated his courage, and inflamed his zeal."[113] Such aspersions seemed to embolden Wesley's commitment to piety. Bourne seemed to be an individual attracted to those in history persecuted for their faith or for applying their principles unapologetically. It is certainly possible that Bourne understood his persecution in the Presbyterian Church in such a light, which in turn strengthened his religious commitments, including his unwavering opposition to slavery. Bourne himself wanted to emulate this great Protestant figure, who with "all the spirit and labor of Luther, and with apostolic gravity and energy persisted in his career, inattentive to contempt or applause, and alike careless both of popularity and persecution."[114]

As an "imagined" concept, "nationhood" is a reality produced discursively by material and ideological forces.[115] The creation of a system of government, finally distilled in the Constitution, was not the only means by which a sense of a unified nation was formed. Social and political activism, the challenge of creating a strong economy, and cultural performances, including commemorative celebrations of events or of people, in the Early Republic played a critical role in giving shape to a collective national self.[116] Nationhood is not a simplistic teleological development from a kind of intrinsic *volkgeist*. Instead, its creation comes from multiple, discursive directions that depend more so on compromise and competition. "Nation-building," writes Ziesche, "is itself a political program based on comparisons and distinctions . . . if we shift attention from the locus of innovation to the process of imitation, we find that nationalists have always constructed their national communities by implicit and explicit comparison with other nations."[117] A nation is built through claims of legitimacy; that is, who can claim the title of citizen. Indeed, the universal language embodied in the country's founding document, the Declaration of Independence, made it nearly impossible to trace restrictive boundaries around those who had the right to life, liberty, and the pursuit of happiness. "American of all kinds," Eustace and Teute argue, "fought for country on the battleground of belonging": "Many articulations of national character in the first decades of the nineteenth century came out of contests over choices, opportunities, and self-definition among different segments of the domestic population."[118]

Nations, for Bourne, required heroes, dynamic figures formed in tandem with the nation itself. Biographer Paul Johnson defines a hero as one "who has been widely, persistently over long periods, and enthusiastically regarded as heroic by a reasonable person, or even an unreasonable one." As the cliché goes, heroes are made, not born; that is, they are contingent realities. Napoleon was the creation of an emerging French Revolution; Wesley was born not so much out of an established religious tradition but as an individual concerned for the regaining of a primitive faith. Legitimizing a nation or, as in the case of Wesley, a religious organization includes a recognition of key "founders," who are often a mixture of artifact and artifice. Bourne's biographies do not provide a philosophical concept of a hero or that of a great figure (the *great* is taken for granted), though he believed strongly in how important events create such individuals. He nonetheless believed that an emergent nation demanded that members of society study important historical figures who understood the importance of living an exemplary life for the purposes of preserving the conditions created by revolution. Napoleon Bonaparte and John Wesley were not only representatives of those radicals who sought to protect the freedom of conscience, the press, religious expression, an educated citizenry, and a republican form of government, but also those who courageously attempted to make such ideals a reality. Heroes like Bonaparte and Wesley were necessary icons for members of society to mimic in the process of their own emergence as "citizens."

These early works of Bourne speak to the fascination with biography in nineteenth-century America. They also show the development of Bourne's own activism, which is why they are included in this intellectual biography. Bourne's appreciation for how heroic figures sought to apply republicanism and a pure religion in an effort to shape a robust notion of liberty—in this case a unique American liberty—was the most consistent thread that shaped his mind and activism. Heroism, republicanism, and true faith were central to his battle not only against slavery and Catholicism but against the corrupt leaders that supported such institutions. An individual committed to a certain cause was in part justified, he believed, not only by the soundness of that individual's polemics but by the great cloud of heroic historical figures that motivated those who sought to change the world. He would later find himself as such a figure: a lone individual who stood by his principles in the face of great opposition, a reformer (but also a republican) in a young nation.

But given the reality of what Bourne was known for (viz., immediate emancipation and anti-Catholicism) among not only his contemporaries but also contemporary historians, I must briefly note the absence in the biographies not so much of anti-Catholicism, which he turned to in earnest by the 1820s, but of slavery. A direct answer to such lacuna is that his hostility toward human chattel bondage had not taken an irrevocable hold on his heart during his time in Baltimore. He was not, in an explicit manner, the pioneering immediatist that nineteenth-century reformers would come to see him as. Bourne's first major biography, written by his son Theodore in 1882, mentions that his father began his initial engagement with slavery while in England, maintaining consistent correspondence with the likes of Thomas Clarkson and William Wilberforce. Yet it is difficult to affirm Theodore's claim given the absence of extant evidence. We have nothing but Theodore's testimony on this point. This was noted by Bourne's later biographers John Christie and Dwight Dumond in 1969, both of whom called Theodore's biography "demonstrably inaccurate."[119] While I think such a description of Theodore's entire biography of his father is a bit hyperbolic, I tend to agree with Christie and Dumond on the timing of Bourne's turn to antislavery. Nothing in Bourne's early works, including the biographies, suggests that he opposed slavery prior to 1812, around the time he began writing *The Book and Slavery Irreconcilable.* No mention is made of Napoleon's freeing nearly two thousand slaves in Malta in 1798, a few years after the National Convention outlawed slavery, on his way to Egypt. (Of course, Napoleon said and did nothing about slavery in Egypt.) Likewise, Bourne is silent on Napoleon's reinstatement of slavery and the slave trade (though he abolished the slave trade after his Elba exile) in Martinique and other West Indies colonies in 1802. He is also conspicuously silent on Napoleon's racist claim that blacks were inherently incapable of governing themselves in accordance with the revolutionary ideals of liberty. The only mention of slavery in the Napoleon biography is a reference to social and political slavery of the Old Regime in France and that the French Revolution had brought liberty to the captives, French citizens. In other words, Bourne's understanding of slavery did not include race or Africans.

The absence of a discussion on slavery in Bourne's *Life of Wesley* is even more troubling. The only statement on the issue in the nearly three-hundred-page biography is this: "[Wesley] wrote a very great number of pamphlets on various subjects: among the rest, one entitled 'Thoughts on Slavery.' He was one of the earliest writers on this subject, and has treated it, in a moral and religious view; but with great spirit and impartiality."[120] This tells us nothing, however, about

Bourne's attitude toward slavery as an institution or certainly as a theological problem. Over a decade and a half later, Bourne, along with Charles Denison and William Lloyd Garrison, was commissioned to compile sources on the official declarations on slavery made by the leaders of both the Presbyterian and Methodist denominations for the purposes of indicting the two denominations for perpetuating the institution. They were also commissioned to publish (with commentary) excerpts from Wesley's "Thoughts on Slavery." Bourne was an obvious choice for the assignment, given his knowledge of the history of both denominations, including specifically his experience as a Presbyterian and his biography of the founder of Methodism. Drawing on his insights on Wesley, American Methodism, and Presbyterianism, Bourne did the majority of the writing and commentary in what eventually became *Picture of Slavery in the United States of America,* published in 1834. Throughout *Picture,* Wesley's opinions on slavery align with Bourne's. "Manstealers!" Bourne quoted Wesley. "The worst of all thieves; in comparison of whom, highway robbers and house-breakers are innocent! What then are traders in negroes, and procurers of servants for America."[121]

Given the source challenges related to Bourne's life, historians can only speculate over the timing of his turn to immediatism. From what is obvious (the lack of any statement on slavery), we could conclude that slavery or Catholicism were not important enough issues for Bourne to address at the time. Christie and Dumond speculate that "a partial source" of Bourne's radical conversion came from his acting upon the capacious reading he had done in Baltimore importing and selling "British publications." "The content of those books and magazines," the authors write, "kept him in continuous touch with the progress of the British and antislavery movement."[122] This is certainly plausible. Bourne could have read quite a bit on the issue but may not have been convinced at the time or even ready to launch an assault against the institution. Indeed, *Book and Slavery* draws on what those in England like Thomas Clarkson and William Wilberforce said about slavery. What is more, his work on the biographies may have temporarily suspended the development of his thoughts on the subject. But the historical connection made by Christie and Dumond between the content of *Book and Slavery* and when, prior the book's publication, Bourne became convinced of immediacy is considerably weak.

What is beyond doubt, however, is that a few years after the publication of his Wesley biography, Bourne became known for his uncompromising hostility toward slavery. The public revelation of his position against slavery began sometime before he moved to Virginia to begin a printing partnership with Andrew B. Davidson. Bourne could no longer be silent on what he saw of the institution firsthand. He seemed to have reached a breaking point. Anyone living in the South, especially recent migrants like Bourne, according to Christie and Dumond, "might defend [slavery] or learn to live within the framework of its restraints, but not ignore it."[123] Indeed, his transition from Baltimore to Virginia *was* a concurrent turn to immediate antislavery. But in terms of understanding the developments of antislavery radicalism, the precise time in which Bourne came to adopt a hostility toward the institution is not as important as the focused reaction against him. It was the opposition that Bourne faced for his views that helped steer the course of immediacy. As I show in the next chapter, the condemnation of Bourne coincided with and was essential to efforts to prevent the voices of immediacy from gaining the high ground in the debates over slavery. Silencing this early voice of immediacy, however, had the reverse effect of motivating an entire generation of radical abolitionists.

CHAPTER 2

THE CHURCH, IMMEDIACY, AND THE TRIALS OF BOURNE

Is he a Christian, then, who holds in bonds his brethren?

—GEORGE BOURNE, *Picture of Slavery in the United States of America*

The absence of any discussion of slavery in Bourne's earliest works can be frustrating for the modern historian. From Bourne's own writings before 1816, one might conclude that slavery and Catholicism were not important-enough issues for him to address at the time. But when he and his family settled in Virginia, just a few years after the Wesley biography, Bourne was firmly committed to the cause of immediate emancipation. Perhaps he had been spending time quietly mulling over the issue, given the sensitive nature of it even in the early decades of the nineteenth century, before committing his thoughts to pen. He certainly felt anxious about making his thoughts public. In an 1815 letter to Andrew B. Davidson, Bourne wrote, "I have a volume nearly ready for the press, which I expect will satisfy every man who wishes to know the truth of the impracticability of reconciling Slavery and the Gospel; but which I suppose I scarcely dare publish."[1] Overcoming his trepidation, Bourne published *The Book and Slavery Irreconcilable* in 1816, a work that historian David Brion Davis has referred to as "the most radical abolitionist tract yet to appear in America."[2] Bourne's conversion, represented indubitably in this his most famous work, was not only an important moment in the transformation of his own identity, but also played a role in pushing the movement to end chattel bondage toward its more radical phase.

This chapter focuses on a crucial step taken by the ecclesiastically and politically influential Presbyterian Church in the first decade of the nineteenth century in addressing the problem of slavery and that of the emancipated slave. Presbyterian leaders pushed their church to accept colonization and the American Colonization Society as the best means to deal with the issues of slavery and emancipation. Such efforts, supporters of colonization believed, were hampered by Bourne's opposition, especially his *Book and Slavery.* Few wanted to deal with slavery through what was believed to be the more radical and destructive means proposed by reformers like Bourne. Convincing members of the denomination to support colonization required the removal from among its leadership the antislavery clamoring of this English transplant. By working to remove those who supposedly threatened national stability or impeded the goals of moderate antislavery, represented particularly in the colonization movement, Presbyterian leaders, according to Bourne, conscientiously nullified "their own avowed creed, their own infallible doctrines, and . . . constitution of their church, expressly that they might propitiate the southern men-stealers."[3]

Opposition to Bourne and to *The Book and Slavery Irreconcilable,* which did not spring from a fear of northern aggression, not only deepened the denomination's wariness of immediacy but also coincided with efforts to popularize the removal of blacks from the American republic. In this way, Bourne believed, the church had abdicated its responsibility to God and the world. According to Christie and Dumond, the idea that the South's defense of slavery came as a response to northern abolitionist aggression "is a monstrous fiction," an ideological pretext that covered the interests of the slaveowning class.[4] The proslavery contingency had been gaining ground against antislavery for much of the Early Republican period. A handful of early abolitionists like David Barrow, George Smith, James Gilliland, Samuel Doak, John Rankin, Levi Coffin, and Gideon Blackburn had been forced to move to other parts of the country in the late eighteenth and early nineteenth centuries, which strengthened the proslavery position in the United States.[5] Relentless in his opposition to slavery, Bourne was among this cohort of early antislavery advocates. His "attack upon slavery was bold," according to Dumond: "Some would say that it was extreme, but no one knew better than he the relentless fashion in which the slave power was silencing its critics, and he retaliated in kind."[6]

The battle against slavery was well underway years before Bourne and his family left England to take up residency in the young American republic. Upon his first visit to New York in 1802, nearly every northern state had enacted gradual emancipation bills, but complete freedom for northern slaves would not come for quite some time. Certain religious organizations had a hand in the fight from the beginning. The earliest antislavery activism from a religious community came from the Quakers. The efforts of Quaker leaders such as Benjamin Lay, John Woolman, and Anthony Benezet laid the groundwork for transatlantic abolitionism and a condemnation of both the slave trade and slavery at the annual Quaker meeting in Philadelphia in 1758. Other radical religious groups—including Freewill Baptists, Covenanters (Scottish Reformed Presbyterians), and the Associate Reformed—continued to put pressure on those unwilling to act directly against slavery.[7] Unfortunately, however, most of the major denominations in America, writes John McKivigan, "had come to terms with slavery by the 1830s."[8]

By the time of the American Revolution, movements toward greater freedom, drawing on the implications of the Revolution itself, were certainly being made. Some like James Dane in 1790 expressed confidence in the type of radicalism gained from the colonists' war against Britain: "Our late warfare was expressly founded on such principles as these: 'All men are created equal: They are endowed by their Creator with certain unalienable rights; among these are life, liberty, and the pursuit of happiness.' Admitting these just principles, we need not puzzle ourselves with the question, whether a black complexion is a token of God's wrath."[9] But the battle against slavery could not be achieved by the force of rhetoric alone. Indeed, early antislavery activists faced what seemed to be an insurmountable challenge of overcoming the momentum that would lead to greater support for the institution in a revolutionary age. Many became convinced that slavery could be preserved in a liberty-loving republic, highlighting, among other things, not only the socializing benefits of slavery but also the much more dangerous bloodbath between the races that would inevitably come if immediate emancipation won the day. While the existence of slavery, according to those of Bourne's ilk, conflicted with the social and ideological gains of the American Revolution, emancipation took an unnecessarily long time in coming. Indeed, the political, economic, and social consequences of the Revolution, "ambiguous in the extreme" according to James Brewer Stewart, "would prove serviceable to all participants" in the debates over slavery.[10] Politically charged rhetoric is consistently found on opposite ends of a controversial issues. Gradualism was tantamount to protecting slavery.

A handful of other factors were involved in maintaining—and thus strengthening—slavery in the decades after the Revolution. Governing elites, especially those at the Constitutional Convention, quickly helped to secure the future growth of slavery. National union was central to the Philadelphia delegates in the summer of 1787. Regardless of the feelings toward slavery, northern and southern delegates came to the realization that a strong central government was impossible without making peace with human chattel bondage. The approval of items like the 3/5ths compromise, the 1808 slave trade clause, and Article IV's fugitive slave clause did not at all leave slavery to itself (or to its own demise), but rather accelerated its expansion. Such acts by the framers provided an adrenaline boost to the power of the planter class, a power needed to protect slavery and one that continued well into the antebellum period. By the time Bourne settled down in Baltimore, sectional lines had already been drawn.

A growing uneasiness over the existence of slavery ran apace with the growth of the institution itself. Such uneasiness, ironically, served to strengthen slavery in the years after America's second war against England.[11] When Bourne became a minister in the Presbyterian Church and around the time of the publication of his *Book and Slavery,* the young republic was still aglow with a celebratory nationalism after its conflict with Britain in the War of 1812. The war "marked a new search for identity on the part of the American population as a whole," writes David Brion Davis.[12] An important part of the anxiety in entering a new evolutionary phase of America's national identity had to do with the challenge of not only slavery but also race. White Americans' anxiety over involuntary servitude in an ideally free republic was outweighed by a growing hostility toward immediate emancipation. The postwar "Era of Good Feelings," accompanied by the mollifying of political partisanship at the federal level as well as the coming of a market revolution, would, many believed, transform America's economic, political, and cultural identity and stimulate a nationalistic spirit that would heal a divided nation. A "public renunciation of partisanship," David Waldsreicher has observed, was the order of the day.[13] Attaining this idealistic nationalism depended on the avoidance of a mixed-race citizenry, which consequently demanded the exclusion of others, leading to a period of "bad feelings" for many.[14] Indeed, the republic witnessed a rise in racism after the war. Two groups in particular stood in the way of a distinctly Euro-American nationalism. The conflicts with the Indians in the Great Lakes region, which reached its peak during the War of 1812, strained relationships between Euro-American whites and Native Americans, making it difficult for the two to cohabitate. By the 1830s and by coordinated political actions at both the state and federal level, notwithstanding the ultimately effete opinions of the Supreme Court, southern Indians were literally removed from any association with an American identity. Likewise, whites, zealous to contain the political ramifications of liberty while protecting the economic expansion of slavery, saw African Americans as an obstacle to this rejuvenated patriotism.

The anxieties over a mixed-raced society were often made worse by accounts of slave revolts. When such accounts circulated, Americans faced a dilemma: either free the slaves, since slavery, many thought, was the cause of such revolts, or intensify the terror of the institution to dissuade those who would participate in such uprisings. In the wake of the Haitian Revolution, the Gabriel Prosser conspiracy, and the German Coast Uprising, many whites feared the real possibility of more insurrections. These could be caused by protecting slavery through terror, which did in fact occur, or by manumissions that would increase the presence of free blacks in the republic. A free black population opened up the thornier issue of not only the socioeconomic status of all blacks but also the permissible inclusion of "blackness" into American identity. Whichever course national leaders traveled, the specter of a race war, which many feared, forced Americans to discuss the future of slavery. Seeing the freeing of slaves as a greater danger, national leaders, with the support of those in the religious sector, actively withheld the blessing of liberty from free blacks and slaves and silenced those who called for an instant end to the peculiar institution, since such a call would have brought greater disaster upon society then if African Americans remained in chains. This was the tumultuous political climate that Bourne entered when he migrated to the United States. Bourne's participation in such hotly debated issues intensified when he became a minister in the Presbyterian Church.

Leading statesmen, including the author of independence, Thomas Jefferson, advanced the scientific racist theory that blacks by nature were "inferior to the whites in the endowments of both body and mind" and that their hostilities toward whites for the violence of slavery would inevitably end in a race war if universal emancipation became a reality: "ten thousand recollections, by the blacks, of the injuries they have sustained . . . will produce convulsions which will probably never end but in the extermination of the one of the other race."[15] Many also seemed to agree with James Madison that deep-seated racial prejudice precluded "a compleat [*sic*] incorporation" of ex-slaves and free blacks into American society. Such a racial apocalypse, coming as a result of emancipation, would be a detriment to the country. Elias Caldwell, one of the founders of the

American Society for the Colonization of Free People of Color in the United States, "considered impossible" the "enjoyment of 'inalienable rights'" between whites and blacks.[16] One benevolent alternative was, in the words of yet another major proponent of colonization, Ferdinando Fairfax, "distance from this [American] country."[17] A number of state legislatures, including Bourne's Virginia at the turn of the nineteenth century, sought "to get rid of the free negroes, who were considered as not only useless members of society, but as exercising a very pernicious influence on the character of the slaves."[18] Colonization seemed to be the best means to deal with the problem of slavery, for it would not only lead to the gradual end of the peculiar institution, but it would also stave off what some feared would be the inevitable bloodshed brought by immediate emancipation.

Contemporary historians have argued quite convincingly that the push toward colonization gave rise to immediate abolitionism. To say it differently, unconditional emancipation was born out of a hatred of colonization. Yet it is unclear as to whether such a causal explanation can be easily applied to Bourne. Bourne was aware of the racism behind discussions of slavery, emancipation, and citizenship, but he did not write about its complexity at any great length. Examining his early writings on slavery, one should note that Bourne opposed colonization from the beginning, but the historical record is unclear as to the exact moment he became convinced of immediate abolition. His son Theodore suggested that his father's radical antislavery surfaced while a student at Homerton College. It would be hard to deny that Bourne was ignorant of the hotly debated issues of slavery in both England and the United States. By the time of Bourne's birth in 1780, the battle against the slave trade and slavery in England and its empire had been well underway. Indeed, the movement was taking on its international character as contemporary historians have now recast it. As Manisha Sinha has recently written, "The long British campaign against the slave trade gave birth to transnational abolitionism."[19] Converted slave trader John Newton published "Amazing Grace" the year before Bourne's birth. Early English abolitionists, especially among the Quakers, founded anti-slave-trade and antislavery societies, wrote pamphlets, and petitioned Parliament already in the late eighteenth century. James Ramsey published *Essay on the Treatment and Conversion of African Slaves in the British Sugar Colonies* (1784) and *An Enquiry into the Effects of Putting a Stop to the African Slave Trade* (1784), both of which spent much of their pages providing gruesome eyewitness accounts of the brutalities of slavery, as did Alexander Falconbridge in his *Account of the Slave Trade on the Coast of Africa* (1788). And it had been only a few years since William Wilberforce's successful campaign to end the British slave trade that Bourne journeyed to the United States. Thus it is hard to believe that Bourne would have been distant from one of the most hotly debated issues of his day. But what should interest the historian is the impact of Bourne's conversion to immediacy.[20]

As mentioned above, John Christie and Dwight Dumond, in their 1969 biography, express skepticism that Bourne turned to immediate abolition during his time in England, for there is nothing in his writings that would suggest this. When relocating to the United States in 1804–05, the Bourne family settled down in Baltimore, the fourth largest city in the nation at the time. Baltimore was a kind of overlapping middle ground between the worlds of northern freedom and southern slavery, and it quickly became a destination for runaway slaves and a sizable place for free black settlement.[21] Unfortunately, the antislavery presence in Baltimore was in slow decline, eventually by the 1820s sealed off from having any greater influence. The Protection Society of Maryland, founded at the time of Bourne's initial trial, existed to confront the morality of the slave trade, kidnapping, and human trafficking. The society reported that it had "rescued more than sixty human beings from the grasp of lawless oppression, and restored a number of legal slaves to their proper masters."[22] One of the main goals of the society was to protect free blacks from being kidnapped and resold into slavery. A number of forces, including a major economic panic in 1819, kept the society from flourishing, again showing the difficulty of increasing efforts to hold back the growth of proslavery power. During Bourne's final trial and with the strong support of the state's former congressman Robert Goodloe Harper, Maryland's legislature fully endorsed colonization. For Harper, utilizing the familiar justification in a letter to American Colonization Society secretary Elias Caldwell, colonization had the greatest benefits for whites, for it would rid the American population of the "idle and useless, and too often vicious and mischievous." Black citizenry was unthinkable, in Harper's mind, since "good conduct . . . is a stranger to his breast."[23] Despite the indefatigable yet brief lightning bolt of Benjamin Lundy's more aggressive *Genius of Universal Emancipation,* which gave a much-needed professional boost to a young William Lloyd Garrison, the forces of the more militant branch of the abolitionist movement had left Maryland by 1830.

Christie and Dumond make a plausible case that Bourne's opposition to slavery came during his time in Baltimore, where he began reading the antislavery works of John Woolman, Anthony Benezet, Thomas Clarkson, David Rice, Samuel Hopkins, Benjamin Rush, George Mason, James Wilson, and Thomas Branagan. He also studied Thomas Scott's "strongly antislavery" *Commentary on the Bible* (1806).[24] Bourne had revealed to Davidson that while in Baltimore he at one time utilized the labor of a slave but, around the same time, quickly repented of such sin and encouraged Davidson to do the same: "That I did wrong in *hiring* a slave I *contritely* admit. I have repented; I have *made restitution;* and now I endeavor to counteract the influence of my former example. 'Go and do likewise.'"[25] Christie and Dumond pinpoint Bourne's adoption of abolitionism around 1809–10. This is corroborated by Theodore Dwight Weld's *American Slavery As It Is,* where abolitionist John Nelson of Ohio testified that during those precise years (1809–10) he "became a student of Rev. George Bourne." Bourne, Nelson continued, "was the first abolitionist I had ever seen, and the first I had ever heard pray or plead for the oppressed, which gave me the first misgivings about the *innocence* of slaveholding."[26]

Regardless of the exact moment of his turn to immediatism, the presence of abolitionism in Baltimore, and the full-steam development of the slave economy in the South, Bourne's entrenched opposition to involuntary servitude and moderate reform crystallized when he left Baltimore to become a minister in the Virginia branch of the Presbyterian Church. In fact, he and Davidson eventually had a falling out over the issue of slavery. The latter did not approve of the developing immediatism of the former. Bourne and his family moved to Virginia at a time when abolitionism, as it had been in Baltimore, became increasingly unwelcome. The fear generated from the Haitian Revolution intensified the opposition to manumissions. Most critics of slavery, including those who did not attack the system directly, were forced to remove themselves from the area. Not only did supporters of immediate emancipation face opposition from specific individuals and groups, they also faced suffocating legislative restrictions that helped to strengthen the institution. Virginia's revised 1806 manumission law severely hampered any effort toward emancipation, legislating a strict time for how long manumitted slaves could stay in the state. And by 1832, a year after Nat Turner's revolt, which intensified the opposition to abolition among most citizens, the Virginia legislature placed a gag order on any discussions on emancipation.[27]

As mentioned in the previous chapter, Bourne was a traditionalist, a conservative moved by the doctrines of the Reformation. The approved doctrinal standards of Protestantism, coming from the Reformed Presbyterian and continental traditions, shaped his radicalism. Part of the requirement for ministerial candidacy in the Presbyterian Church was the adoption of the Westminster Confession of Faith (WCF), a seventeenth-century summary of Calvinistic biblical theology, and its Larger and Shorter Catechisms. The church in North America adopted the entire confession in 1792. Two years later, a committee of presbyters, which included Ashbel Green and William Tennant, annexed the biblical proofs to the WCF, the Catechism, and the Directory for Public Worship, which were subsequently published and distributed to each congregation.[28] Members submitted to its authority, and each prospective minister had to have an adequate knowledge of it for ordination. The American Presbyterian Church was thus "cemented by a compact."[29] The WCF comprised, according to theologian, gradual abolitionist, and president of Princeton Theological Seminary Samuel Stanhope Smith, "the most complete development of the entire system of our holy religion."[30] After his examination in theology, ecclesiology, and homiletics by the Lexington Presbytery, Bourne was sustained, licensed to preach, and called to the small South River Church at Port Republic, Virginia, in 1812. His ministerial duties put him in contact with a number of southern Presbyterian leaders. He was elected by his local presbytery in 1813 and 1814 to be a commissioner to the General Assembly, a gathering of ministers that met annually to discuss the well-being of the national church, he preached at Conrad Speece's installation service, and he was elected clerk of the presbytery. Bourne was primed for a successful career as a Presbyterian minister. Yet the denomination, through its leadership, specifically what leaders were confessionally bound to, was in need of considerable reform. Slavery had corrupted the church; Bourne was poised, then, to initiate a new Reformation.

Question 142 of the WCF's Larger Catechism—"What are the sins forbidden in the eighth commandment?"—played a definitive role in Bourne's turn to radicalism.[31] He knew the confession well, and 142, part of a series of questions related to the requirements of the Ten Commandments, troubled him. The eighth commandment condemned, as exposited by the catechism, "theft, robbery, *man-stealing,* and receiving anything that is stolen . . . and all other unjust or sinful ways of taking or withholding from our neighbors what belongs to him, or enriching ourselves." The supporting scriptural proof the General

Assembly adopted in the late eighteenth century, 1 Timothy 1:10, stated that God's law was made for "man-stealers." The synods of Philadelphia and New York in the early eighteenth century had defined "man-stealing" as "all who are concerned in bringing any of the human race into slavery, or in retaining them in it. . . . Stealers of men are all those who bring off slaves or freemen, and keep, sell, or buy them."[32] Ignoring this, most members believed that "man-stealing" referred to the Atlantic slave trade, but not necessarily to the keeping of slaves in such an economic state indefinitely. Many were not convinced that sin somehow removed itself when it came to holding slaves in their current state. By the early nineteenth century, western presbyteries, mainly in the Ohio and Kentucky regions, sent overtures to the General Assembly asking to resolve the dilemma between slave trading and permanent slaveholding. They needed only to look to their own ecclesiastical history, Bourne thought, and the testimony of the scriptures: "he that stealeth a man, and selleth him, or if he be found in his hand, he shall surely be put to death" (Exodus 21:16, KJV). "Found in his hand" was broad enough for Bourne to include those who "held" slaves.

In 1815, Bourne was once again nominated by the presbytery to attend the General Assembly. Taking the opportunity to confront the issue of involuntary servitude, Bourne planned to present an overture to a committee regarding the issue of whether a minister could own a slave, partake of communion, and still be called a Christian. Attempting to live consistently with the doctrines of the church, Bourne had already suspended the sacraments from slaveholding members of his own congregation. The committee did not hear him, so he spoke directly on the floor of the assembly. After citing question 142 and its scriptural note, Bourne boldly exposed "the horrors of slavery as practiced in Virginia even by Members of the Church and Ministers themselves."[33] He cited a number of instances of abuse by church leaders, but at the time refused to name names. Returning to Port Republic, the newly ordained minister, according to the Lexington Presbytery, continued to make "several unwarranted and unchristian charges against many members of the Presbyterian Church in relation to slavery."[34] He soon found himself charged with slander and, after the publication of *Book and Slavery,* libel. And so began the prosecution of George Bourne.

The letters written between Bourne and Davidson during the late summer of 1815 (mentioned at the beginning of this chapter), which included the announcement of *Book and Slavery,* were the most condemning evidence used by the prosecution.[35] (How the presbytery got hold of the letters is unknown.) Prior to the initial trial and before their fallout over immediacy, Davidson and Bourne developed a friendship. Around 1812, they helped organize the Virginia Tract Society and established a printing house in Harrisonburg. Success was immediate and at times overwhelming. In 1813, Bourne and Davidson published *Marriage Indissoluble and Divorce Unscriptural,* a book written by Bourne that highlighted the importance of marriage and family in fostering a healthy society, and *The Mountain Muse,* a patriotic narrative that recounted the adventures of Daniel Boone (not written by Bourne).[36] The consumer demand for the latter work may have kept Bourne from his ministerial duties, according to Christie and Dumond. At any rate, Davidson and Bourne's time together allowed them to discuss important political and religious issues, which undoubtedly included slaveholding. Although sharing many of Bourne's ideas, Davidson vacillated over the issue of Christianity and slaveholding. Bourne came to accept immediate emancipation before Davidson did. Davidson owned a slave named "Uncle Joe." When Joe's day of jubilee drew near (i.e., when his term of service ended, promised to him by Davidson), Davidson reneged and refused to free his slave. Consequently, in an act of defiance, Joe cut off his own thumbs, rendering himself useless for manual labor. Bourne harshly reprimanded Davidson for his failure to free Joe, and he also took the opportunity to show how slavery hurt all involved, black and white. Nothing more is known about Joe or the aftermath of his self-mutilation. But the incident certainly contributed to Bourne's growing hatred of the institution.

The letters used in Bourne's first trial revealed the central tenets of what later became *The Book and Slavery Irreconcilable,* predicated "upon the word of God and [the] Confession of Faith." Bourne wrote to Davidson that slaveholding represented an "impious usurpation of the government of God."[37] Owners were guilty of nullifying Presbyterianism, the moral maxims of the scriptures, and the confession that clearly forbid the practice. Such theological impertinence corrupted civil and ecclesiastical society. Slaveholding ministers were liars, thieves, and hypocrites, but worst of all, they were not Christians. This was the heart of Bourne's argument and the reason for the church's anger toward him. "A Slaveholder's pretensions to Christianity," Bourne wrote, "were no better than Satan's." At the first trial, Robert Herron testified that Bourne "believed it to be impossible that anyone could be a Christian and a Slave holder."[38] Such a position ignited the fulminations of the Lexington clergy, who then indicted Bourne for "making injurious impressions in the Assembly against the Presbyterian Clergy in Virginia."[39] The presbyter deposed him from the ministry in December of the same year.

This initial prosecution by the presbytery induced Bourne to publish *The Book and Slavery Irreconcilable.* The primary intent of the book, as the title aptly indicates, was to demonstrate that biblical Christianity and slavery could not be reconciled. A failure to recognize slavery as hostile to authentic Christianity was a willful suppression of biblical doctrine, a tacit acceptance that "divine revelation is not our sole infallible directory."[40] Slavery extinguishes "all capacity for the fulfillment of terrestrial duties [and] nullifies the evangelical law of love and equity"; anyone who supported such an institution could not use the moniker "Christian."[41] The unconverted heart steeps itself in all kinds of immoral behavior, behavior that leads to the castigation of God's word for selfish "present world" idolatries. Slavery is symptomatic of "idolatry, lust, and worldly materialism," according to Bourne. The life of the Christian, however, was a constant struggle between following the righteousness of God or succumbing to the enticements of the world, the flesh, and the devil. The worldly idolatry of slaveowners negatively impacted slaves. For Bourne, slaves were made in the image of God like all humans; they were "rational, responsible beings," but under slavery they had become abject in mind and broken in heart.

Bourne spent much of the book challenging a host of proslavery Bible arguments: that slavery had been around since antiquity and thus permissible, that it derived its origins in the curse of Canaan and his descendants, that Christianity's Hebrew forefathers owned slaves, that the New Testament was silent on the issue. As proslavery evangelical arguments reached greater sophistication by the 1830s, Bourne provided a more detailed theological exegesis in *A Condensed Anti-Slavery Bible Argument* (taken up in chapter 3 in this volume), published the year of his death. This latter polemic, however, drew on a few of the antislavery Bible and commonsense arguments in *Book and Slavery.* For instance, biblical language in both the Old and New Testaments that included words such as "buy," "sell," "bondsman," "servant," "master," and "slave" suggested not a race-based involuntary labor relationship, but a contractual or indentured one. Equally, no historical or exegetical evidence supported the racist claim that Africans were descendants of Canaan and thus destined to continuous servitude. And the New Testament explicitly condemned both "man-stealing" and the transformation of humans into articles of property. Specific passages, as well as the general spirit of the Bible, Bourne wrote, "proclaim that *slave-holding* is an abomination in the sight of God."[42] The Bible could not support American slavery. In many ways, *Book and Slavery* was a precursor to later antislavery Bible arguments published between the 1830s and 1850s.

Another strong aspect of the book related to how it answered a few of the practical arguments advanced by Presbyterian leaders. First, there was the issue of compensating masters for their loss. Bourne opposed even the mention of financial reimbursement, which would have legitimized the buying and selling of humans in the first place, a criticism most gradualists faced. What right did humans have in owning other humans as chattel? What value did the slaves have that kidnappers could morally claim as their own? Human law that supported compensation was not to be "obeyed when it contravenes the divine command." And because slavery represented "all iniquity," any law protecting it would force every citizen, including nonslaveholders, "to participate in its corruption."[43] If arguments regarding compensation should have been taken seriously, Bourne reasoned, it would behoove man-stealers to compensate their slaves for taking away the fruits of their labor and, more importantly, the life-changing message of the gospel. Second, Bourne offered a response to the argument from origins: the position that made an ethical distinction between slavery in its beginning (viz., the West African slave trade) and slavery in its continuation.[44] Princeton seminary theologian and Presbyterian Samuel Stanhope Smith, a leading race scholar of his day, weighed in on these two questions in his "Lectures on the Subjects of Moral and Political Philosophy," which Bourne answered in a separate essay published in the appendix to *Book and Slavery.* Smith believed that kidnapping slaves was sinful but retaining the offspring of those slaves was not. The unfortunate institution was thrust upon nineteenth-century Americans by the immoral actions of their ancestors.[45] Smith represented the majority opinion of the Presbyterian Church. Bourne contended that such an excuse defied common sense. A stolen item remained stolen regardless of how many times it changed hands: "The wealth of every Slave-holder in the World is as obviously, an unjust acquisition, as if he had entered a Bank and escaped with a load of its notes."[46] A slave would have faced stiff punishment if he had initially stolen something and subsequently passed it on to another. Undeterred by such absurd logic, Bourne simply reminded his readers of their confessional commitments. Question 142 of the WCF condemned "receiving anything" stolen. Smith, like the rest of his denomination, willfully rejected, Bourne believed, "the *self-evident* verities of his own Confession of Faith!"[47]

As to the second—though most important—goal of *Book and Slavery,* Bourne sought to confront "the most obdurate adherents of slavery": religious leaders. Hardly an advocate of a purely democratic Christianity and in no way anticlerical, Bourne's evangelicalism and its relationship to the strength of the nation rested on his ecclesiology. Ministers held the responsibility of taking up the work of emancipation. "Christian Instructors," Bourne wrote, "cannot be silent upon man-stealing, much less excuse, defend, or engage in it."[48] Slave-holding ministers of the gospel "neglected the teachings of pure Christianity," smothering the light of redemption by misinterpreting both the letter and the spirit of the Bible: "They only quote the scriptures, Satan-like, to falsify their meaning."[49] The minister was the guardian and cultivator of the faith. His failure in this area contributed to the religious decline of society. If the Church collapsed, the nation soon followed. For Bourne, Presbyterian ministers who supported slavery deserved the "severest castigation" since they made a travesty of Christian love, suppressed the dictates of their own confession, and "endeavoured to intimidate and silence the promulgers of the truth."[50] Every man-stealing reverend lacked Christian sincerity, for he was "disguised in a hypocritical garb of exterior decorum."[51] And a heart that tended toward "every moral obliquity" would inevitably "*change the truth of God into a lie.*"[52] Such leaders were not even "nominal Christian believers": "How can a person pretend to be a disciple of the crucified Jesus, who hinders his worship and contravenes his commands; in whom all evangelical charity is extinct; and who will neither enter the kingdom of heaven nor permit those to approach who would crave admission at the gate?"[53]

While Bourne was chiefly interested in a defense of the Bible and the church, he also addressed the spiritual foundations of America's social order. Along with the incompatibility of the Bible with the institution of slavery was the irreconcilability of slavery with "republican principles." Slavery contradicted the "public formularies [*sic*] of the United States," both at the state and federal levels, most of which affirm that all men were created "free and equal."[54] Sadly, as Bourne wrote in the revised 1834 edition of *The Book and Slavery Irreconcilable,* retitled *Picture of Slavery in the United States of America,* "the law of Virginia" and those of the South in general changed "to the law of the slave-holding states."[55] Bourne's attack on the clergy and his effort to show

how slavery contradicted republicanism was a shared criticism among abolitionists. It was not uncommon for abolitionists to call out American ministers for their religious failings in not taking an immediate stand against chattel bondage; ministers likewise failed by allowing such an institution that contradicted the republican principles laid out in America's founding documents. The first report of the American Anti-Slavery Society in 1833 compelled the church to take the lead in ending chattel bondage, echoing Bourne's words nearly two decades earlier: "[T]he American Church is stained with the blood of 'the saints of the poor innocents,' and holds the keys of the great prison of oppression; and that she can never go forth to millennial triumph until she shall wash her hands from blood—open the prison door—and let the oppressed go free."[56] The spirit and letter of the scriptures not only detailed the story of redemption and offered guidelines for Christian morality, but also, when properly understood, provided a basis for a just political order. This was unique among American Biblicists. Not only did the "Laws of nature and Revelation exactly harmonize," Bourne wrote, but the Bible plainly taught "a preference of the republican form" of government "over all others."[57] In a recent study, historian Mark Noll writes that pre- and post-Revolutionary Americans "took for granted a fundamental compatibility between orthodox Protestant religion and republican principles of government."[58] Traditional continental republicans like John Milton, James Harrington, Thomas Paine, John Trenchard, and Thomas Gordon showed a faith in individual empirical and deductive reason, classical Greek history and politics, and either a skepticism or outright rejection of Christian—especially Calvinistic—orthodoxy (e.g., the Trinity, the infallibility of the Bible, the reality of free will, and the bodily resurrection of Christ, to name a few). Yet only in America, Noll argues, did the ethics of republicanism (virtue, liberty, resistance to tyranny, independence) and the epistemology often associated with it (common sense, induction, empiricism, moral intuition) undergo a process of Christianization that had begun during the First Great Awakening and the French and Indian War. It was after the Revolution that Enlightenment republicanism and orthodox Christian beliefs were sealed.

Bourne unquestionably accepted the relationship between the teachings of the Bible and the political philosophy of his day. As a case in point, *Book and Slavery* incorporated the religious republicanism of Kentucky Presbyterian David Rice (the most quoted author in *Book and Slavery*). Rice had been converted to Presbyterianism through Samuel Davies, a moderate abolitionist

Presbyterian minister who began missionary work to southern slaves. After spending a short period in Virginia, Rice moved to Kentucky and was later involved in the Kentucky Abolition Society (KAS), founded in 1808. The KAS had connections with the Pennsylvania Abolition Society. Bourne quoted a speech Rice gave in 1792 at the Kentucky Constitutional Convention, later published as *Slavery Inconsistent with Justice and Good Policy,* in which he argued that slavery was inconsistent with the general peace and well-being of society. In fact, as he wrote in *A Kentucky Protest against Slavery,* slavery represented a "standing monument" of the American government's tyranny that, in essence, nullified universal justice for any race: "If I have no sense of obligation to do justice to a black man, I can have little to do justice to a white man."[59] His faith in the universal injustice at the heart of human chattel bondage rested on a kind of commonsense moral insight: "there is an honest SOMETHING in our breasts, that bears testimony against [slavery] as unreasonable and wicked."[60] Unfortunately, the Presbyterians in Kentucky, aware of Rice's efforts and the efforts of the KAS, fell back on a 1794 decision that the issue of ending slavery was left up to a decision of the civil magistrate in consultation with individual slaveowners. In this way the church distanced itself from any moral failings. Bourne's own presbytery was unwilling to confront slaveholding ministers and by the 1820s came to adopt colonization, following the decision of the General Assembly in 1818. In the year of Bourne's death (1845), the General Assembly of the Presbyterian Church adopted a resolution from a Kentucky minister and decided that it could not legislate on those things that were not addressed or acted directly upon by Christ and his disciples. Again, slavery grew stronger while abolitionism grew weaker by the inaction of the clergy.

A properly biblical society was a republic based on the rule of law, justice, and social virtue, which in turn were shaped by the Bible. Yet slavery directly assaulted, the author wrote, "Republicanism and Christianity": "Revealed religion is predicated upon the natural equality, the individual responsibility, the reciprocal duties of the human family, and the paramount claims of the most high God to the services, and the obedience of all his creatures." An affinity existed between God's special revelation and the natural order: "[S]lavery does not merely diminish the energy, and mitigate the obligation of the sacred scriptures, but it totally nullifies all the fundamental principles" derived from Christianity.[61] Slavery negated the individual's innate moral capacity that forged affectionate bonds among humans. Pride, which sought to elevate the self over others, an anti-Christian and antirepublican aim, dethroned God and threatened public virtue. Bourne frequently reminded readers—as later abolitionists would do—of the glaring language of liberty in America's founding document, the Declaration of Independence: "We hold these truths to be self evident, that all men are created equal, that they are endowed by their Creator with certain inalienable rights, that among these are life, liberty and the pursuit of happiness." In the same way, Bourne continued, a number of state constitutions testified to the same universal language of liberty: New Hampshire, Massachusetts, Pennsylvania, Delaware, Virginia, Vermont, the Northwestern Territory, and Ohio.[62] The iniquity of slavery, "ten-fold more than Egyptian servitude," made a mockery of a country that prized freedom: "A free people, and hold slaves? Republicans, and traffic their fellow-creatures? Democrats, and enslave those who are born with natural, inherent and inalienable rights! and *Christians all!*—No: such persons are enemies of the republic, humanity, religion and God."[63]

The antislavery Bible arguments, compensation arguments, and the argument from origins divided Presbyterians and thus opened another ethical dilemma that Bourne addressed in *Book and Slavery:* the moral weight of immediate versus gradual emancipation, a lesser of two evils squabble. Smith argued that it was "of high public concern that slavery should be gradually corrected, and, at length, if possible, entirely extinguished; for whatever it is incorporated with the institutions of a republic it will be productive of many moral, and political evils."[64] At the same time, however, he assumed that "the public safety necessarily prevents a speedy accomplishment of the emancipation of the colored population." For the church—and the nation as a whole—immediate emancipation would affect an ill on society much greater than if masters kept their servants in a state of slavery. Bourne then responded with a question: "Which is most unjust, to manumit a slave unrighteously doomed and detained for servitude, or to sanction the endless deprivation of all his hopes and enjoyments?"[65] Slavery severed all earthly ties and negated religious instruction and piety: "A slave-holder's justice defrauds his neighbor, of his wife, his children, and their labour, deprives them of all religious instruction, and robs them of every terrestrial comfort." A fractured family and the irreligion of its members would be a worse evil in the eyes of God and much more of a detriment to the health of society and the church. Since slaveholding was a greater evil, the only remedy was "immediate abolition."[66]

Taken as a whole, *The Book and Slavery Irreconcilable* reads like a pastorally polemical sermon. It begins with a prayer for spiritual liberation—"SPIRIT OF THE LORD JESUS OF NAZARETH, TO PREACH DELIVERANCE TO THE CAPTIVES: O, ILLUMINE! O, REGENERATE! BLIND, CORRUPT OPPRESSORS"—and ends by reminding religious leaders of their duties as guardians of the Bible's teachings: "Remember, Church-Officers, your awful responsibility: with the illumination of the sacred volume around you, can you rest in peace, with the conviction, that men are deluded, and you enlighten them not." As Garrison later testified in the *Liberator,* Bourne preached against slavery "like one having authority."[67] The goal was not to denounce or reject the church, but to convert the clergy: "repentance, reformation, and restitution" was the only remedy for man-stealers.[68]

While *Book and Slavery,* according Manisha Sinha, "anticipated antebellum abolition," it was not the only work of its kind, though it was the most radical.[69] There were a handful of similar works published around the same time. Jarvis Brewster of New Jersey published in 1815 *Exposition of the Treatment of Slaves in the Southern States,* which focused on the need to recognize and protect the rights of slaves. Laws passed to protect slaves, he noted, were disregarded. Unlike Bourne's, Brewster's intent had more to do with showing the abuses of the system of slavery. It was far from an aggressive attack against slaveholders themselves. John Kenrick's *Horrors of Slavery,* written in 1817, published the works of a number of abolition advocates in England and the United States. This was closer to Bourne's immediatism. As Sinha writes, "the long title of [Kenrick's] pamphlet encapsulates immediatist rhetoric."[70] Also like Bourne, Kenrick, in part II of the book, demonstrates how slavery is inherently "*impolitic, antirepublican, unchristian and highly criminal.*" And finally, the author of *Portrait of Domestic Slavery in the United States* in 1817, Charles Torrey, sought to separate himself from "unconditional emancipation" while critical of the negative aspects of slavery. It is certainly possible that anti-immediatist ministers in the General Assembly were aware of these works, which intensified their hostility to antislavery.

According to Molly Oshatz, Bourne "took the step that previous antislavery Protestants had been unwilling to take—he called slavery a sin."[71] This is what troubled the Presbyterian establishment. Bourne, leaders of the denominational establishment believed, was sowing the seeds of discord, threatening the stability of the church within a fragile national context. For the most part, moderate antislavery advocates viewed slavery as contrary to both nature and God's word, but virtually no one would refer to the institution as a sin nor slaveholders as sinners. But for Bourne the situation was much more terrible given that because ministers refused to see slavery as a sin they became complicit in protecting its growth. Fellow Lexington Presbytery elders Robert Doak and Capt. John Humphries came to Bourne after the first trial and confessed that "they had no quarrel with him on the subject of slavery," but they encouraged him to allay the militant nature of antislavery rhetoric and "use language more consistent with harmony."[72] They wished him to speak moderately. Found guilty by the presbytery for making "strong marks of contempt," Bourne sent an apology letter before the second trial in hopes that the presbytery would forgive "everything which they [construed] to be justly offensive to them." He admitted that his "irritable temper," "undecorous expressions," and "actions incompatible with the charitable sensibilities" of the gospel were unjustified.[73] Yet he "did not regret using the language" that called for the eradication of racial bondage. "I rail at no person," Bourne wrote in an early letter to Davidson, "but if it be reviling I affirm, that Preachers traffic slaves, like horses; and *your* Confession of Faith, says, that all such men are guilty 'of the highest kind of theft,' I must be a reviler as long as they continue in the iniquitous practice."[74] Not surprisingly, Lexington rejected the apology.

Of course, the inconsistency of the presbytery in failing to prosecute all slanderous speech revealed its true motives. For instance, in the same way as Bourne, Davidson "denounced all Slaveholders as *Negro-stealers* [and] the *Devil's Dogs and Children.*"[75] But the question is why Davidson escaped prosecution when he himself spurned proslavery ministers. Likewise, although Bourne initially refused to comply with the General Assembly's wishes to print the names of those he accused, most of the names were later printed in Theodore Weld's *American Slavery as It Is: A Testimony of a Thousand Witnesses.*[76] Yet even before Weld's 1839 *American Slavery,* Bourne did identify a slaveholding elder. John McCue, questioned by Bourne during the first trial, admitted that he had purchased "two Negro men, one woman and two children" and occasionally whipped them on the Sabbath. For the prosecution, this single testimony was not enough to clear Bourne of slander. Bourne concluded that the presbytery was not interested in civility in addressing slavery. The presbytery in his mind were moved by a different end: a hatred of his radical reform.

When Bourne left Virginia for a pastorate in Germantown, Pennsylvania, he appealed the local presbytery's ruling to the General Assembly. Reviewing the case at its 1817 meeting, the assembly decided in favor of Bourne, stating in the minutes "that the charges were not fully substantiated, and if they had been, the sentence was too severe."[77] He was to be tried again by his Virginia peers as was the requirement of a reversal by the higher court. But before the second trial began, the assembly attempted to take its own action—albeit indirectly—against what Bourne brought to the floor two years earlier. In the mind of the assembly, the scriptural notes attached to each question and answer of the Larger Catechism, adopted in 1794, which included 1 Timothy 1:10 to question 142, were separate from the constitution and thus "subject to alterations, amendments, or a total erasure." Knowing full well what they were doing, Bourne writes, the church body omitted "the note connected with the Scripture proofs in answer to the question in the Larger Catechism, what is forbidden in the eight commandment, in which the nature of the crime of man-stealing, and slavery is dilated upon."[78] The consequence of such action was not only to suppress church history, but also to delete from memory the haunting voice of a militant confessional abolitionist.

When the new trial began in the summer of 1817, the original charges of slander were reinstated along with four additional ones, which included a seemingly bogus charge of purchasing a horse on the Sabbath. Tried in absence, Bourne was stripped of his ministerial qualifications.[79] Once again he appealed to the General Assembly. But unlike 1817, the Presbyterian assembly in 1818 confirmed the six charges of the presbytery without an explanation, "declaring [Bourne] deposed from the Gospel ministry."[80] An important question needs to be asked at this point: What caused the General Assembly to change its position? It is quite possible that a majority of the delegates to the 1818 assembly had read *The Book and Slavery Irreconcilable,* published between the trials, and thus turned against Bourne for his now published (and public) assault against them.

Bourne's tirade against slave-supporting religious leaders undercut the denomination's attempt to end slavery moderately and reduce the growing presence of blacks in America. The removal of African Americans, which was essential in shaping early republican nationalism, was frequently couched in the language of benevolence. The nation witnessed a spate of voluntary organizations that combined the language of republican virtue, evangelical benevolence, and racist imperialism. No other organization, however, captured the country's insidious nationalistic ethos more than the American Colonization Society (ACS). The ACS, according to Sean Wilentz, "merged two distinct, and in some ways contradictory, points of view: first, a philanthropic antislavery reformism that aimed to eliminate slavery gradually and allow the ex-slaves the chance to return voluntarily to Africa; and, second, a growing fear among slaveholders that the nation's two hundred thousand free blacks were potential fomenters of slave rebellions."[81] Chartered in the final month of 1816, the ACS was organized by prominent politicians and religious leaders including Robert Finley, Charles Mercer, Henry Clay, William Crawford, and Bushrod Washington, to name a few.[82] As Paul Goodman has written, the ACS represented the "most important effort to construct a *Herrenvolk* republic."[83] Colonization provided a way to deal indirectly with the problem of slavery and to avoid the stickier question of nonwhite American citizenship. This is not to negate influential characters like Benjamin Coates, who supported colonization as a way to provide an economic alternative that would indeed attack the heart of the peculiar institution, or to negate the different ways colonization was envisioned by influential African American leaders like Paul Cuffee to create a pan-African nationalism among African Americans themselves.[84]

Since its founding in New York and Philadelphia, the Presbyterian denomination leaned heavily toward gradualism, and colonization quickly became a favorite among conservative Old School Presbyterians, the dominant ruling faction in the denomination. New Jersey Presbyterian minister Robert Finley, a former student of Samuel Stanhope Smith, was a principal founder of the ACS and worked successfully to convince northern whites of the advantages of removing blacks to a distant land. Finley's justification for removal echoed that of a number of principal statesmen: "Their number [Free Blacks] increases greatly, and their wretchedness too as appears to me. Everything connected with their condition, including their colour, is against them; nor is there much prospect that their state can ever be greatly ameliorated, while they shall continue among us. . . . We should be cleared of them:—we should send to Africa a population partially civilized and christianized for its benefit:—our blacks themselves would be put in a better situation."[85] He believed he was acting in a benevolent manner and that the blessings of national patriotism, manliness, and progress—all of a different sort—could not be acquired by such an "unhappy people" if they remained in the United States: "The people of colour, observing the constant emigration of the whites, would soon feel the common impulse, if they could see a place where they might remove, and which they could fondly call their own. . . . Their local attachments are no stronger than those of other men, their ambition no less than that of any other colour. But it is vain that we believe them capable of improvement, or that we are convinced that they are equal to the task of governing themselves, unless this unhappy people are separated from their former masters. . . . The hope of place and power will soon create the feeling that they are men."[86] Large support for black expatriation came from the church's intellectual elite at Princeton. Archibald Alexander, former president of Hampden-Sydney College and pastor of Third Presbyterian Church in Philadelphia, became the first professor of didactic and polemic theology at the seminary and one of the first to write a complete history of the colonization movement in 1846, *A History of Colonization on the Western Coast of Africa.* For Alexander, colonization removed a group of people who, if left in America, would only excite white hostilities. But it also offered an excuse to provide evangelical training among blacks so that they could be sent to West Africa.

The denomination's decision to support colonization came in the same year that the assembly made its final decision against Bourne. The committee that reviewed the Port Royal minister's second appeal—made up of Ashbel Green, Dyer Burgess, and George Baxter, a member of the Lexington Presbytery and one of Bourne's chief opponents—was commissioned to write a statement representing the general consensus of the church regarding slavery, slaveholding, and abolition. The outcome of the committee's work, the 1818 declaration on slavery, was subsequently adopted by the assembly. The declaration first denounced slavery as a "gross violation" of the "sacred rights of human nature" and declared that involuntary servitude was indeed "incompatible with the spirit and principles of the gospel of Christ."[87] The document then listed some of the consequences of slavery on the slave. While the institution degraded both the mind and moral actions of slaves and threatened the unity and stability of the family, the assembly agreed that not every moral evil was committed by owners and that slavery itself was not a sin. Nonetheless the decision encouraged slaveholding members "to use their honest, earnest, and unwearied endeavors, to correct the errors of former times, and as speedily as possible to efface this blot on our holy religion, and to obtain the complete abolition of slavery throughout Christendom, and if possible the world."[88] Yet this was not to be done immediately: the "number of slaves, their ignorance, and their vicious habits generally, render an immediate and universal emancipation inconsistent, alike, with the safety and happiness of the master and slave."[89] In keeping with the opinion of a number of colonization organizers, Presbyterians admitted that white Americans had "inflicted a most grievous injury" upon the Africans, but freeing them without moderation would "add a second injury to the first." Because of their ignorance and the animosity toward the enslaving (white) community, manumitted blacks would likely "destroy themselves or others."[90]

The committee's report offered a few recommendations for the assembly's consideration. First and foremost, to dismantle chattel bondage in a decent and orderly fashion, Presbyterian leaders called members "to patronize and encourage the [ACS], lately formed, for colonizing in Africa, the land of their ancestors, the free people of color in our country." Second, while masters and slaves waited patiently for manumissions to materialize, ministers were expected to provide religious instruction "in the principles and duties of the Christian religion; by granting the liberty to attend on the preaching of the gospel; by favouring the instruction of them in Sabbath Schools . . . and by giving them all other proper advantages for acquiring the knowledge of their duty to both God and man." They dismissed the belief among some that religious instruction would incite "insubordination and insurrection." Third, ministers compelled members to avoid acts of cruelty including "separating husband and wife, parents and children" and slave trafficking. The punishment for violating the latter, especially against a slave in good standing in the church, would lead to the suspension of a minister's duties until he repented. The final recommendation was undoubtedly directed toward Bourne and those potentially persuaded by him: "*And we, at the same time, exhort others* to forebear harsh censures, and uncharitable reflections on their brethren, who unhappily live among slaves, whom they cannot immediately set free; but who, at the same time, are really using all their influence, and all their endeavors, to bring them into a state of freedom, as soon as a door for it can safely be opened."[91] "Harsh censures" like that offered by Bourne produced schism and disrupted the bonds of ecclesiastical unity. (Bourne later defined "schism" as not a division over secondary or, as Bourne himself labeled them, "*non-essential*" doctrinal issues—like the mode of baptism—but a complete "alienation of heart from Christ's institutions."[92] As unbelievers, slaveholders, and not Bourne, necessarily severed Christian unity.) There is no doubt that at least one leading architect of colonization, Robert Finley, objected directly to Bourne's immediatism. In 1833, Finley gave a speech in New York where he "publicly accused leading abolitionists with the design of exciting the negroes to insurrection." As reported by the *Liberator*, when asked "to whom [Finley] applied these charges and epithets," Finley named "George Bourne," along with two others, "Simeon Jocelyn," Connecticut reformer and educator, who helped defend the rights of the Africans in the Amistad case, and "Charles Denison."[93]

The committee's recommendations were in no way "strongly antislavery" and thus failed to initiate "strong action" by both laity and clergy.[94] The *Southern Christian Herald* called it a "dead letter."[95] Christie and Dumond described it as "a masterpiece of equivocation" for "studiously evading the fateful question about manstealing."[96] Bourne returned to Green, Burgess, and Baxter's "appalling delineation" in 1834 and systematically denounced each duplicitous and irreverent point, made "to cloak over their own ungodliness."[97] Bourne had already written in *Book and Slavery* that colonization was "totally impracticable."[98] By 1831, he repeated his position in William Lloyd Garrison's *Liberator:* "The system is so entirely corrupt, that it admits of no cure but by a TOTAL and IMMEDIATE abolition. For a gradual emancipation is a virtual recognition of the right, and establishes the rectitude of the practice. If it be just for one moment, it is hallowed for ever; and if it be inequitable, not a day should it be tolerated."[99] At an 1833 Providence Anti-Slavery Society meeting, Bourne supported a resolution rejecting as "false and unfounded" the antislavery claims of the ACS. He also proclaimed that anyone who was convinced of its efficiency was "either a deceiver or stark mad."[100] Likewise, Garrison, Bourne's close associate, interpreted "the Colonization scheme as inadequate in its design, injurious in its operation, and contrary to sound principle; and the more scrupulously I examines its pretensions, the stronger is my conviction of its sinfulness."[101] Abolitionist James G. Birney rightly captured the true nature of colonization: "an opiate to the conscience."[102] As an alternative between extremes, colonization assuaged the moral and spiritual dilemma that unnerved ministers, allowing them to silence radicalism and retain their slaves while paying lip service to the ultimate collapse of the peculiar institution.

After his first trial, Bourne was willing to amend any slanderous accusations. But the 1818 decision only hardened what he described in *Book and Slavery* as a self-appointed "fanaticism." He came to believe such flaming righteousness was the central impetus of a rejection of ungodliness, the defense of the gospel, and the reformation of church and society. Elijah and Jeremiah of the Old Testament, Peter and Stephen of the New Testament, and Martin Luther and John Knox of the Reformation exhibited the traits of turbulent and misrepresenting fanatics. Bourne celebrated these passionate liberators and called for more: "O for more *'Misrepresenters,'* who have the boldness to display the abominations of *Negro-Tanners!* O for more *'Exaggerators'* who will heap confusion upon *pretended* Christians, by lucidly developing their constant violations of the eighth commandment! O for more *turbulent* and *factious souls,* who will not connive at Officers and Members of the Church, *stealing men,* with impunity, and without censures! O God, grant us all the exuberance of that spirit which impelled the reformers, the Martyrs, the Prophets, and the Apostles of Jesus Christ! AMEN."[103] Bourne saw himself as coming from a long line of courageous "fanatics" of true religion.

Bourne stood at a critical juncture in the history of the antislavery movement. It must be noted that although he played an important role in convincing reformers of the morality of immediate and universal abolitionism, the groundswell opposition of one of America's marginalized groups pushed antislavery to its more radical phase. According to Goodman, colonization "mobilized black opposition," creating the "modern biracial abolitionist movement."[104] "The roots of antebellum abolition," for Sinha, "lay in the virtually unanimous rejection by blacks of the program of the American Colonization Society."[105] Colonization convinced a number of leaders to lay claim to their own American identity and to forge a union among all blacks in America. Richard Allen, founder of the African Methodist Episcopal Church, challenged the exclusion of African Americans from American citizenship: "The land that we have watered with our tears and our blood is now OUR MOTHER COUNTRY."[106] Other leading African American opponents of colonization, including James Forten, John Brown Russwurm, Samul Eli Cornish, and David Walker, confronted America's failure to deal with its deep-rooted racism, highlighting the hypocrisy of white Americans who failed to live consistently with their own founding documents and encouraged a courageous agitation among blacks for civil rights. The participants at a meeting in Philadelphia's Bethel Church in 1817 made a historical leap by linking the plight of free blacks to black slaves. "[W]e will," the resolutions pronounced, "never separate ourselves voluntary from the slave population of this country; they are our brethren by the ties of consanguinity, of suffering and of wrong."[107] By challenging America's pursuit of racial hegemony, blacks pressed the issue of race and racial equality and thus "compelled whites to clarify and make explicit their understanding of American republicanism as the white race's exclusive gift."[108] Many white abolitionists were persuaded by the efforts of the black community to extend the boundaries of American national identity. Bourne's opposition to slavery coincided with the various forms of resistance employed by African Americans, free and slave alike. Yet in his polemics, Bourne did not engage African American agitation, the creatively furtive activities of blacks in dealing with slavery and racism. The same was true of Bourne's comments on colonization. Historians have convincingly shown the myriad understandings and uses of colonization, challenging, in particular, the limited view of colonization as simply a racist scheme to deal with an unwanted group in America. While certainly seen by some as a way to remove African Americans from a "white" America or truly as a benevolent (though nonetheless racist) plan to ameliorate the plight of American Americans, especially slaves, many viewed colonization as a way to escape the racism inherent in the creation of a new nation. Colonization was understood by some as a first step in the creation of an African nationalism (or pan-African nationalism), at least before the Philadelphia meeting in 1817. Bourne's position on colonization, however, did not account for such complexities. For him, colonization was, plainly and simply, a failure to deal directly with the sin of slavery. The error of colonization rested on the fact that it did not end the practice of slavery. For someone like Bourne, as well as other radicals, especially those impacted by Finneyite revivalism, sin was not something to gradually end nor ameliorate. The issue, in his mind, was straightforward: slavery was sin that should not be tolerated. The organizers of the American Society for Free Persons of Color in Philadelphia likewise believed that "the problems of slavery and racism could be addressed only on American soil."[109]

Not much is known about Bourne's involvement in abolitionism in the years between his removal from the Presbyterian Church in 1818 and his return to radicalism in creating the American Anti-Slavery Society in 1833. In 1885, forty years after Bourne's death, Oliver Johnson wrote in *Boston Commonwealth* that when Bourne left Virginia his antislavery activities ceased. Bourne, Johnson noted, did not take part in the "Missouri Struggle," for instance.[110] Bourne's youngest son William Oland Bourne offered a response in the same newspaper saying that his father had less time to devote to antislavery after leaving Virginia because his "literary and parochial duties demanded his time and labors." Yet his father never ignored his commitment to antislavery and by 1830, William writes, "he returned to the contest fully harnessed, when Mr. Garrison . . . again sounded the appeal that has made our country free."[111] When Bourne returned to the cause of antislavery, nearly twenty years after his first trial, he, with the help of Charles Denison and William Lloyd Garrison, republished *Book and Slavery* under a different title, *Picture of Slavery in the United States of America.* Bourne's original 1816 argument remained unchanged in its "amended reprint." Bourne returned to the "contest with the kidnappers" in its "existing, definite and tangible form."[112] *The Genius of Universal Emancipation* praised the new edition and stated that it "should be in the hands of every religious professor, at least, in the slaveholding section of the United States and the West Indies."[113] *The Liberator* also lauded the revised work: "Next to the bible we are indebted to this work for our views of the system of slavery. We pronounce it the most faithful and conclusive exposition of the cruelty and sin of holding the slaves in bondage, that we have ever seen. The more we read it, the higher does our admiration of its author rise."[114] *Picture of Slavery* became an important resource for a number of antislavery works, including Weld's *American Slavery As It Is,* a work that put together a number of eyewitness accounts of the southern institution. Bourne incorporated into *Picture of Slavery* additional experiences as a resident in the land of slavery. Many of the accounts were so appalling, Lewis Tappan wrote in *The Independent,* "that most people believed them to be fictions of the imagination. . . . Even many abolitionists thought them exaggerated descriptions; although they have since learned by Weld's 'Testimony of a Thousand Witnesses,' Mrs. Stowe's works, the testimonies of fugitive slaves, and the confessions of repentant slaveholders, that they are veritable facts."[115] *Picture of Slavery* was printed in the United States in 1835 and in England in 1835 and 1845, the year of Bourne's death. According to Margaret Abruzzo, *Picture of Slavery* "participated in the 'explosion of print and visual culture' in the 1830s that 'allowed slavery's critics to recreate the immediacy of both enslaved suffering and the corresponding obligation to relieve it.'"[116]

Among its notable edits, *Picture of Slavery* subtly raised the issue of race and nationhood.[117] In the early work, Bourne used the term "Negro" in reference to slaves, but in *Picture of Slavery* the same term was changed throughout to "Americans," "American citizens," or "neighbors," and he explicitly acknowledged that African Americans, including slaves, should be given the same rights guaranteed by the nation's laws and thus to own the title "American."

Bourne's use of "citizen" to describe slaves, according to Martha Cutter, eroded the "verbal distinctions between black and white citizens," forwarding, she continues, "a practice of intersubjectivity in which it became increasingly difficult to disentangle the enslaved from the citizen proper."[118] By the 1830s, therefore, Bourne did not follow the direction of the nation in seeing blackness as an impediment to national identity.

The label "abolitionist" encompasses quite a bit, as does "immediatism." There were those who opposed the institution but made little or no effort to end the system immediately. Eventually, however, as passions intensified, abolitionist qualifiers mattered little: slaveholders began to identify any and all forms of antislavery as threatening to the nation, civil society, the economy, and religion. Even those who sought to abide by the General Assembly's 1818 recommendations, especially as it related to colonization, were construed as fanatical abolitionists and thus faced the wrath of proslavery religious forces.[119] Baptist minister John Lankford suspended the sacrament of communion, precisely what Bourne advised, to slaveholding members. He was expelled from his pulpit in 1826. A glaring example of the hypocrisy of the church came in the experience of Virginian Presbyterian John Paxton, an acquaintance of Bourne. In an attempt to comply with the recommendations of the General Assembly, Paxton, who inherited slaves through marriage, sent a small number of slaves to Liberia. He was quickly accused of being "an imprudent extremist" and removed as pastor from his Cumberland County church.[120] After his relocation to Danville, Kentucky, Paxton reflected on the 1818 report and its recommendations: "The grand error was that while the church declared to the world the great sin and guilt under which the church and country lay, no corresponding effort was made in the church or through the church, to put an end to the evil and lead to repentance and reformation."[121]

In his now classic *Story of Religion in America,* William Warren Sweet argued that "the friends of slavery" came to the 1818 assembly primarily "to effect the deposition" of George Bourne. After the final decision against Bourne in 1818, a majority of Presbyterian delegates left the assembly to begin their long journey home. And having "accomplished their design in expelling the obnoxious Bourne, they were now willing to let the antislavery resolutions pass with the nominal sanction of the whole Presbyterian Church." "These facts," Sweet concluded, "raise a large question as to the sincerity and real significance" of the

1818 declaration.[122] Bourne too believed that the church acted in a hypocritical manner. The deepening hostility toward colonization and the rise of radical and immediate abolition among whites and blacks were made possible partly by the actions of a nationally influential denomination against a minister who simply sought to live faithfully with the church's biblical doctrines and confessional standards. Failing to take the lead in dismantling slavery, the Presbyterian denomination unwittingly motivated a more intense radicalism. The case against Bourne was the crack that would eventually lead to the fracturing of the major denominations in the entire country. In 1806, George Baxter, who later helped author the 1818 declaration, admitted "with sincerity" that he considered slaves "an unfortunate people" and that anyone "who would want only to add to their misery, must possess a bad heart."[123] But Baxter's benevolence was later cancelled out by his hostility toward abolitionism. Baxter's turn to antiabolition may have germinated after his experience with Bourne. Growing tired of the intensification of abolition in the 1830s, the Old School–dominated assembly in 1837 removed New School presbyteries—the Western Reserve, Utica, Geneva, and Genesee—for their divisive opinions concerning slavery. The Presbyterian division of 1837, in the words of Baxter, "will put an end to the abolition question and disturbance in the Presbyterian Church." "If the separation begun should be carried out," Baxter continued, "the Presbyterian Church by getting clear of the New School, will at the same time get clear of abolition."[124] Offering a resolution to the West Hanover Presbytery in 1838, this Old School southern minister described abolition as "fanatical in its spirit" and "directly contrary to the Holy Scriptures." He then encouraged leaders to "oppose abolition principle[s]" by withdrawing as a body whenever "any part should get the ascendancy in one church, which would introduce abolition discussion and abuse into the General Assembly." The "abolition character" threatened "the laws of our State and the peace of our country."[125] By the 1840s the nation's two other largest denomination, Methodists (split in 1844) and Baptists (split in 1845, the year of Bourne's death), were also divided between antislavery and antiabolitionist forces.[126] Another split over slavery occurred in the New School Presbyterian denomination in 1856. For antislavery Protestants, writes Oshatz, "there was no constructive, Christian method of advocating emancipation. National and ecclesiastical unity required tactics of conciliation and compromise. Holding to the moral purity of the higher law of liberty and equality would invite destructive conflicts, personal abuse, and isolation."[127] Some blamed these church splits on abolitionists. For Bourne, the opposite was true. The destruction of the republican ideals of the nation as well as the pure doctrines of the church rested on the shoulders of ministers who failed to preach deliverance to the captives.

CHAPTER 3

THE MATURATION OF BOURNE'S ANTISLAVERY BIBLE ARGUMENT

God will eventually deliver the slaves, whether we repent of the sin of enslaving them or not; but the whole analogical teaching of the Scriptures, as well as the promises of God, teach us that He will do so by our own national destruction, unless we seasonably repent and reform from the sin of slavery by voluntary abolition.

—GEORGE BOURNE, *Condensed Anti-Slavery Bible Argument*

Around 1806, a few years before his move to Virginia from Baltimore and the same year as *History of Napoleon,* Bourne had a brief encounter with the famous (or, for many, infamous) political revolutionary Thomas Paine, author of *Common Sense,* at a small merchant store in Baltimore. Bourne eagerly engaged Paine's recently published *Age of Reason,* a work that challenged the historicity of Christian doctrine. The book sent shock waves throughout the young republic; its author went from being a revered patriot of liberty to a blasphemous pagan. Although complimenting the author's expertise on political philosophy, Bourne gently reprimanded Paine for his lack of knowledge in both ancient language and history, which ill-equipped him as an authority on the Judeo-Christian religion. This particular incident offers a glimpse of Bourne's willingness to engage those who directly (or indirectly) undermined the veracity of revealed religion.[1] Yet Paine's harsh criticism of the Bible was less threatening than those who endeavored to destroy the faith under the guise of religious piety. It was one thing to reject Christian orthodoxy outright, but it was quite another to provide biblical justification for clearly unbiblical ideas and habits. Bourne spent a large portion of his life defending the sacred text against the twisted interpretations of irreligious clergymen, the guardians of southern slavery. Such an engagement required a more critical reading of the Bible.

After the revolutionary period, abolitionists found themselves facing a variety of arguments employed by the defenders of slavery: arguments defending the peculiar institution on the basis of the inherent inferiority of blacks; the environment-related physical, intellectual, and cultural differences between people and races that made some fit for liberty and others not; slavery as a civilizing and ostensibly benevolent institution; slavery as a contrasting economic arrangement to counter the threat of the competitive capitalist North; and the urgency to tighten the chains of bondage given the fears over slave revolts. Added to these was the increasing use of the Bible by slavery's apologists. Debates over the Bible's position on slavery intensified by the 1830s. The "early antislavery movement," David Brion Davis wrote in *The Problem of Slavery in the Age of Revolution,* "coincided in time with the beginnings of serious Biblical criticism on historical as well as philological grounds."[2] The slave controversy complicated the Bible's message concerning slavery and race and created contradictory interpretations between advocates and opponents of abolition, thus stimulating hermeneutical engagements that helped structure a unique form of textual analysis in nineteenth-century America. Radical immediatists like Gerrit Smith and William Lloyd Garrison, the latter of whom often attended intellectual conferences that focused on the textual integrity of the Bible, preferred moral intuition and commonsense rationalism over that of a literal reading of the Bible, the first step toward heresy according to anti-abolitionists. Moderate antislavery and proslavery Biblicists often unfairly labeled "fanatical" abolitionists as unorthodox because of their association with a radical few, failing to take into account the diverse perspectives within the antislavery movement. While some radical antislavery activists distanced themselves from the accusations of the proslavery faction and confidentially traveled the iconoclastic route of a more freethinking skepticism, others recognized the need to sharpen their commitments to a plain and literal reading of the Bible, regardless of their doctrinal idiosyncrasies.

By the late eighteenth century, "the biblical proslavery argument was already common currency," Molly Oshatz reminds her readers.[3] A handful of popular antislavery Bible arguments countered those who identified radicals as those who rejected revealed religion. And Bourne's *Condensed Anti-Slavery Bible Argument,* although not wholly original in terms of its argument, stands out among similar works in revealing how differing hermeneutical attitudes toward the authority of the Bible did not necessarily detract from a shared belief on what the biblical text said about slavery. With this in mind, historians are correct in affirming that the existence of slavery created a significant challenge to hermeneutics, but it is not easy to conclude, as Oshatz intimates in *Slavery as Sin,* that slavery complicated the plain meaning of the Bible's message, shifting hermeneutics away from a stricter literalism. A survey of a few popular antislavery arguments—including Theodore Weld's *The Bible against Slavery,* John Rankin's *Letters on Slavery,* Angelina Grimké's *Appeal to the Christian Women of the South,* which repeats the arguments laid out by Weld, LaRoy Sunderland's *The Testimony of God against Slavery,* Albert Barnes's *Inquiry on the Scriptural Views of Slavery,* Elizur Wright's *Does the Bible Sanction Slavery,* and Bourne's *Bible Argument*—shows that despite doctrinal presuppositions or exegetical aptitude, most antislavery arguments advanced the idea that America's form of chattel bondage, including its attachment to race, could not be supported by appealing to either the Old or New Testament. On the issue of the Bible and slavery, John Rankin captures in a poetic manner the exegetical consensus of these writers, all of whom came from different faith traditions: "The whole Bible is opposed to slavery. The sacred volume is one grand scheme of benevolence. Beams of love and mercy emanate from every page, while the voice of justice denounces the oppressor, and speaks to his awful doom."[4] Bourne, while closer to Rankin's form of Protestantism, echoed the conclusions made by Weld, a Finneyite; Grimké, a former Quaker; Sunderland, a Methodist-turned mesmerist; Barnes, a minister prosecuted for his Arminian beliefs; and Wright, who underwent his own secular shift away from "the dogma of the church and the pietism of early immediatism."[5] The point is that Weld, Grimké, Barnes, and Wright, while sharing or at least benefiting from an active moral evangelicalism that was inherently hostile to traditional, especially Calvinistic, faith, all agreed on the Bible's position on slavery. Bourne, as was clear from his ecclesiastical trial, was more loyal to the historic confessions of Protestantism. His *Condensed Anti-Slavery Bible Argument* shows how traditional religion and antislavery were not necessarily antithetical to one another.

Innovations in print production, advanced further by steam power and the widening of the means of distribution in the early part of the nineteenth century, contributed to America's national culture. Faith played a central role in the printing industry. The distribution of the Bible from numerous tract and reform societies throughout the country was of the highest priority and thus "dwarfed all other literary enterprises," according to Mark Noll and Nathan Hatch.[6] More than three thousand copies of the ancient text, which included twenty-seven editions, were published annually from 1830 to 1865 by leading religious societies—the American Bible Society (1816), the American Sunday School Union (1824), and the American Tract Society (1825)—"innovators," writes David Paul Nord, "in modern print technologies and distribution strategies."[7] The goal was to place this depository of timeless moral and theological truths in every home, imprint them on every mind, and shape the habits of American citizens in a competitive and rootless society.

The democratization of Christianity and its alliance with market entrepreneurialism not only accelerated the growth of the press but also spurred the rise of a number of independent religious communities, creating the backdrop against which Americans interpreted biblical theology. Citizens encountered God's word without the mediation of historical tradition or outside authority (clerical elites or confessions). They were free to shape the message of the divine to fit their own social, regional, and economic contexts. Although leading religious groups—Methodists, Baptists, Disciples, Presbyterians, and Congregationalists—fought over issues related to church government, strategies of evangelizing, predestination versus free will, the authenticity of revivalism, the use of traditional creeds and confessions, and even the class status of the truly faithful, they each expressed an allegiance to a plain literal reading of the Bible, a commitment to the Reformation doctrine of *sola Scriptura* (the Bible alone) as the only source of religious authority in the area of faith and practice.[8] But it was America's democratic-market ethos that worked to perennially undermine a unified consensus over the Bible's teaching. Traditional doctrines or specialized theological arguments in the American context, according to Noll, have "rarely been able to overcome the inertia behind institutions and practices sanctioned by the evolving usages of a voluntaristic, democratic consumerist culture."[9]

As the market further entrenched the human chattel system, an unrelated intellectual trend, slowly gaining strength in American institutions of higher learning, would have a profound effect on the religious debates regarding the morality of slavery. American theologians became acquainted with European higher criticism after reading Johann Gottfried Eichhorn's *Einleitung ins Alte Testament,* which ushered in to America, in the opinion of E. Brooks Holifield, "a new kind of biblical study."[10] Classical scholars like Moses Stuart at Andover Seminary and Andrews Norton at Harvard, a few leading northern Unitarians—William Ellery Channing, William Henry Furness, and George Noyes—and a number of theological journals published in the 1830s interacted with this cutting-edge theology. For Eichhorn, a lower critical analysis dealt with the "problem of reconstituting the ancient biblical texts," that is, comparing and contrasting different ancient manuscripts in order to find patterns of consistency and authenticity. The higher method, on the other hand, applied contemporary theories related to the social and cultural position of the original authors and subsequent translators, asking in the broadest sense "a series of historical questions."[11] This latter method troubled traditional doctrinarians, for it tended to demythologize the supernatural elements of the scriptures, clearing the way for a rejection of certain unreasonable or even immoral teachings that did not stand up to the scrutiny of modern thought. In the United States, higher critical scholarship was largely ignored outside the academic and Unitarian communities. The fight over slavery, however, "pushed biblical exegesis toward a critical hermeneutic," writes J. Albert Harrill, author of *Slaves in the New Testament: Literary, Social, and Moral Dimensions.* Harrill suggests that the road was paved for the entrance of a more advanced European-shaped higher criticism since educated "Americans were already accustomed to a more sophisticated kind of biblical criticism if they had followed the literature of antislavery and abolitionism."[12]

Although not directly engaged in Europe's changing intellectual fashions, the theological arguments made by Bourne in his *Condensed Anti-Slavery Bible Argument* followed the mood of religious leaders in their efforts to provide a tighter analysis of the Bible's message. Bourne's own work—and the work of his reformist colleagues—echoed the new criticism in its emphasis on original languages and the historical context of the ancient biblical text. His intent was to strengthen the Bible's authenticity. Unlike *The Book and Slavery Irreconcilable* and its reprint, *Picture of Slavery in the United States of America,* Bourne's *Bible Argument* was a more detailed exegetical examination of the Bible's teachings on slavery. And, for the purpose of this chapter, the book provides a detailed analysis of the favorite Bible passages used by abolitionists.

Bourne, who intensified his opinions regarding the relationship between slavery and the Bible by the 1830s, never abandoned traditional Protestant theology. In fact, as was seen during his trial, his approach to biblical interpretation was more explicitly confessional than other abolitionists. His method of interpretation included a circular Reformed hermeneutic, as stated succinctly in chapter 1, section 9, of the Westminster Confession: "when there is a question about the true and full sense of any Scripture (which is not manifold, but one) it must be searched and known by other Places that speak more clearly." The meaning of one passage, in other words, could not be fully understood in isolation, but in the context of the whole. A balanced harmony existed between the letter and the spirit. The structure of Bourne's argument matched that of the new literary scholarship, even though he made no comments regarding it. Furthermore, the book can be easily associated with what came to be known as the "historical-grammatical" method, first popularized in America by Andover Seminary's Moses Stuart in the 1820s.[13] Such an approach focused on the language and historical context of the biblical writers "rather than modern science or philosophy." "The aim," in the words of E. Brooks Holifield, "was to guard against reading present-day meanings into the biblical texts."[14]

Bible Argument began with a working definition of America's form of slavery. This was done to contrast it with the system found in the Bible. Slavery represented a total deprivation of human rights and the reduction of human beings to the condition of property. Bourne defined a "right" as "the privilege or liberty of being, doing, having or suffering something at our own pleasure and discretion without the interference, interruption or hindrance of others" and a "wrong" as "any voluntary act which disturbs, interrupts, hinders, or destroys the free exercise of the rights of others." The infringement of one's self-sovereignty, the reprehensible means of making a human being into an item of property, was "strictly forbidden by the law of God" but was the very essence of American slavery. On this point Bourne cites a passage from Weld's *Bible against Slavery:* "Not robbing a man of privileges, but of himself; not loading him with burdens, but making him a beast of burden; not restraining liberty, but subverting it; not curtailing rights, but abolishing them; not inflicting personal cruelty, but annihilating personality; not exacting involuntary labor, but sinking man into an implement of labor; not abridging human comforts, but abrogating human nature; not depriving an animal of immunities, but despoiling a rational being of attributes, *uncreating* A MAN to make room for a thing!"[15]

After providing a definition of American slavery, Bourne returned to and explored more fully the word that first inspired his abolitionism (and removal from the church): "man-stealing." In his letter to a young minister, the apostle

Paul included "man-stealing" among the unsaved to which the law of God was to be applied. What is more, the name was not limited to the slave trade, but included "making merchandise" of humans (2 Peter 2:3) by trafficking them like any other commodity—silk, iron, cinnamon, frankincense, sheep, beasts, etc.—as listed in Revelation 18:10–13, a chapter decrying the materialism of a godless Babylon. Slaveholders failed to see the merchandise or chattel-making process of institutional bondage. The move from West Africa was part of the Atlantic trade system. The Middle Passage, in essence, transformed humans into commodities. Africans held in perpetual slavery—which, as opposed to slave trafficking, was not wrong in the minds of southerners—never forfeited their propertied status.

Man-stealing also included the exploitation of free labor. Jeremiah 22:13 ("Woe unto him . . . that uses his neighbor's service without wages, and giveth him not for work") and James 5:4 ("the hire of labourers . . . kept back by fraud, crieth: and the cries of them which have reaped have entered into the ears of the Lord of sabaoth") chastised those who failed to pay workers. In the coming years of the Civil War, southern theologians advanced the argument that a slaveowner did not own the humanity of slaves, just their labor. By failing to pay for labor, according to Bourne, masters kept their servants in poverty and veritably enslaved them: "depriving the poor and helpless of the wages justly due them for labor and other services performed, is everywhere denounced in the Scriptures as one of the greatest sins that men can commit, and as sure to be punished with the utter destruction of the criminals and their families and posterity."[16]

Although he never publicly supported the interests of organized labor, Bourne intimated opposition to egocentric monopolistic capitalism, the root of America's chattel system: "God forbade all human monopoly. . . . He never made a grant to one class of men of any other class."[17] The treatment of servants in both the Old and New Testaments was not to support the prerogatives of wealth, but to prevent the tyranny of the rich. God gave to all men, not just the wealthy elite, "dominion of ownership or property in the earth and its production" (Genesis 1:26–28; 9:1; Psalm 8:6–8): "one individual of the human race has just as good natural and divine right to the earth and its productions, as any other individual has, of which rights every kind of monopoly is a direct infringement and breach of the moral law of God."[18] The labor structure of the slave system in tension with the emerging movement to "dignify and honor

[free] labor" that the United States inherited from British abolitionism laid the foundation of modern capitalism.[19] Bourne was aware of the economic root of the peculiar institution but showed no interest in entering discussions related to the wider meaning of labor in the nineteenth century.

After these preliminary remarks, Bourne commenced his exegetical foray by first separating the doctrines of the Bible into two categories: "first, those which are matters of faith or belief only, and secondly, those that are matters of faith and practice both." Concerning the former—"the doctrines of the Creation, the fall of man, the Nature of Christ, the nature of Inspiration, [and] the nature of the future state"—theologians have room to debate, but when it came to the latter—"the rules of the Decalogue, the New birth, the Law of Love, the Golden Rule, and all other practical precepts" (i.e., the practical aspects of doctrine)—the scriptures were without ambiguity. An error in one's theology did not necessarily manifest itself in a sinful practice, but sinful practice necessarily meant a deficiency in one's theology. "It is everywhere contended by the friends of the slave," Bourne concluded, "that the Bible doctrines in relation to human slavery and its abolition belong entirely to the latter class, being so plainly and perspicuously revealed in the Scriptures."[20]

He then considered the problem of relating specific passages with the general message of special revelation, harmonizing, that is, the letter with the spirit. Masters perverted the scriptures by severing the relationship between the letter and the spirit, making "the Almighty say what He has not said, and to mean what He did not mean."[21] They focused too much on only a few passages and entirely neglected "the spirit of the Scriptures." The "spirit" of the word taken with the "intent of other parts" showed slavery to be "contrary to the universal rule of ethical construction." They failed therefore to "promote the harmony of the whole code."[22] As the Westminster Confession itself testified, God's overall message laid out in scripture was "not manifold, but one."

The bond between the parts and the whole was perhaps best illustrated in God's moral law found in both the Old and New Testaments, which southern masters egregiously flouted. The first five commandments of the Decalogue focus on the duties of the Hebrews to God. Slavery transgressed the first commandment (allegiance to one God) and the second (prohibiting the worship of other gods) by forcing slaves to recognize their masters as God, "compelling them to obey their owners' will in every case." Next, those who suffered under the lash were often tempted to infringe the third commandment by using "the most profane language" against providence. Masters took away their slaves' right to the Sabbath (fourth commandment), "inducing a general neglect and disregard in all slave societies to the ordinances to be attended to on that day." Since owners demanded direct obedience, they prohibited "slave children from honoring and obeying their own parents" (fifth commandment).[23] The latter five commandments focused on the ethical responsibilities regulating the relationship between Hebrews. Concerning the sixth commandment, masters, regardless of their own impunity in getting away with murder, instilled a desire for revenge in the hearts and minds of their slaves. Driven by their own lusts, masters ignored the seventh commandment by either "prohibiting marriage to their slaves, and producing criminal concubinage and licentiousness among them" or forcibly severing all family connections. They also trampled their own marriage commitments. Finally, of the ninth, the chattel institution tended "to produce the habit of falsehood and lying in both masters and slaves—in the former for the purpose of deceiving and abusing their slaves, in the latter to deceive their oppressors and avoid punishment for slave offences."[24]

Christ simplified the old covenant law in the New Testament by dividing it into two all-encompassing principles: to love God and to love one's neighbor. The logic is straightforward. If someone claims to love God, then he or she will necessarily love his or her neighbor. The latter part of the biblical ethic shares a resemblance to the Golden Rule, a favorite among abolitionists: "do unto others as you would have them do unto you" (Luke 6:31). If southerners followed this imperative, the prerequisite of which required a true love of God, then the slave system, Bourne emphasized, would immediately collapse. If a southerner desired freedom of choice, labor, and the pursuit of property for himself, he should have the same desire for his servant. In sum, slavery conflicted with a love of God and neighbor, and a true love for one's slaves would have led to a swift end of slavery.

In order to maintain union between the letter and spirit and to avoid the interpretive errors of proslavery theology, Bourne carefully put forward "certain rules of critical construction" that began with a systematic comparative analysis of biblical language and then moved to the various moral codes:

> I. That the letter of a statute or other law be so construed, whenever it has different meanings in different uses and connections, as to harmonize

with the spirit or general and collective meaning of the whole connection to which it belongs.

II. Where a double or different construction of the letter is admissible, that shall always be preferred which is most consistent with natural liberty, justice and righteousness, provided the general spirit of the law permit such construction.

III. All parts of every code or collection of laws or system of ethics are to be thus harmonized by construction, unless the express letter as well as the general spirit of the same prevent such harmony by such construction, in which case alone we are to allow that there is a conflict of laws in such code or collection. It is to be presumed that no fault will be found with these just and equitable rules, nor with their just and equitable application to the present important subject matter *now under consideration.*[25]

Initially, antislavery Bible expositors tried to show that no word in the ancient text corresponded to the actual meaning of slavery in the American context. American slavery was organized and systemic, touching economics, politics, and culture—the whole of American society, North and South—by the 1840s. Modern slavery, capitalistic and race-based, clashed with the contingent variations of slavery—neither capitalistic nor raced-based—presented in the Bible. Without a critical reflection, slaveholders pushed the notion that the words "buy" and "sell," as it related to "customary legal Hebrew servitudes," suggested a "slavish" system. As Bourne pointed out, the closest example to American slavery from the Old Testament was the experience of Joseph: (1) Joseph had been kidnapped and sold without his consent; (2) he received no compensation for his sale or his labor; (3) he had been converted into a commodity, "as suitable for subsequent traffic and merchandise in."[26] But not even slaveowners cited the example of Joseph in defending southern slavery, for Joseph's enslavement was the result of immoral actions. It was not a benevolent good for Joseph.

Bourne, however, showed by "critical examination and comparison of several passages" that the Bible exhibited "two different purchases and sales of human beings, both entirely opposite to each other in their moral and political nature."[27] This was, as he called it, the "Key to Inquiry," the pivot on which the understanding of slavery turned. Southerners failed to distinguish between regulations having to do with "buying the services of men for a limited period" (Genesis 27:12–27) and servants like Joseph who were "said to be sold or stolen" (Genesis 37:27–26; 42:21–22). It is true that certain selections (e.g., Genesis 37:27–36; Exodus 21:16; Deuteronomy 24:7) used terms like "selling" in reference to involuntary slavery, but the same words were also used to describe free service (Genesis 42:19–23; 1 Kings 21:20–25; 2 Kings 17:17; Acts 20:28; Romans 7:14; 1 Corinthians 6:20, 7:23; 2 Peter 2:1). Genesis 47 delineates the condition and rights of voluntary servants: (1) "that the persons sold were thus treated at their own earnest request," (2) that those who "sold themselves" did so by making a "contract with the purchaser," (3) that they received just (i.e., agreed upon) compensation for their sale, (4) that such laborers were in actuality rented tenants, (5) that the "whole transaction was perfectly moral and virtuous in its own nature, and just as free and equal as common leasing and hiring now are," (6) that such rented servants could "freely hold property of their own" as detailed in Leviticus 26:49 and Nehemiah 5:5, (7) that the sale of one's labor was appropriate for the "payment of previous debts" as intimated in Leviticus 25:27 and Nehemiah 5:8, and finally (8) from passages like Genesis 47, Deuteronomy 24, John 8, and Galatians 4, those who sold themselves often "received their pay *before* their services were to commence" or when they were called "hired servants," paid *after* services were rendered.[28] At any rate, a servant was always compensated. Thus, from Bourne's perspective, references to slavery in the Bible referred to voluntary servitude.

An important aspect of the emerging biblical scholarship was an examination of the hidden motives and possible errors made by Bible translators. Bourne indicted the 1611 King James translators for their linguistic blunders and sloppy translations on the terminology related to biblical servitude, "which they thought bore the strongest resemblance to the then popular practice of Negro slavery . . . without any regard to the literal import of the words in the Hebrew text, or the real doctrine intended to be inculcated by the latter."[29] On this point, Bourne relied heavily on Weld's *Bible against Slavery,* an essay, according Robert Abzug, not of exegesis but of "translation and semantics."[30] Bourne wrote that Weld was one of the first "to call the whole of these absurd perversions into question." *The Bible against Slavery,* first published in 1838, nearly seven years before Bourne's work, focused exclusively on the Old Testament (hence the book's subtitle, *An Inquiry Into the Patriarchal and Mosaic Systems on the Subject of Human Rights*). *Bible Argument,* on the other hand, was not only more harshly critical of the King James translators but also a more complete examination of both the Old and New Testaments. Bourne believed that both his and Weld's study would "now extensively" shake the foundation of the peculiar institution.[31]

King James Bible translators often obfuscated the language of the ancient text. The Hebrew words *evedh* and *amau* in Leviticus 25:44–46 were falsely translated "bond men" and "bond maids." They literally meant "servant" and "maid." Similarly, the word *quaunah,* "buy" as in Genesis 12:5, could denote "to get," "gain," render," "procure," "acquire," or "obtain," while *nauhal,* rendered "possess," was often correctly understood as "inherit," or "redeem." *Quanah* and *kaurau,* "to buy or purchase" also had spiritual meanings and could have related to the acquisition of souls for the true religion. Likewise, *gnabad,* meaning "servant," was used five times in the Old Testament as a proper name—once used to describe David's grandfather, *gnabad* Edom (the servant of Edom), *gnabad* Yahovauzh (the servant of Jehovah), Abednego or *gnabad nago* (the servant of light), and *gnabad malik,* Ebedmelik (the servant of the king). The root of *gnabad* meant "to labor" (or "labor for"), "to serve," "to be tributary," and "to cultivate," as in the case of Adam, who was to till the earth and cultivate it. Neither noun nor verb suggested forced enslavement. Man was created not to be a slave but to be a servant of God by ruling over (not lording over for selfish gain) the earth.

Beyond the linguistic problems slavery's defenders faced, the historical record did not support a system of enslavement among the Old Testament saints. "If ever, therefore, the Jews had practised human slavery," Bourne wondered, "even in violation of the Levitical law, they would have left an historical tradition of it, the same as the Greeks and Romans have of their history—while the entire absence of any such history is the strongest negative testimony that can exist, that the Jews never had any such practice or custom among them." Even ancient religious historians, including Josephus, identify "no such custom."[32] In fact, just the opposite had been the case; God swiftly punished both Hebrew and non-Hebrew nations for establishing involuntary slavery (2 Chronicles 28:8–13; Nehemiah 5: 5–15; Joel 3:3–8; Amos 2:6–7; Obadiah 11; Nahum 3:10; Zechariah 11:5). After its long Babylonian captivity (Jeremiah 34:11–17), the ancient Jewish nation faced judgment for "the sin of human oppression," which included placing their brethren in slavery. Deliverance from Egyptian and Babylonian bondage foreshadowed the ultimate spiritual liberation by God offered through the coming messiah (Matthew 20:28, 26:28; Acts 20:28; Romans 7:14; 1 Corinthians 6:20, 7:23; 1 Peter 1:18–19; 2 Peter 2:1–3; Revelation 5:9; Galatians 4:1–5; Hebrews 9:9, 10:1).[33] A perennial slavish institution would have run counter to Israel's identity as an emancipated people.

A more problematic issue than the actual language of the Bible was a theological justification of "race." The Old Testament never endorsed racial slavery. On this point, Bourne took a closer look at a couple of popular historical-exegetical arguments: the curses of Cain and Canaan in Genesis 4:15 and Genesis 9:20–27 respectively. Such passages were crucial in reinforcing the myth of the black body and its supposedly natural association with the lowest form of labor ("hewers of wood and drawers of water"). Cain, the son of Adam and Eve, was a tiller of the ground, a farmer. At one point, he offered a sacrifice to God composed of agricultural produce. God found such a sacrifice to be profane and therefore repudiated the gift. A separate meat sacrifice given by Cain's brother Abel, however, was accepted. Outraged at God's rejection, Cain murdered his brother in a fit of jealousy. After confronting him for his sin, God made Cain a cursed vagabond; the land into which he would travel and subsequently cultivate would eventually become spoiled. Since the curse affected the land Cain entered, causing the people around him to suffer from his curse, God placed "a mark" (4:15) upon him so that he could be distinguished from others and his life protected from vengeful neighbors. Proponents of slavery asserted that the mark was to be understood as "the black color," which was so absurd to Bourne that he expressed "no disposition to interfere" with the argument. Even moderate antislavery and proslavery biblical scholars found such a view exegetically untenable. Noah's curse against Ham's son in Genesis 9 was a bit more compelling.[34] After his famous journey in the ark, Noah became drunk on the wine made from his own vineyard. Seeing his father in a drunk and naked state, Ham failed to literally clothe his father's shame. Noah's two older sons, Shem and Japheth, covered Noah but did so with their backs turned in order to avoid witnessing his nakedness. When Noah recovered, he cursed Ham's son Canaan by making him "a servant of servants" (9:25) to the sons of Shem and Japheth (9:26–27).

The point of disagreement among Bible readers was the limit of the curse: Did it apply to Canaan's descendants in perpetuity? Boston's Samuel Sewall, who published one of the first antislavery tracts in America, *The Selling of Joseph,* in 1700, and southern Baptist David Barrow, in his 1808 *Involuntary, Unmerited, Perpetual, Absolute, Hereditary Slavery, Examined,* believed it did not. Following in a similar direction, Bourne answered those who "contend that the Negroes descended from Canaan."[35] First, nothing supported the notion that Canaan's children were also to be lowly servants. According to Genesis 10:5–20, Canaan became the ancestor of whole tribes and nations (the Jebusites, Amorites, Girgashites, to name a few) "apparently as free as others." Second, Bourne wrote, "we have no account in the Scriptures, or in any other history, that any of the posterity of Canaan ever settled in Africa." On the contrary, passages from Genesis 10:15–19, 13:12, 15:18–21, and 17:8 show that the posterity of Canaan settled in that part of Asia then called the "Land of Canaan," near Sodom and Gomorrah. The inhabitants of nineteenth-century Syria were closer to the Canaanite lineage. Africans, Bourne conjectured, came from the line of Cush, Mizraim, and Phut, the other sons of Ham. Third, Noah's malediction had been fulfilled when the Jews conquered the land of Canaan (Numbers 24:2–12; Joshua 12:7–8). For the most part, however, proslavery theologians, including leading erudites Robert Lewis Dabney and James Henley Thornwell, "acknowledged the weakness of the racial interpretation of the curse of Canaan and refused to employ the text to justify racial slavery. The curse of Canaan was the weakest of the proslavery biblical arguments."[36]

Additional proslavery historical arguments pointed to the godly example of the patriarchs, many of whom owned servants, and the Mosaic Law that regulated (and hence did not oppose) slaveowning.[37] But according to Bourne such appeals ironically strengthened the antislavery position. From Abraham to Moses, Hebrew servants were (1) circumcised, which brought fellowship with God (Deuteronomy 29:10–13) by means of the covenant and offered, therefore, all the privileges of the Hebrew system (Genesis 17:13–27; Exodus 12:44–48), including a religious education (Genesis 18:19; Joshua 8:33–35), participation in the Passover, the privileges of the Sabbath, various other feasts (Exodus 12:44–49, 23:12; Leviticus 22:11, 25:1–6, 8, 35; Exodus 20:10; Leviticus 25:6), and the "civil rights of periodical freedom of service" during the year of Jubilee (Exodus 21:2; Leviticus 25:10; Deuteronomy 15:12; Nehemiah 5:11; Jeremiah 34:14–17); (2)

given liberal wages, making them the equivalent of hired servants (Leviticus 19:13, 25:35–41; Deuteronomy 24:13–14; Jeremiah 22:13, 34:14–17); (3) governed by the same laws (i.e., the children and heirs of masters had no "greater privileges," wrote Bourne, than did servants) (Exodus 12:49; Deuteronomy 16:18–19; Joshua 8:33–35; 2 Kings 23:2; 2 Chronicles 34:30); (4) able to become heirs of their masters (Genesis 15:3; Proverbs 17:2), exercise the highest offices (Genesis 15:2, 24:2; Proverbs 17:2), marry within their owner's family (Exodus 21:8–9; 1 Chronicles 2:34–35), and hold property and servants of their own (Leviticus 25:49; 2 Samuel 16:4); (5) at times armed militiamen (Genesis 14:14); and (6) free to leave when inflicted with physical violence by their owner (Exodus 21:26–27; Deuteronomy 23:15–16; 1 Samuel 9:22).[38]

A more complicated issue was the specific Old Testament places in which God allowed for Hebrew servitude and non-Hebrew enslavement. This was not a problem for Bourne, however. Placing a fellow Israelite in bondage was a capital offense, yet Leviticus 25:39–44 allowed for poorer Hebrews to be indentured for a time by their brethren. They were to be taken in by a more financially stable member of the Hebrew community. The manager was forbidden to treat his newly acquired servant as a "bondsman," and the service was limited to a six-year term, which could be renewed (Exodus 21:6; Deuteronomy 15:12–18). For example, 2 Kings 4:1 tells the story of a Hebrew woman who came to Elisha and expressed fear that the creditors to whom her husband owed money would take her two sons as servants. If her sons were Hebrews, they could not have been enslaved. The servants needed to be paid in order to absolve their own or their parents' debt. Servitude was a reality for those who owed money, but what did the African owe to the Southern master? Southern slaveholders were unable to offer an explicit command from the Bible justifying the enslavement of anyone. To test the proslavery position even further, it was possible to cite a number of cases in the Old Testament where servants had accumulated money, held property, and even owned servants themselves. As Weld illustrated, "Ziba, the servant of Mephibosheth, . . . had twenty servants [2 Samuel 16:1]"; "Arza, the servant of Elah, was the *owner of a house* [1 Samuel 9:8]"; in the "case of the Gibeonites, who, after becoming servants, still occupied their cities" (Genesis 29:15, 18; 30:28–33); and "of the 150,000 Canaanites, the *servants* of Solomon, who worked out their 'tribute of bond-service' in levies."[39]

Bourne paid closer attention to Leviticus 25:45–46, noting two verses that would have been particularly troubling for antislavery theologians:

> the children of the strangers that do sojourn among you, of them shall ye buy, and of their families that are with you, which they begat in your land: and they shall be your possession. And ye shall take them as an inheritance for your children after you, to inherit them for a possession; they shall be your bondmen forever: but over your brethren the children of Israel, ye shall not rule one over another with rigour.

Agreeing that they should not enslave their own cultural kin, southerners believed that this stipulation protected the right to purchase a bondsman from among the heathen. Once again for Bourne, this was not enough to support the kidnapping of presumed "heathen" Africans. First, the Hebrew word *edh,* in reference to the length of servitude, did not mean perpetual, but rather a set time; the term *olaum,* on the contrary, did.[40] Nonetheless, the King James Version authors translated *edh* to "forever." Second, as shown above, circumcision was required for even foreign servants (Genesis 17:13–27; Exodus 12:44–48; Deuteronomy 29:10–13), which brought them into fellowship with the Hebrew nation and the Hebrew God. Third, Leviticus 25:47–48 showed that a possible reversal of fortune could have occurred between the stranger and the Hebrew overseer: "if a sojourner or stranger wax rich by thee, and thy brothers that dwelleth with him wax poor, and sell himself unto the stranger or sojourner, or to the stock of the stranger's family . . . he may be redeemed again." In order to become rich, the "stranger" must have been paid by the original Hebrew overseer in order to accumulate wealth. Furthermore, the Hebrew who became indebted to the stranger could be redeemed (along with his property) by a family member, suggesting that the servitude between strangers and Hebrews—and thus servitude in general—was neither fixed nor generational. The "purchase" of such foreign servants, as in the case of Abraham, was to protect the "poor foreigners and strangers" from economic exploitation and compel them to adopt the true religion.[41] Such an inheritance of foreigners was given not to individual Israelites but to the covenant and corporate body. Taking captives from among the heathen was encouraged for evangelical reasons.

American slaveholders ignored two further aspects of the Old Testament standards. The first had to do with specifications regarding runaways. The law forbade returning fugitives: "Thou shalt not deliver unto his master the servant which is escaped from his master unto thee. He shall dwell with thee" (Deuteronomy 23:15–16). Despite the *prima facie* reading against slavery, this was not an interpretive difficulty for moderate and proslavery exegetes. According to Moses Stuart, for instance, the rule concerning runaways related only to foreign slaves. An absconded Hebrew servant, on the other hand, was to be returned to his brethren. Bourne was unconvinced. As mentioned earlier, the penalty for enslaving Hebrews was death (Exodus 21:16; Deuteronomy 24:7). Thus, an escapee, according to Bourne, had to have been a voluntary or contractual servant, for if he were a propertied slave he could not be returned to a master who was to be executed anyway. The second related to the requirements of circumcision. Strangers entered the Hebrew community and were offered fellowship with God through this ceremonial act. Circumcision erased distinctions between Hebrews and non-Hebrews. Leviticus 19:34 was clear: "But the stranger that dwelleth with you shall be unto you as one born among you, and thou shalt love him as thyself." Foreign servants lost their heathen identity and became family members when they ceremonially entered the covenant community. Thus, masters had to respect and maintain the well-being of their servants as their own kin; otherwise, the latter could freely choose to leave the service of a tyrannical master.

Another governing proviso ignored by antebellum theologians, Bourne argued, was the Jubilee year found in Leviticus 25:8–10:

> And thou shalt number seven sabbaths of years unto thee, seven times seven years; and the space of the seven sabbaths of years shall be unto thee forty and nine years. Then shalt thou cause the trumpet of the jubilee to sound on the tenth day of the seventh month, in the day of atonement shall ye make the trumpet sound throughout all your land. And ye shall hallow the fiftieth year, and proclaim liberty throughout all the land unto all the inhabitants thereof: it shall be a jubilee unto you; and ye shall return every man unto his possession, and ye shall return every man unto his family.

In the fiftieth year of one's service, a proclamation of liberty, signaled by the blowing of a ram's horn, sounded "throughout all the land unto all the inhabitants thereof" (Hebrew and non-Hebrew). Jubilee was a celebratory cessation of all work, a Sabbath, a period of familial reunion and property reclamation, and a time to reflect on redemption and atonement. By it, owners were deterred from keeping their servants, including foreigners, in a continuous state of servitude. But where was the jubilee proclamation among southerners?

The final portion of *Bible Argument* examines the handful of New Testament sections connected to slavery. Bourne first addressed the "naked and obvious untruth" often asserted by proslavery theologians that Jesus was silent on slavery, since he did not directly condemn it. This was hardly a strong argument; Christ was silent on a number of ethical issues: "we have no account whatever that Christ and his apostles preached against piracy, arson, forgery, counterfeiting, etc, . . . they must have connived at and approbated the practice of those crimes, and thereby left us their Christian sanction to practice the same."[42] But he did condemn slavery insofar as he reaffirmed and in some places tightened the Old Testament legal code: "It would be just as absurd and false to pretend that Christ did not by such ratification and confirmation [of the Old Testament law] directly condemn murder, robbery, theft, and the other crimes specifically condemned in the moral law of the Levitical code, as that he did not directly condemn manstealing or slavery by it."[43] What is more, Christ and his apostles gave numerous speeches not recorded in the New Testament (Acts 1), which made it even more difficult to purport with certainty that they never condemned slavery. Rather, Bourne speculated, Christ did not shy away from teaching "*all* the counsel of God": "'he was pure from the blood of all men,' and as he, in Eph. iv. 20, 21, and other passages, requested the prayers of the brethren for special grace to preach the gospel boldly, which he could not have done without faithfully preaching against slavery or man-stealing, we may confidently conclude that he and all the other apostolic preachers did so."[44]

Another New Testament proslavery argument came from those sections of scripture that bound Christians to live in submission to earthly authorities. Why did Paul in Romans 13, asked antiabolitionist leaders, encourage obedience to imperialistic Rome even though he knew that the empire relied on slavery? Earlier exegetes like Jonathan Edwards's protégé, Samuel Hopkins, believed that for Paul to preach against slavery would have incited the Roman authorities to persecute a nascent religious community. Paul was silent on the issue given the fears that Roman authorities had in potential revolts. Yet his silence on the subject, like that of Christ's, could not be construed as an affirmation of the practice. Although he agreed that a public denunciation of slavery would have been dangerous, Bourne focused on the limits of earthly authority. First, Paul never dealt with the morality of the ancient chattel institution as such, but the ethical conduct of an individual who was in a socioeconomic and political situation; that is, citizens' obedience to God did not morally support a slavish institution. Second, terrestrial authority was by nature service-oriented and not despotically authoritarian. The civil magistrate had a specific duty: he was a servant (literally, in Greek, a "deacon") of God not for evil, but for good (Romans 13:1–4). Christians abided by earthly government to the extent that the magistrate acted in accordance with God's law. They could—and at times did—ignore earthly legislators if they contradicted God's word by serving their own selfish interests. Peter legitimized civil disobedience in Acts 5:29, for example, when he was commanded by the civil authorities not to preach the gospel, which compelled a pious and defiant response: "We ought to obey God rather than man." The duties and boundaries of earthly rulers applied also to relationships at the micro level: between wives and husbands (Ephesians 5), children and parents (Ephesians 6), and masters and slaves (Ephesians 6:5–9; Colossians 3:22–25, 4:1; Titus 2:9–10; 2 Peter 18–20).

A more difficult passage centered on "believing masters" in the early church (Ephesians 6:5–9; Colossians 3:22–25). "It has been sagaciously inferred in behalf of slavery," Bourne defiantly stated, "that Paul fellowshipped with slaveholders, not only as Christian brethren, but as members of the Christian church."[45] A crucial question was how "believing masters" squared with Paul's letter to Timothy condemning "man-stealing." Bourne speculated that no evidence was available to affirm the fact that these believing masters were church members, for the meaning of "believing master" was indeterminate. Perhaps it related to one's past life as in the case of a "converted *Infidel*," "reformed *drunkard*," or other customary scriptural phrases, such as "the blind *see*," "the deaf *hear*," or "the lame *walk*." In these cases, he concluded, "nobody supposes that *converted infidels* and *reformed drunkards* retain the vicious practices they have been converted and reformed from." It could also have referred to the time between conversion and the subsequent casting off of a sinful life: Mary Magdalene was still a prostitute when Jesus saved her, Matthew ceased from being a tax collector only after Christ called him to discipleship, and Paul ended his murderous duties after his conversion experience on the road to Damascus. But whatever their spiritual state, such individuals were identified by what the messiah delivered them from. Despite what the term meant, "it is unreasonable as well as unscriptural to suppose that 'believing' or converted slaveholders in the apostles' time, continued in the practice of slavery after they discovered the sinfulness of it, though it is highly probable that many of them did before they made that important discovery."[46] Additionally, given the passages in the

Old Testament, the term "master" could have referred generally to a temporary employer.

The closing chapter of *Bible Argument* offers an attentive response to the strongest proslavery New Testament argument most appealed to by slave-owners: the case of Philemon's runaway servant, Onesimus.[47] Paul counseled Onesimus to submissively return to his owner and encouraged Philemon to graciously receive back Onesimus. According to antiabolitionists, the letter never condemned the general system under which Onesimus had been enslaved to begin with. Furthermore, the injunction for Onesimus to return to his owner was grounds for members of American churches to support fugitive slave legislation, the most severe of which came in 1850. Bourne scrutinized both word and context. The Greek word for slave, *doulos,* in verse 16, used to describe Onesimus, did not necessarily mean an involuntary slave. Toward the end of the epistle Onesimus is called *oiketes,* meaning house or domestic servant. Since *doulos* and *oiketes* were interchangeable, Onesimus's status was indeterminate. On a related note, *douloi* was regularly used to describe the disciples of Jesus, who, as Lord (*kurioi*) and master, was in no sense a wealth-seeking tyrant of the ancient or nineteenth-century kind. The closest phrase to involuntary bondage in the New Testament, Bourne suggested, came from 1 Timothy 1:6, which described "servants under the yoke." Onesimus was nowhere described in this way.

Since Onesimus's condition was difficult to pin down, Bourne reasoned about the letter's context, which intimated a familial or spiritual relationship between servant and master. Paul reminds Philemon that he had a relationship with Onesimus "in the flesh and in the Lord." If they were fraternal brothers or fellow Jews, then Philemon had egregiously violated Old Testament statutes, and Onesimus had no obligation to return. Paul, a scholar of the Jewish law, would never have ignored Deuteronomy 23:15–16 by returning a fugitive. The same principle applied if they were brothers by faith. Paul calls Philemon a "fellow labourer" and Onesimus "a beloved brother"; both were somehow related to the spread of the gospel ministry. In this way, they were spiritual brothers, an association that would have also condemned enslavement.

No information is given for Onesimus's absence. He may have left for a season or for unjustly injuring Philemon (v. 15). But a key point in understanding the situation comes in verses 18 and 19. Onesimus "owed" something to Philemon, and Paul offered to repay "it." But the payment could not have been

Onesimus himself. For if it was, why would Paul make the additional request for Onesimus to return? Looking forward to the American context, since the master stole labor and wages in order to keep their slaves poor, what did the slave owe to the master? As Bourne wrote in his earlier *The Book and Slavery Irreconcilable,* it was the American man-stealer that needed to financially compensate his slave. If Onesimus was "a servant under the yoke," he would have owed nothing and Paul could not have paid Philemon anything. This confirmed, in Bourne's mind, the fact that Onesimus was an indentured servant.

Each counterargument presented in *Bible Argument* is placed within a holistic interpretive grid presupposed by the author. A key characteristic of antislavery hermeneutics was an emphasis on the historical progression of revelation from the Old to the New Testament. This approach is often difficult to verify by single isolated interpretations. Accordingly, practices in the old Hebrew regime such as polygamy or divorce, although not necessarily approved by God, were done away with when the fulfillment of God's revelation came in Jesus Christ. The New Testament was the age of fulfillment, when all things passed away and were made new. Salvation, for instance, in the Old Testament was incomplete until the coming of Christ in the New Testament. The same was true for a variety of practices. Although punished when they "fell into great errors or sins," the members of the old covenant, Bourne assumed, had more of an excuse than nineteenth-century Christians, for they lived under the "dim and uncertain light" of nature.[48] Nineteenth-century slavery was a much greater crime in the post–New Testament age. This falls in line with what J. Albert Harrill calls the "seed growing secretly" hermeneutic.

Part of the "seed growing secretly" interpretation was the way in which the things in the Old Testament acted as shadows of things to come in the New Testament. The Jubilee, for instance, foreshadowed and anticipated the ultimate spiritual jubilee with the coming of the messiah. Bourne specifically cited Abraham and Christ to present the relationship between image and reality. The patriarch was a prefigure or incomplete type of the messiah, and the references to his purchasing individuals to be under his authority was to be seen as part of God's unfolding plan to gather a people unto himself as promised in Genesis 17. The same sense of being "bought" or "purchased with blood" and "with a price," as in the case of Abraham, was attached to Christ and his "overseers," the disciples, in Acts 20:28 and 1 Corinthians 6:20–7:23. Yet not even slaveholders thought that Christ or his disciples were owners of human property. The functional titles of the messiah figure—a prophet, a priest, and a king—were present but in seed form in the person of Abraham. Bourne explained how Abraham filled, in an incomplete sense, the duties of a prophet (Genesis 20:7), a priest (Genesis 12:7–8, 12:4), and a king (Genesis 23:6). Christ fulfilled these offices in the new covenant. But none of the messiah titles were analogous to American man-stealers. In contradistinction, the true messiah was one who took on the form of a lowly servant.[49] A key to understanding this interpretation was to distinguish "types" from "examples." According to E. Brooks Holifield, the latter "bore their meanings on the surface," while the former "were outward signs" or a kind of anticipatory form "of future spiritual realities."[50] This is to say that Abraham was not an example for contemporary Christians to follow but was a form of the future Christ.

The New Testament likewise redefined "foreigners" or "strangers," first introduced in Leviticus 25, from which slaves could be acquired. The messiah extended salvation to the whole world, not just to a specific ethnic community. According to Galatians 3:28, there existed no spiritual foreigners or heathens; all were one in Christ. The spiritual aspect of redemption, in its full New Testament bloom, superseded and thus nullified physical distinctions. Tayler Lewis, who began his academic tenure teaching Greek at the University of New York in 1838, once wrote, "We [antebellum Americans] still speak of the heathen, using the term geographically, and, to some extent, ethnologically; but theologically, ecclesiastically, Christianly, there are no heathen."[51]

Southern and antiabolitionist theologians eagerly exploited the inherent irreligion of abolition, seeking to make themselves the representatives of a pure Christianity. They pointed to the invectives of William Lloyd Garrison, the voice of antitheological antislavery. At a women's rights convention in Philadelphia ten years after the death of his mentor, Boston's fiery liberator took a stand against traditional orthodoxy: "[T]he Bible never settled any question. It has filled the world with theological discussion, growing out of the various interpretations given to the book. *The human soul is greater than any book.* If there is truth in the Bible, we take it; if error, we discard it."[52] Garrison appealed to the heart, not the literal letter, of the Bible. "Radical abolitionists," Oshatz highlights, "appealed to the law of God, engraved on the conscience, over and against the biblical word." In 1845, the year of Bourne's death, Garrison proclaimed that instead of using the words of scripture to form their consciences, moral men and women should use their consciences to judge the contents of the Bible. "To say that everything in the Bible is to be believed, simply because it is to be found in that volume," wrote Garrison, was "absurd and pernicious."[53] Gerritt Smith, who had a slightly higher view of the Bible, likewise elevated human character: "All this talk that the Bible is the charter of man's rights is nonsense. His nature is that charter; and his rights are the rights of his nature . . . every book to the contrary not withstanding."[54] If the Bible was authoritative and infallible, Garrisonians wondered, why then could it not settle one of the most divisive issues of the nineteenth century? Radical abolitionism came to be symptomatic of heresy. Not all agreed, however, with such an association. Bourne's nearly one-hundred-page *Condensed Anti-Slavery Bible Argument* was a double-edged sword: it attacked those who perverted the Bible to support their own self-centered interests, and it inadvertently engaged those who thought that the Bible, given its use by the friends of slavery, needed to be abandoned.[55]

Placing the American nation within a redemptive historical drama, Bourne ended his theological argument, as he did *Book and Slavery,* with a call to repentance and reformation in order to escape the impending wrath of God: "It is most true that God will eventually deliver the slaves, whether we repent of the sin of enslaving them or not; but the whole analogical teaching of the Scriptures, as well as the promises of God teach us, that He will do so by our own national destruction, unless we seasonably repent and reform from the sin of slavery by voluntary abolition. . . . That the Lord, in his infinite goodness, may grant us the disposition to [end slavery], is the prayer of the writer of these pages."[56] Bourne's exegetically detailed argument only strengthened the religious case in favor of antislavery and further indicted those who ignored the authoritative and inherently liberating message of the Bible.

By the time of the Civil War, the theological debates over the Bible and slavery reached what many considered an irreconcilable crisis point. In his second inaugural address, President Abraham Lincoln highlighted the crisis in an acute and unsettling manner. Both sides read the same Bible, he said, but both could not be right. Bourne, and other antislavery slavery Bible writers, believed that their reading of the Bible was the correct reading. Regardless, slavery and the war had a profound impact on the authority of the Bible in postbellum American life. As contemporary historians note, the Bible arguments against slavery put into question the whole of Protestant theology. According to E. Brooks Holifield, a closer examination of the historical conditions of the development of theology undermined the stability of Protestant theology in general.[57] Eugene and Elizabeth Fox-Genovese argue dogmatically that antislavery Protestants had to abandon orthodoxy in constructing abolitionist polemics.[58] Molly Oshatz writes, "Proslavery Protestants succeeded in focusing the debate on the question of slavery in the abstract. Making a biblical case against slavery in the abstract required an enormous departure not just from antebellum literal hermeneutics, but from the entire Protestant understanding of revelation, that is, of God's relationship to humanity. The slavery debates posed fundamental challenges to Protestant theology."[59] What is more, after the slavery debate, settled ultimately not by debate but by war, "marked a beginning—that is, the beginning of Protestant awareness of the role of history and experience in shaping truth and morality."[60] Given the difficulty of employing a biblical argument to settle the question of slavery once and for all, biblical hermeneutics opened itself to less restrictive views on divine revelation. Antislavery Protestants, she writes, "came to rely on a new, liberal understanding of Christian truth," and the very existence of slavery "gave rise to the ideas that would become the hallmarks of liberal Protestant theology: God's revelation unfolded progressively through human history, moral action had to be considered in its historical and social context, and the ultimate source of Protestant truth was the shared experience of believers rather than the letter of the biblical text."[61] By 1864, the conservative Old School Presbyterians came to admit God's moral revelations in history as "manifest tokens that the time has at length come, in the providence of God, when it is His will that every vestige of human slavery among us should be effaced."[62] The biblical debates over slavery, Oshatz concludes, "contributed to the transformation of American intellectual life. . . . The Bible was no longer a transparent record of the moral law, and being a good Christian required determining the meaning of Christian revelation for one's own time."

Yet I wonder if historians and theologians examining the Bible and slavery have anticipated a future liberalism that faults the biblical text itself. Historians should avoid an argument of inevitability, namely that the hermeneutical challenges led to an abolitionist relegation of the Bible's authority. There was no lack of consensus among abolitionists from various faith traditions as to what the Bible said about institutional slavery. Indeed, if any group lacked consensus—as well as consistency—it was the defenders of slavery as well as moderate antislavery advocates. In this way, antislavery Bible polemicists like

Bourne cannot be culpable for later theological developments; certainly not in Bourne's case, for he did not see a dilemma between scripture and slavery. Even those like Garrison who rejected the authority of scripture could agree with the various hermeneutical strands among abolitionism. One final note to make is that Bourne highlighted the posture of those who rejected a robust antislavery Bible argument, namely that human beings can willfully suppress the truth, or in the case of slavery utilize sophisticated arguments to distract from their sordid agendas. The source of the textual problem, according to Bourne, had to do less with the Bible itself and more with those reading it and twisting the text to support the sinful institution of slavery. Proslavery arguments were formulated and propagated by those whose eyes had not been illuminated by the redemption of Christ, hence the reason why Bourne consistently proclaimed liberty to the captives.

CHAPTER 4

CATHOLIC SLAVERY AND PROTESTANT FREEDOM IN BOURNE'S *Lorette*

> I am not my own director, you know who manages my concerns, I never did.
>
> —GEORGE BOURNE, *Lorette*

As demonstrated in the previous chapters, Bourne's hostility toward slavery rested on a kind of ultra-Protestantism, which inevitably moved him beyond strictly physical enslavement and toward a higher concept of liberty, liberation that incorporated an individual's body *and* soul. Many abolitionists shared a similar mindset: freedom was absolute. This is why hostility toward Catholicism was not uncommon among abolitionists, especially for Bourne. William Lloyd Garrison once wrote that the "main pillars" of "man-enslaving religion" were partially infected by "Popery."[1] Dublin printer Richard Webb, a frequent reporter for the *Liberator* and close friend of its editor, stated at one time that "the rampant, audacious, Ultramontanism of the Romish clergy" was identical with the "kindred spirit of chattel slavery."[2] George Cheever, Congregational minister and correspondent for the *New York Evangelist,* considered the political and social tyranny of southern slavery as "Romish and Romanist." For abolitionist and women's rights advocate Jane Swisshelm, "to be a minister of the Roman church was to be a friend of Southern interests."[3] Elijah Lovejoy, commemorated as a courageous martyr of the abolitionist crusade, attributed the rising opposition against his antislavery newspaper, the *St. Louis Observer,* not to southern slaveocracy, but to popery: "The fire that is now blazing and crackling [against his paper] was kindled on Papish altars and has been assiduously blown up by Jesuit breath."[4]

Few reformers, however, worked as hard as George Bourne in combating southern slavery and Roman Catholicism, "the two foes of the Republic and of a pure Christianity."[5] In his mind, American slavery rested on the institutionalization of false religion, derived from a distortion of true doctrine by ecclesiastical elites who, through the suppression of the Bible, elevated themselves to a status reserved only for God. They enslaved bodies and souls, crushed true piety, impeded spiritual enlightenment, and severed communal relationships. By 1830, Bourne made a similar observation about Catholicism, which had grown significantly in America by that time. The same organizational structure and social consequences found in slavery were at the base of the Roman Catholic Church. Institutionally, the churches of "Negro-Thieving preachers," Bourne wrote, were like those of Jesuit priests: "genuine Synagogues of Satan."[6] And like "Popish lessons," the beliefs and practices of man-stealers were of "little more value than the rays of the sun during a total eclipse."[7] By 1830, Bourne had widened his perspective of freedom by linking slavery and popery.

Hysteria over "popish" plots in North America sprang up erratically in the middle to late seventeenth and eighteenth centuries, but it was not until the early nineteenth—due in large part to the conservatism sweeping Europe after the demise of Napoleon, the success of Pius VII in elevating Baltimore to the status of archdiocese with satellite dioceses in Philadelphia, New York, Boston, and Bardstown (Kentucky), and the later waves of Irish Catholic immigrants—that a virulent (and violent) "no-popery" impulse reached a high point.[8] And according to Bourne, it was popular religious print, particularly "theological discussion and missionary intelligence," that effectively warned the republic of the growing threat of a papal takeover.[9] Although dedicated largely to theological polemic, Bourne, for the first and only time in his life, used evangelical fiction to battle this "Man of Sin." In the same year that he helped organize the American Anti-Slavery Society, Bourne popularized a new genre in American literature. His first and only novel, *Lorette: A History of Louise, Daughter of a Canadian Nun, Exhibiting the Interior of Female Convents,* a runner-up bestseller in 1833, was, according to historian David Reynolds, the "prototype of the most popular type of post-1835 anti-Catholic fiction—the exposé of convents." Through *Lorette,* Bourne "set the pattern for anti-Catholic fiction in America" and paved the literary way for the immensely successful *Six Months in a Convent* (1835) by Rebecca Reed and *Awful Disclosures of the Hotel Dieu Nunnery of Montreal* (1836), the "Uncle Tom's Cabin" of American nativism, by Maria Monk.[10]

Lorette—which had been dedicated as "a tribute of respect" to friend and fellow reformer Arthur Tappan, "for his Christian Philanthropy and zeal, on behalf of the Blind and Wretched"—represented an important moment in Bourne's reformist development. *Lorette* launched Bourne as an authority on anti-Catholicism. Indeed, Marie Anne Pagliarini has argued that given the similarities between *Lorette* and Monk's *Awful Disclosures,* Bourne, one among a handful of Protestant "advisers" to Monk, was the primary author of the latter.[11] The anti-Catholic overtones in the novel were crucial in the additions made in his later antislavery writings, figuring prominently in *Picture of Slavery in the United States of America* (1834) (chap. 2) and *Slavery Illustrated in Effects on Woman and Domestic Society* (1837) (chap. 5). Both of the later works uncovered the shared religious root and social consequences that undergirded southern and Romish tyranny.

The secondary literature on anti-Catholicism in America has focused largely on issues related to immigration, labor, and political formations within the context of the market revolution and an expanding democracy. Contemporary cultural scholars like Jenny Franchot and Marie Anne Pagliarini have devoted a considerable amount of time discussing how the cultural images in the ex-nun (e.g., the presence of a lustful priestly class, raped nuns, the collapse of marriage, the evil that lurked in the private Catholic sphere, and the need for middle-class patriarchal protection, themes that bore a striking resemblance to the escaped slave narratives) "voiced the tensions of mainstream Protestant culture."[12] Much less attention, however, has been given to the important theological emphases that structured earlier no-popery works. In *Roads to Rome,* Jenny Franchot, one of the leading historians of American nativism to come after Ray Billington, admittedly lumps the "not so interesting waters of theological polemic" with the "more contemporary psychological terrains of the comic or the pathologically hostile."[13] There is a subtle presentism in the way contemporary scholars dismiss as neurotic beliefs that sharply conflict with our modern sentiments. Such dismissive psychological arguments have a tendency to elevate the present by disparaging the past. Writing around the same time as Franchot, Richard Carwardine offers an indirect critique of this conceptual approach: "the power of evangelicals' anti-Catholicism is misunderstood when it is seen principally as a vehicle or a cover for more 'real' economic or social concerns." Scholars often lose "sight of the reality of the religious confrontation."[14]

Bourne's anti-Catholicism should be understood as a functioning part of his rationalized worldview. While never shying away from nineteenth-century literary constructs, his central goal in revealing the false religion of Catholicism (as with slavery) was to present a picture of true Bible-centered Protestantism. The theological interacted with changing cultural understandings of the self in society and played a leading role in Bourne's concept of absolute freedom. His views on Catholicism reflected his pursuit of articulating a universal freedom, one that took into consideration both body and soul. Bourne writes in the preface that *Lorette* "may enhance the love of freedom, intelligence, purity and truth: and also render that triple alliance, ignorance, error, and corruption, more odious and repugnant."[15] Truth, purity, and freedom were all protected by a vigilant and active Protestantism. The goal of this chapter, then, is to consider *Lorette* as an evangelical theological drama that presents the author's concept of freedom as a product of the relationship between biblical faith, church authority, and family cohesion. The characters' search for an authentic religion leads to the breaking away of abusive ecclesial power and the restoration of their identity within the family context, exposing the irreligious nature of Catholic intrigue in its attempt, according to Bourne, to invert "proper" gender roles, destroy marriage, and undermine male headship.

Bourne's attitude toward the papacy paralleled the evolving nativism that shaped the political scene in the North. After his removal from the Presbyterian Church, Bourne spent a few years as a schoolteacher in Mount Pleasant, New York.[16] In New York particularly, as Jason Duncan argues in *Citizens or Papists?*, Catholics had been involved in community development long before the influx of Irish immigrants. Wealthier New York Catholic families succeeded in the business community, helped establish schools, worked to provide a safe haven for Catholic immigrants, and even engaged in public service.[17] Yet at the same time, from the colonial period to the early 1820s, opposition to the papacy followed Catholic growth and played a central role in New York's political culture.

Between 1823 and 1829, perhaps because of financial hardships he and other New Yorkers faced as a result of the Panic of 1819, one of the first major economic depressions to hit the United States, Bourne and his family relocated for a brief time to Quebec. Along with his ministerial duties, which included acquiring three separate pastorates, Bourne continued to work with a number of reform agencies. In 1825 he was elected secretary of the Quebec Bible Society; four years later he became "Librarian and Keeper of the Cabinet" of the Literary and Historical Society of Quebec.[18] When he returned to New York with his family in 1829 to take up a call at the North Street Third Dutch Reformed

Church, the Catholic Church was in the midst of its own internal upheaval in the lay trustee controversy, one in which the church, like other Protestant denominations, underwent a kind of democratization. A few Protestants, for a time, supported the actions of the laity to maintain their right to local sovereignty, which included regulating their property and choosing their own ministers.[19] But following the political changes occurring in nineteenth-century Europe, papal leaders increasingly took local control away from the laity, bringing American Catholics closer to a new conservative Rome. Such a power struggle, many contemporaries believed, seemed to echo what England had done in ignoring local colonial rule, a major cause of the American Revolution. The lack of a major revolt on the part of American Catholics to the dictates of Rome suggested that Catholics, based on their religious nature, were willing subjects of abusive power. From the Protestant perspective, then, Catholicism was quickly becoming an unassimilable, foreign, anti-Revolutionary, and *un*-American presence.[20]

Before writing *Lorette,* Bourne attempted to establish his own no-popery newspaper. Concerned over the influence of Catholics in New York, he began publication of *The Protestant* in January 1830, "the first journal published in America devoted to the Antipapal controversy," according to Ray Billington.[21] Theodore Bourne, commending his father for taking the "early lead" in the papal conflict, wrote that the *The Protestant* "awoke the sleeping genius of Protestantism."[22] The goal of the paper, as outlined in its prospectus, was "to inculcate Gospel doctrines against Romish corruptions"; "maintain the purity and sufficiency of the Holy Scriptures against Monkish tradition"; exemplify the watchful care of Immanuel over the church; continue in the history of those who defended the Christian tradition from error (e.g., Luther, Calvin, Zwingli, Cranmer, Knox, Baxter, Owen, Whitefield, and Wesley); and denounce the creed of Pope Pius IV and the Council of Trent.[23] Leading evangelical newspapers including the *Western Recorder,* the *Rochester Observer,* the *Baptist Register,* and the *New York Evangelist,* each known for its anti-Catholic tirades, endorsed Bourne's *Protestant* upon its appearance in 1830.[24] Religious reformers like Nathaniel Beman and Joshua Leavitt found Bourne's work beneficial to the cause of righteousness. Garrison likewise praised the paper and even encouraged African Americans, "as far as their means allow, to patronize this grand 'Expositor of Popery'" in gratitude to the author's efforts in antislavery.[25]

The Protestant had, for Garrison, "a claim to public patronage not surpassed by any other publication" in America; it was the initial unifying step in the clergy's battle against "Jesuitism."[26]

Concurrently, conservative Catholic writers, many of whom denounced all forms of fanaticism, including radical abolition, worked to discredit Bourne, characterizing *The Protestant* as "a lamentable ignorance" produced by "the cupidity of [a] brainless mendicant" who had a "bigoted attachment to falsehood."[27] As Billington informs us, Bourne was eventually removed as editor-in-chief for not exposing a series of articles written by Bishop John Hughes, one of the most outspoken nineteenth-century American Catholics. Under the pseudonym "Cranmer," Hughes sarcastically mocked the tenets of the Catholic Church, inciting Protestant and nativist readers. He later revealed his plot in the Catholic *Truth Teller.*[28] But an underlying issue was that the board of editors of *The Protestant* disliked the theological focus of Bourne and used the Hughes controversy to remove him. Bourne's associate, William Craig Brownlee, another famous anti-Catholic editor and member of the Dutch Reformed Church, took over the paper, but he too was removed in 1832. These theologically focused writers failed to arouse the interest of the public and thus garner large numbers of subscriptions. Hardly discouraged from their removal from the paper, both reformers established the New York Protestant Association and later the Protestant Reformation Society, which eventually merged with another organization to become the ultra-Protestant American Foreign Christian Union.[29]

As mentioned above, Bourne's "no-popery" writings were more theological in orientation, emphasizing the doctrines of biblical authority, salvation (specifically the Protestant doctrine of justification by faith alone, which was also emphasized in his biography of Wesley), and evangelical persuasion in the pursuit of social reform. The anti-immigration elements that show up in later nativistic works are largely absent from his. There are a couple of references to the Irish and one comment on the "debasement of Ireland" in his later *American Text-book of Popery,* but presumably not in the sense that the Irish themselves posed a threat, for even they—led as slaves by their master, the pope—could be redeemed through faith. Lacking an explicitly political nativism, Bourne's battle against Catholicism was more theological in perspective: he never abandoned his commitment to the centrality of historical Protestantism in maintaining a healthy society. False religion, manifested in the systems of both Catholicism and proslavery evangelicalism, not only undermined an individual's divinely ordained economic, political, and cultural duties, but also the very foundation of piety itself.

Antebellum religious novels like *Lorette* offered spiritual realities that tapped into much earlier Protestant understandings of the sacred and the secular. From its inception in the sixteenth century, Protestantism challenged the idea that certain activities were inherently sacred or secular and that the truly pious Christian had to escape the mendacity of the everyday world—renounce mother and father, brother and sister—for sustained spiritual contemplation. In reaction to this separation between the pious and the mundane, what Bourne referred to as "monastic mummery," many reformers came to affirm that all of life was sacred. Christians in both Europe and America could now maintain an intimate relationship with the divine even in their everyday ordinary lives. According to Alistair McGrath, "The Reformation witnessed a remarkable turnabout in attitudes towards the secular order . . . the real vocation of a Christian came in serving God in this world . . . in the cities, marketplaces and council chambers of the secular world."[30] Secular activities were given sacred meaning. The truly faithful, Protestant reformers believed, worked within the world with a sincere heart before God and, therefore, yielded greater spiritual wealth.[31]

This sacralization of the secular sharpened cultural distinctions as well, especially those related to domesticity and the cult of true womanhood. Reformer Martin Luther elevated housework over hermetic meditation: although having no "appearance of holiness, yet these very household chores are more to be valued than all the works of monks and nuns." Similarly, English reformer William Tyndale also closed the gap between domestic and ecclesiastical labor: "washing dishes and preaching the word of God," although vastly different, were "as touching to please God."[32] And America's market revolution reinforced this sacred-through-the-secular mentality. The spatial division between work and home, accelerated as a result of the market revolution, restructured the sacred and secular nature of such spaces that consequently fashioned the identities and duties of the people within them.[33] Popular novels of the 1830s linked domestic chores with spiritual rebirth, showing "evidence of saving grace by sweeping the cottage floors and doing the laundry." Duty and practice reflected one's faith, but it was the character of the feminine mother that instilled such faith. The nineteenth-century middle-class mother became a key avenue toward salvation. In her analysis of this type of literature, Jane Tompkins emphasizes the idea that many early nineteenth-century writers illustrated "the story of salvation through motherly love."[34] A spate of evangelical Protestants identified the analogy between the earthly family as "the aptest [*sic*] illustration" of the heavenly home, placing the wife and mother as its "chief minister."[35]

Presenting images of the self in a commercial society in accordance with "separate sphere" ideology contributed to what historian David Reynolds called the "fictionalization" of American evangelicalism. Such a process was a move away from the more metaphysically abstruse discourses of late eighteenth- and early nineteenth-century Calvinist ecclesiastics. For many, Old World Protestantism and the realm of the sacred seemed distant or elitist, but with the democratization and feminization of Christianity in the post-Revolutionary period and the explosion of cheap print, according to Reynolds, there came a wider appreciation for religious fiction that stressed secular morality, sentimental piety, and a more "friendly" and "affectionate" (feminine qualities) redeemer, themes that represented increased hostility to older (and colder) Calvinistic theological discourse.[36]

Fictionalization revived individual practical morality as the litmus test for true faith, placing orthopraxy over orthodoxy. Acts of piety were interwoven and often conflated with earthly duties and cultural distinctiveness. Henry Ware's *Formation of the Christian Character,* published the same year as the first installment of Garrison's *Liberator,* related religious storytelling with the language of the popular mind: "The World is the theatre on which you are to prove yourself a Christian. . . . We must enter the crowd and distractions of common life." Such "common language" was used to "engage in common and secular affairs."[37] Antebellum writers and reformers, as Reynolds suggests, "reflected a confidence that individual regeneration and social change were linked and that preachers could help speed conversion by addressing topical social issues in sermons containing concrete illustrations of success or failure in common life."[38] The religious and cultural alterations in popular print assisted Bourne in presenting the doctrines of Protestant Christianity. If Reynolds's observation is at all helpful, Bourne's novel can be situated between the changes in American religious literature. *Lorette* reflected the cultural imagery of nineteenth-century literature but retained a connection with the theological discourse of older religious writings.

In setting the backdrop for *Lorette,* Bourne relied on the bucolic scenery in the area surrounding Quebec and how it revealed God's "beauteous and fascinating material operations."[39] In 1829, with the help of James Smillie, the "first pictorial engraver" in Quebec and a famous New York painter, Bourne published *Picture of Quebec and Its Vicinity,* a guidebook for visitors to northern Canada.[40] One section of the booklet described the small town of Lorette near Quebec. Upon entering, guests would first encounter Lake St. Charles, an "enchanting picture" that "developes [*sic*] imagery little inferior in natural beauty, which history and poetry have consecrated to perennial remembrance." After passing an Indian village near the lake, visitors would come to an old hermitage built by an intendant of the French government "for the secluded residence of a Lady."[41] The lady's husband, as one rumor had it, thought his wife so beautiful that he hid her in the house. Bourne, however, saw this as unlikely, for the "swarms of mosquitoes and gnats" during the summer months "must have rendered the Hermitage anything but an abode of rest."[42] Another explanation was that the intendant, who wanted to live with his family at Beauport, built the abode for his mistress. Regardless of the history of the hermitage and its inhabitant, it is highly probable that the rumors served Bourne's imagination in creating the narrative's central character, Louise.

What is most striking about *Picture of Quebec* is the absence of any harsh anti-Catholicism. According to Bourne, tourists would have been edified by Quebec's scenery, which included numerous French Catholic establishments. He described the artwork in a number of Roman churches—the nativity, the virgin and child, the vision of St. Therese, and a meditating St. Bruneau—with no Protestant commentary that linked such images to idolatry or the "son of perdition." Equally, he portrayed the infamous Hotel Dieu as "a capacious edifice," taking up a large portion of the northern part of the interior of Quebec between Couillard and Palace streets.[43] In fact, the interior and exterior of the Ursuline convent was conducive to the domestic arts, for it was, as Bourne wrote, established "to promote female education," which included things like "needlework." The Duchess of Aiguillon built the institution in 1637 for works of charity for "the reception and care of the sick." The presence of benevolence or the domestic crafts like needlework linked the convent to traits associated with female virtue.[44] When discussing the Hotel Dieu, therefore, Bourne offered no warning of a Catholic threat to the United States, no scenes of torture, no lustful priests, and no slavish nuns. His descriptions of the nunnery were nowhere near the horrific gothic scenes most readers would come to be familiar with after reading Reed and Monk.

Nonetheless, Bourne presented Catholic Quebec as a kind of Old World artifact, a lifeless society tied to an expiring religion, intimating the inherent nature of Catholicism as a religion of barbarity and inevitable decline. The author describes Lorette as a "dilapidated memento of anterior times."[45] Paradoxically, Bourne's admiration of the past may have been offered as a kind of celebration of its demise, inculcating in the mind of his readers a greater appreciation for the progressivism of a Protestant civilization. His descriptions of an older unenlightened environment made so by false religion mirrored his picture of the non-Protestant (i.e., non-Christian) slave plantation in both *Picture of Slavery* and *Slavery Illustrated* as barbaric and uncivilized.

In the introduction to *Lorette,* Bourne related an experience he had while writing *Picture of Quebec.* During his tour of Canada, he met up with an elderly gentleman by the name of Diganu, the name of an important character in *Lorette,* who accompanied the author to Montmorenci, Lorette, and Lake St. Charles. When they came to Lorette, Diganu told Bourne of the "affecting occurrences" of the place and gave the author a sealed package that contained "the record of some past events and characters." The packet was not to be viewed until after Diganu's death. When he finally perused the document, Bourne was shocked to read the harrowing account of an escaped nun. The incident confirmed in his mind the satanic undertones of Canada's religious and social conditions and rekindled his anti-Catholicism: "The peculiar characteristics of society there elude a slight regard; and to comprehend the state of religious principles, the tone of domestic morals, the mental vassalage, and the profound debasement of the *habitans* [*sic*] of that province, numerous difficulties and obstructions must be surmounted." The events described by Diganu, which detailed his relationship with an ex-nun named Louise, stirred Bourne to write a fictional account about the events. He assured his readers that Diganu, who changed the names of the real characters, affirmed the accounts to be true. For Bourne, this was a true story about human nature placed in a fictional setting: "man as he is, not as fiction describes him," presenting the essence of each person in the story in the "unadorned drapery of truth."[46]

The main character and heroine of *Lorette,* Louise, breaks away from the clutches of a lecherous priest after reading the Bible and accepting the tenets of the Protestant faith. Two young men, Diganu and Chretien, rescue a pale Louise near Lake St. Charles immediately after her escape. The squaws of the local Indian village nurture her back to health. After Louise regains her strength, she tells her male rescuers and close confidants of her life under a despotic priest. She also discusses her conversion to Protestant Christianity, which had inspired her to run away in the first place. Diganu and Chretien express dismay when Louise disavows Catholicism. Explaining in detail her religious transformation, Louise eventually produces a change in the hearts of her companions, encouraging them to "snap the chain" of Jesuitism that fettered their mind.[47]

During her recovery and interaction with Diganu and Chretien, Louise's former master, a Jesuit priest, works to recapture his prized possession. Accepting that Louise has renounced the life of a celibate nun, Diganu offers her patriarchal protection through the bonds of marriage, a victimized woman's only safe harbor from a dissolute and, thus, unmanly tyrant who cares little for the well-being of the "weaker vessel." The two agree to a secret ceremony, but before its commencement the priest enters the scene, stops the wedding, and makes the most startling announcement: Diganu and Louise are in actuality siblings. Readers could only assume that such images of incest were not used to condemn the betrothed (for they were ignorant of their actions) but to denounce the priest for not educating the two in the proper understanding of courtship and marriage. This type of sexual perversion was the consequent of false religion. After the wedding, the priest imprisons Louise once again as a heretic. She continues to correspond with her brother, who busily works to find ways to free his sister, which include working closely with a lawyer. Louise endures the sexual advances of her captor, but her new faith—the protector of her soul—allows her to withstand the theological errors and immoral practices that flow naturally from the Jesuit religion. Although never physically freed from her physical imprisonment, which seems to work against the escaped nun genre, Louise's acceptance of the true faith after an encounter with Christ and his word suggests the very nature of ultimate freedom.

While imprisoned, the former nun meets up with another heretic, Therese, who, the reader comes to find out, is Louise's mother. It is at this point in the story that Bourne's theological and evangelical perspective becomes most salient. As they regularly interact, Louise takes the opportunity to tutor her estranged mother in Protestant doctrine. Central to their discussions is the authority of the scriptures. When an uninformed Therese asks where one could find true Christianity, her daughter offers a standard reformed response: "The Scriptures are given to us as a rule by which to try our spiritual condition."[48] It is only through a direct reading of the Bible and not the words of a priest that salvation came. In fact, everything related to the errors of Romanism stemmed from a refusal to search the scriptures: "The whole fabric, called Popery, is founded upon an impenetrable ignorance of the gospel of Christ."[49] But despite the work of those who suppressed the truth, Louise argues, the Bible maintained its integrity throughout history as a result of the miraculous work of the Holy Spirit.

According to Bourne, suppressing the word of God was the initial step in securing papal dominance and creating slaves: "[T]he Pope established himself above all law, arrogated the god-like attributes of holiness and infallibility and demanded and enforced obedience to his decreetals." Not only did he project himself higher than any earthly or heavenly law, but he arrogantly "exalteth himself above that [which] is called God or that [which] is worshipped, so that as God [he] sitteth in the temple of God, shewing himself that he is God" (2 Thessalonians 2:4). Priests accomplished this task by convincing their followers that their word was "greater than the word of God."[50] Allowing the members of the Catholic Church to read the scriptures for themselves would have threatened priestly authority. Consequently, such leaders determined the meaning of "the sacred scriptures," demanding "belief or rejection of them in conformity with the papal decision."[51] "[B]y grasping and concealing the divine word," Romanists became "unlimited and supreme."[52] They deprived "men of the true law of their sanctification [and] the progressive holiness which the Gospel demands."[53]

From there, in a kind of evangelical Socratic dialogue, Louise and Therese discuss the errors of Catholicism as they relate to faith and works in salvation. Bourne's thoughts on this issue were later articulated in greater detail in his *American Text-book of Popery* (chap. 6). The doctrines of Rome negated the importance of Christ's obedience, death, and resurrection unto salvation. Contrary to reformed theology, then, Catholics divided "the work of salvation between man and Christ."[54] The church rejected the Protestant doctrine of "justification by faith alone": "Faith doth not justify as an instrument . . . [it is] not the only cause of justification, but also hope, charity, alms, deeds, and other virtues."[55] Because additional "works are necessary as efficient causes" for salvation, Rome, according to Bourne, enabled individuals to save themselves by their own efforts.[56] If salvation were a matter of human action, then the sacrificial atonement of Christ would not have been necessary. "Thus the Romanists do not acknowledge the Lord Jesus Christ to be the only and exclusive cause of eternal salvation [Isaiah 45:21–25; Matthew 11:28; John 3:16, 36; Acts 4:12]; and therefore their doctrine is contrary to the essential design of the Gospel, because they have devised other means of redeeming sinful men than Christ and genuine faith in him."[57] Bourne integrated into the story the Protestant doctrine of justification by faith alone, whereby a penitent rested on the active work of Christ in imputing righteousness to sinners. Romanism could not be "Christian" because the work of Christ was removed from salvation.

Convinced of Rome's theological errors, Therese is finally instructed to personally apply the Bible—its doctrines, commandments, and the lives of the many biblical heroes—with a sincere heart directly onto her conscience; otherwise it "will be of no permanent advantage."[58] It is at this stage that the reader would recognize the contrast between the Protestant cultural emphasis on inner sincerity and the shallow exterior of Catholicism. Catholics, like the Pharisees during Jesus' day, paraded their piety in public. Christ condemned such hypocrisy. Coming to an understanding of the doctrines of salvation, Therese asks whether she herself had "experienced godly sorrow," realizing, contrary to Catholic piety, that "religion is more a personal thing of the heart."[59] Sincerity before God mattered more than outward practices; for, as Karen Halttunen suggests, Protestants who inquired as to whether they were truly saved were, in actuality, questioning their sincerity.[60] This was perhaps one of the richest literary moments in all of Bourne's writings, for he led his readers to see and thus witness the gradual conversion of Therese, a process that incorporates a knowledge of the true religion, the conviction of individual sin, and the final acceptance of the person and work of the messiah.

Therese's change of heart reminds Louise of her own conversion. During her initial enslavement, Louise interacted with an old woman at Guernsey, Marguerite, who warned the aspiring girl of the error of priests in not allowing the freedom to read the Bible. An individual's transfer from darkness to light required an unmediated reading of the scripture, the source by which one could fully understand human nature and the person of God. In a scene that would have reminded a Protestant of St. Augustine's conversion, the young Louise heeded the advice of the old women to read the Bible for herself. At once, the scales fell from her eyes. "Seeing Jesus," Louise recalled the old woman saying, brought emancipation. The individual encounter with the word, a necessary component of Reformed theology and, more broadly, evangelicalism, transformed Louise, allowing her "to dissipate the mists of error" in which she had been trained.[61] The youthful woman experienced a new birth. This "born again" motif through direct Bible reading remained in only a few nineteenth-century exposés.[62] In a late nineteenth-century ex-nun story, a conflicted nun came into contact with "the ranks of Bible Protestantism, her eyes were open, the scales of dark Romanism, error and superstition had been removed." She became, therefore, "a new creature."[63]

Woven into the storyline of *Lorette* is a Protestant discourse concerning identity transformation through spiritual conversion. The restoration of one's true self—i.e., the new birth—followed on the heels of Protestant conversion. In the Calvinist mind, a true knowledge of one's self demanded a true knowledge of God. A committed Calvinist and student of church history, as evident in his pastoral examination before the Lexington Presbytery and his numerous publications, Bourne was familiar with the writings of John Calvin, a leading architect of the Protestant Reformation. Calvin's opening ontological discussion in book I of the *Institutes of the Christian Religion* underscores the important epistemological link between the individual and God:

> [N]o one can look upon himself without immediately turning his thoughts to the contemplation of God, in whom he "lives and moves" (Acts 17:28).... For what man in all the world would not gladly remain as he is—what man does not remain as he is—so long as he does not know himself, that is, while content with his own gifts, and either ignorant or unmindful of his own misery? Accordingly, the knowledge of ourselves not only arouses us to seek God, but also, as it were, leads us by the hand to find him.... Again, it is certain that man never achieves a clear knowledge of himself unless he has first looked upon God's face, and then descends from contemplating him to scrutinizing himself.[64]

Complementing Calvin's discussion, Bourne seemed to intimate that a true knowledge of God was not only the basis for a true knowledge of the self, but also the foundation for the true (or ideal) family, an earthly institution from which an individual received his or her identity. *Lorette* revealed how false religion fractured family relationships and destroyed individuals' earthly duties. Catholicism detached "one individual from another" and thus severed all social and familial relations.[65] Sent to the Ursuline convent in Quebec at an early age, Louise had been stripped of her identity; she had no knowledge of her age, birthday, or familial line. In a comparative way, Louise's psychological trauma of not knowing her own origins echoed those of real-life slaves in similar circumstances. The only clue linking Louise to a particular identity was the mark "M" on her forehead. Diganu had a similarly placed mark. Her mission—namely, to find her true self—required a search for family members. Without such connections, Louise had been lost, but so too were the other characters in the story. Her ancestral detachment acted as a metaphor of spiritual wanderings. Since both mother and daughter had been "without God," Louise and Therese were "unconscious of the true character" of their actions.[66] As Louise described it, "[Therese] was exactly like a traveler without a guide in a desert; where to stand is impossible, but to move is to storm every conceivable danger." Louise made a similar confession earlier in the story when she confessed to Diganu, "I am not my own director."[67] When they finally recognized their relationship to each other, it was Therese that expressed the deepest remorse: remorse for her failure as a mother. Such realizations and the reunion of mother and daughter, it should be repeated, were preceded by doctrinal discussions. While evangelizing Therese, Louise confessed that there emerged "an indistinct allusion to the possibility of a future personal recognition of each other by associates." And even though the three were unable to spend the remainder of their earthly lives together, they knew that they would one day meet "to enjoy that sanctified undying communion" in heaven.[68]

The absence of the father figure is also a prominent theme throughout *Lorette.* Diganu, like Louise, was Therese's child; his father is the priest, the same one who chased and ultimately recaptured Louise. Louise, on the other hand, had a different father, a different priest. The tragic rape of Therese and the bastardization of Diganu and Louise, heinous acts rooted in Catholic heresy, represented an egregious nullification of a father's appropriate role. The father-child relationship in the novel was never restored, which gave a sense of uneasiness to the reader and suggested the need to restore and protect patriarchal authority. As is clear from the novel, the priest's suppression of masculine protection came by attacking marriage, an institution whereby men sheltered women and secured their status as heads of their household. As Pagliani has argued, the need to protect male headship manifested itself in Protestantism's opposition to celibacy, a papal practice that presented the rejection of marriage and family as a pious act.[69] The interference in the marriage ceremony became the occasion for Diganu to renounce his allegiance to the church and to rebuke the priest's failure as a spiritual father.[70] The problem of the father was central in Rebecca Reed's *Six Months in a Convent,* a narrative that, in part, exposed the efforts of a convent's mother superior to reverse proper gender roles. Equally, the absence of patriarchy not only compelled Reed to escape, but also provoked the actual burning of the Charleston convent.

The reinstating of familial identity after accepting the Protestant faith uncovered the surreptitious endeavors of those who took captive the souls of young women. "The Pope rules the interior and penetrates the heart," Bourne wrote in the *Textbook,* "for *conscience is the seat of his empire.*"[71] Echoing such a statement, a later no-popery author suggested that the Jesuit priest had "mastered . . . the understanding of human nature," prying into "the very core of [a] young girl's heart." Auricular confession, "the fertile source of every possible crime," became the most important tool of enslavement, for it dethroned "reason, intellect and self, entirely, and enthrone[d] the superior as absolute King and guide."[72] Through the dark space of the confessional, "the knowledge of the character, propensities, and circumstances of every individual, with the concealment in which it veils all its mysterious communications and acts, eradicates the shield of virtue, and places every person within the controlling power of the Priest."[73] It involved a "surrender of all personal and mental independence."[74] Capturing the inner self enslaved the whole person. And confession was even more dangerous when offered by a women to an unscrupulous man: "[L]et the female be of what class she may, simple-hearted or lax, the repetition of her dishonor . . . enhances beyond measure when the instincts of nature are violated by making the recital to a man."[75] As a helpless victim, then, the convent nun fell "entirely [into] the hands of her superiors," precluding her from "*all opposition to his commands.*"[76] As Elizabeth Fenton points out, Louise's regaining of her true self meant the restoration of and sovereignty over her own reason, a critical means of coming to God. Louise chose, Fenton writes, "Protestant rationality over Catholic superstition."[77]

The priest, who is never named or "unmasked" to reveal his inner depraved nature, physically and spiritually seduced both Louise and Therese by penetrating their hearts, collapsing any hint of sensibility, disconnecting their family affiliations, and stripping them of sovereignty over their own bodies. Religious slavery transformed women into irreligious beasts. Using the same language to describe the effects of slavery on women, Bourne defined the person of the nun as "a woman abjectly submissive in body, soul, and spirit, to the will of her superior."[78] Priestly control rested not only on the ability to alter a woman's nature, but also to make such "poor creatures" accept their depraved state. "When animated by the demon of Popery," Bourne argued, aspiring nuns, like women who married southern men, became "daring persecutors, exulting in carnage, and surveying with delight streams of Christian blood, and piles of *naked* mangled human bodies."[79]

In essence, therefore, "popery" was totally irreconcilable with true womanhood and domesticity. Nuns could never be true women unless they broke the fetters of their oppressors. Catholic priests "stifle all natural tenderness, and spoil the most amiable dispositions; for gentle and delicate women."[80] Diganu lamented the priest's intent to fracture the family by suppressing the cultivation of feminine feelings: "How is a human creature to show sensibility, who has never enjoyed a relatives' endearments to keep it in exercise; and just when it was beginning to awake and expand itself, who had had its first fresh and green fruits forever blasted."[81] Indeed, Louise's conversion allowed her to experience the duties befitting a woman, becoming herself—if for only a short period—an affectionate mother to Therese. "I was thus remarkably appointed," she wrote to her brother, "to attend and support the enfeebled and dispirited woman by whom we had been ushered into the world."[82]

With its emphasis on how Catholicism corrupts religion, women, and the family, *Lorette* contributed to the basic literary structure of the escaped nun's story, positioning its author as a highly qualified editor for the most famous of this genre: Maria Monk's *Awful Disclosures of the Hotel Dieu Nunnery of Montreal.* Published in 1836, *Awful Disclosures* sold more copies than Rebecca Reed's *Six Months in a Convent,* another popular exposé, and moved to second in sales after Harriet Beecher Stowe's *Uncle Tom's Cabin.* Monk told the story of her Protestant upbringing and her late desire to become a nun. After an elaborate ceremony at the Montreal nunnery, she received the veil and subsequently witnessed the horrors committed in the convent, which included priest-directed rape, murder, and infanticide. Impregnated by a priest and unwilling to comply with her superiors to abort her child, Monk escaped the convent. Convinced "that she had been divinely selected to expose the horrors of Popery," Monk ran toward male protection, calling for a Protestant clergyman to whom she could tell her story.[83] William K. Hoyt, a committed no-popery nativist, aided her escape to the United States and compelled her to write an autobiography. J. J. Slocum, Arthur Tappan, and Theodore Dwight were also involved in editing Monk's report. Dwight, as one report had it, encouraged Bourne to be the "ghost writer" for the exposé.[84] According to Billington, Bourne and Harper Brothers publication took over the book's copyrights, offering none of the profits to Monk.[85] Whether or not Billington is correct in this claim, Bourne recounted his own reading of *Awful Disclosure:* "[N]othing in Maria Monk's pages act to startle my belief; whether I regarded the description of the Nunnery without or that part of the interior with which I had been familiar for so many years."[86] His reading of Maria Monk in light of his knowledge of the Hotel Dieu Nunnery corresponded with Bourne's representation, in his words, of the "true picture of Popery in Canada." The efforts to debunk Monk's account from Catholics and Protestants alike gained the aspersions of Bourne as "strongly and actively prejudiced against Maria Monk."[87] Those who questioned Monk's account should be dismissed in Bourne's estimation, since they "are identical in principle, character, dispositions, and habits" to every other Catholic authority, "publicly denounced by the world as kidnappers and violators of females, and as sacrificing both the offspring of their lusts, and, also the wretched mothers whom they have debased, to their jealousy and revenge. They do not pretend to deny or disprove the facts."[88]

There is a noticeable difference in emphasis, however, between *Lorette* and *Six Months.* The latter focuses more on the frightening, dungeon-like features of the convent, the murderous activities of the nuns, the external hypocrisy of convent leaders, and the damaging effects of the institution on young girls, themes that contemporary historians highlight as the dominant features of such literature. Although similar matters are brought to light in *Lorette, Six Months* does not enter into any extensive discussion regarding the doctrines of the Protestant faith. The Bible is certainly mentioned as an important religious text, but no dialogue occurs over its historical authenticity or the miraculous process by which its doctrines radically change hearts. In an important way, *Lorette* can be read as an apology of the tenets of the Protestant faith, an evangelical message that relies on nineteenth-century cultural constructs.

Centralizing theology as the tool to fight religious despotism mirrored the basic structure of Bourne's antislavery work. *Lorette* lent support to the additions Bourne made to *Picture of Slavery,* published a year after the novel in 1834. This updated antislavery booklet made frequent reference to the relationship between Catholicism and slavery, a subject absent in the original *The Book and Slavery Irreconcilable.* At the heart of both Romish and southern slavery, two institutions that demanded total control over body and soul, was the suppression of the scriptures by dictatorial religious leaders. "Like the Papists," Bourne concluded in *Picture of Slavery,* "[slaveholders] will not permit the coloured citizens to learn to read or to possess the scriptures," which offered "the only appointed and effectual means by which this transformation of the human heart and character can be attained: *for men are sanctified through the word of truth.*"[89] "Romish" slaveowners took "away the key of knowledge, and defraud the coloured citizens of 'the pearl of great price,' and the light of their feet and the lamp of their path." The deceptive work of Jesuitism, Bourne continued, was no less "base and deficient in religious truth than the soul deceiving 'strong delusions' with which the slavites attempt to gull the coloured people."

Furthermore, as the lifeblood of spiritual slavery, counterfeit theology had a direct impact on the family community. The devastating effects on marriage and women, as the characters in *Lorette* understood all too well, represented the full extent of the depravity of absolute oppression. This of course was a crucial matter of discussion in *Slavery Illustrated in its Effects,* published four years after *Lorette.* Both slavery and Catholicism equally eradicated a "wife's affection, the mother's love, and the sister's tenderness, in all their energetic purity."[90] While man-stealers refused to recognize slave marriages, Catholics specifically desecrated the "connubial" covenant through the pseudo-pietistic practice of celibacy, the "occasion of criminalities" that "poison the well springs of domestic virtue."[91] They violated marriage with impunity and made it easier for church members to do penance for sexual sins, especially those against the sanctity of marriage, which suggested that the Roman faith did not require an inward change of the heart in order to be saved. "Rome," as in the case of the South, was "one vast brothel."[92]

Slavery shared, Bourne wrote in *Picture of Slavery,* Catholicism's "theological tragic-farce."[93] Both were manifestations of false religion, both grew out of a misreading of the sacred text and the abuse of church authority, both had enslaving tyrants, and both sought to destroy the foundations of civil society: the family unit, sincere piety, and sexual purity. Among reformers, America's besieging evils were not necessarily equal. Some radicals saw slavery as a worse institution than Catholicism; more moderate antislavery reformers took the opposite position. The *New York Observer* in 1834 showed a greater fear over the potentially rapid growth of the Jesuit population: "The number of negroes imported from Africa in one hundred and fifty years, was less than

300,000—less than the number of Papists we are now importing every five years from Europe! We shall soon have more Papists in the North than they have slaves in the South."[94] Another writer for the *Observer* confessed that "Negro slavery is indeed a curse, but what is it compared with the curse of Popery!"[95] Abolitionist Joseph Berg considered the "poor slave . . . *a freeman,* when compared with the man who breathes the atmosphere of liberty, and yet voluntary fetters his soul, and surrenders himself, bound hand and foot, to the sovereign will and pleasure of a popish priest."[96] The opposite was true, however, for abolitionists like the Grimké sisters. Sarah believed that "if all the horrors of the Inquisition and all the cruelty and oppression exercised by the Church of Rome, could be fully and fairly brought to view and compared with the details of slavery in the United States, the abominations of Catholicism would not surpass those of slavery, while the victims of the latter are tenfold more numerous."[97] As a result, proslavery Protestants, according to Sarah's sister Angelina, were hypocritical and "more criminal" because they deprived slaves of "the Sacred Volume by not allowing them time and opportunity to learn to read, and do not a great majority urge the very same reason for their conduct that the Catholics do for theirs?"[98] Bourne maintained a strategy whereby he could evenly battle the two without taking away from either one. As a foot soldier in a Manichean struggle wherein Christ would trample Satan's demonic hordes and eventually purge the church and the nation of its sins, the pioneer of antislavery and anti-Catholicism remained steadfast in his crusade against the type of bondage that destroyed doctrine and social identity. *Lorette*'s double-edged sword not only intensified evangelical nativism, but also reinforced the cultural arguments related to faith and family used by this radical abolitionist.

CHAPTER 5

ABOLITION AND THE WOMAN QUESTION IN BOURNE'S *Slavery Illustrated in Its Effects on Woman and Domestic Society*

To all the members of female abolitionist societies, with profound solicitude, that those sisters in philanthropy may be stimulated to untiring exertions in behalf of twelve hundred thousand women, who are now chained in the American house of bondage.

—GEORGE BOURNE, *Slavery Illustrated in Its Effects on Woman and Domestic Society*

On May 19, 1840, William Lloyd Garrison embarked on his journey to the World Anti-Slavery Convention, which was to be held the following month in London. This gathering would not only have a tremendous impact on the efforts to end slavery, it would also expand the idea of participatory democracy by giving birth to the women's rights movement. Unfortunately, the *Columbus,* the ship on which Garrison was to travel, had been anchored in New York and was delayed due to inclement weather, making the fiery Bostonian late to the opening session of the convention. While in New York, he wrote to his wife Helen Eliza about the upcoming London gathering and the labors of the American Anti-Slavery Society, now divided over the issue of the "woman question," to send delegates, including Lucretia Mott, to be seated at the convention. He anticipated what would be a hard-fought battle for those, including his wife, who supported women leadership in the antislavery cause. Bourne, who was also in New York at the time, kept company with Garrison on that very day. The two discussed the rights of women. "Father Bourne," Garrison wrote to Eliza, "goes against 'woman's rights' . . . and he predicts, with all confidence, that no woman will be allowed a seat at the Convention. Such a thing, [Bourne] says, was never heard or thought of in any part of Europe."[1] Apparently, Bourne had counseled Garrison against putting his hopes in securing the place of women in the movement. Although encouraging women to get involved in the movement to eradicate slavery, Bourne was certainly not as radical or forward looking on the "woman question" as were other antislavery associates. He did not, however, adopt the position that women's more public leadership role in immediatism was grounds enough for the division that had occurred among American abolitionists. Garrison may have been a bit too quick to judge Bourne's opinion on women's rights.

By 1834, George Bourne included women among the "two classes of persons" (along with ministers) whose duty it was to "combine their energies, cry aloud, spare not and never cease, till the thralldom of American citizens [slaves] has been dismissed to that bottomless pit."[2] His *Slavery Illustrated in Its Effects on Woman and Domestic Society* was published in 1837, a year in which antislavery organizing by northern women reached a high point. According to Beth Salerno, these societies sprang up in rapid succession following the example of the first African American planned Female Antislavery Society of Salem, Massachusetts. Seventeen were established by 1834, "twenty-nine in 1835, forty-one in 1836, and a record forty-five in the peak year of 1837."[3] Bourne dedicated the book "to all the members of female abolitionist societies." Despite the difficulty in determining how many reformers actually took note of *Slavery Illustrated,* with the important exception of Garrison, who desired to see, as he said, "a million copies of the book distributed broadcast," this timely work reveals the problematic nature of the author's views regarding traditional religion, the status of women, and the radicalism of the antislavery movement.[4]

For historian Nancy Cott, the 1830s represented a significant "turning point in women's economic participation, public activities, and social visibility."[5] Women played a crucial role in moral and social reform throughout the nineteenth century. Bourne followed the activities of women in reform and enthusiastically supported their increasingly public presence in antislavery. Ignoring more conservative reformers who criticized his "indelicacy and indecorum" for calling women to united action, Bourne believed that these God-fearing saints were within "their own appropriate sphere" to "take up arms" and sound the trumpet of jubilee "until with their matronly purity and authority they have exterminated this devastating pestilence."[6] "The abolition of slavery," he wrote in the introduction to *Slavery Illustrated,* was "emphatically the duty and privilege of women."[7] He shared the sentiments of radicals like Angelina Grimké, who at the 1837 Anti-Slavery Convention of American Women (ACAW), called women "to move in that sphere which Providence has assigned her." But supporting women in the movement was different from supporting their place as equals in society. When a few leading radicals began pushing for mixed "promiscuous" antislavery gatherings, wherein women could equally perform the duties traditionally reserved for men, they explicitly threatened male leadership and defied deep-rooted gender customs.

Many antislavery women heeded the call of fellow abolitionists and "invaded churches and disrupted Sunday services," according to John McKivigan.[8] The limits of a woman's "appropriate sphere" or what was meant by "cry aloud" and "take up arms" was particularly vague in *Slavery Illustrated.* Bourne plainly incorporated middle-class cultural models into his arguments, especially those related to true womanhood, marriage, and domesticity, the pillars of morality and religion in society, but it is unclear as to whether he advocated active disruption in churches throughout the country. Historians can be fairly certain that Bourne was a supporter of what has become known as the "Cult of Domesticity," as shown in this passage from his 1820 sermon "The Virtuous Woman": "An undomesticated woman is the veriest [*sic*] unnatural sprout in Nature's plantation: because it is a universal rule, without exception, that a female who cannot make the habitation of her father or husband her resting place, so far from being of any benefit, is only a pest at home, and a nuisance abroad."[9] "The management of all the economy attached to the house," he concluded, "is one of the special enactments of Divine Providence for the woman."[10] Women were divinely appointed for the maternal-domestic realm. At the same time, however, Bourne left no comment regarding the implications of gender equality, never split from the American Anti-Slavery Society as many of his close friends did in 1840, and never intimated wariness over how early feminists broadened the parameters of political and cultural identity in nineteenth-century America. So what were his feelings regarding the increasing public leadership and independence of women, especially by the 1840s? He was never one to neglect a controversial issue or what he thought was a controversial issue. What about this one?

Focusing largely on *Slavery Illustrated in Its Effects on Woman and Domestic Society,* this chapter offers a suggestion as to how Bourne would have reconciled his traditional religious commitments with the changes going on in the antislavery movement. For him, the condition of women, however shifting, was secondary—but not necessarily unimportant or troublesome—to the ultimate work of God to eradicate sin in American society and usher in the kingdom. According to Ronald Walters, many abolitionists outside Boston and New York considered the battle over gender equality "as silly and refused to take sides."[11] Perhaps Bourne himself fit into this category. The place of women in leadership and the push for independent civil rights, for him, were not enough to divide reformers. But thinking about it in relation to Bourne's Protestantism, women and men were not created to live in isolation (or to assert their individual sovereignty as an end in itself); they were made for the purposes of marriage, a temporal institution that modeled the heavenly reality, preserved true religion, and pointed toward the Christian millennial era. In other words, the efforts of antislavery reformers in the 1830s were never abstracted from their place in a divine cosmological drama. Bourne identified this in the actions of women, but he never developed a theological argument that defended their independent rights.

Fifteen years after his ecclesiastical trials, Bourne came to the realization that the "definite and intangible" contest between the North and the South was less a political war than a religious one. Slavery "invented a geographical religion," he wrote.[12] The South had become the place of unholy darkness where "the spirit and principles of Christianity in ordinary cases are far less potent in their practical influence."[13] The North, despite those who had long aided the southern institution, remained the bastion of true religion. Bourne understood his part in the crusade against false religion: "*The contest is a war for the extermination of slavery.* . . . We have drawn 'the two-edged sword of the spirit,' and have cast away that vile scabbard, 'the fear of man that bringeth a snare,' in which, alas, it has been too long buried in the hilt."[14] Only the pure gospel, advanced by faithful ministers and pious women, could heal the sin that divided the nation. Bourne's argument over the role of women fits his Protestant vision in the way he ostensibly compelled women to initiate a veritable ecclesiastical coup d'etat. Antislavery women were the true heirs of historic Protestantism, standing in as replacements for their cowardly religious counterparts.

Bourne's major religious works maintained a level of consistency throughout his life. The changes he did make, however, never strayed from his main objective: the defense of Christian doctrine and ecclesiology and the preservation of marriage and the family. These remained core issues. (Even *The Book and Slavery Irreconcilable* discusses obliquely the impact of slavery on the family and female character.) But the former preceded the latter. Marriage and the family were not the sole means toward social and spiritual fulfillment, but rather physical or earthly pictures of the metaphysical that rested on sound theological teachings. Individuals were to consider social and cultural institutions as windows that directed one's perspective heavenward.

This is not to suggest that Bourne was unaware of the shifting economic, social, cultural, and political currents reshaping America; *Slavery Illustrated* reflected these changes. But such alterations were always interpreted from his religious point of view. The nation's rapid shift from an Old World artisan economy to a commercial-based industrial one divided the family, the erstwhile social unit of production, and paved the way for the material separation of the world of work (public) from the world of the home (private) and an ideological separation between the influential spheres of men and women. As an emerging—and slippery—cultural category, the public represented the realm of competitive individualism, a place where men had to use their wisdom, cunning, and rationality to establish a course in an uprooted, morally vacuous, and irreligious environment. In contrast, the market transformed the home as the site of moral instead of economic development.[15] The private domestic space was, in a sense, reborn and came to be viewed as a place of spiritual rest and renewal, characteristically feminine and divine.[16] Wives, mothers, and daughters were "granted unprecedented domestic authority" as protectors of religion and social well-being.[17] A nation's spiritual health rested on motherly affection. In his 1833 bestseller *The Mother at Home,* John Abbott expressed the moral superiority of the Christian mother:

> the female breast is the natural soil of Christianity. . . . Thus far the history of the world has been composed of the narrations of oppression and blood. . . . Where shall we look for the influence which shall change this scene, and fill the earth with the fruits of peace and benevolence? It is to the power of divine truth, to Christianity as taught from a mother's lips. . . . She who was first to transgression, must be yet the principal earthly agent in the restoration. [T]he mothers of our race must be the chief in [the nation's] redemption. The brightest rays of the millennial morn must come from the cradle. O mothers! reflect upon the power your Maker has placed in your hands. God has constituted you the guardians and the controllers of the human family.[18]

And women in general, as historian Charles Sellers writes, "were called upon to provide the love, tranquility, and socially invisible domestic labor needed by men pushing themselves to the limit of effort."[19] Given their special duties to both family and society, middle-class women were motivated to become crucial agents in American reform. They were guardians of morality in both the private and public realms. It was through the channels of antislavery that women came to realize more acutely the paradoxical nature of their sphere: its confining restrictions and powerful possibilities. As Karen Sanchez-Eppler suggests in her book *Touching Liberty,* domesticity constituted the source of a woman's power but also her incarceration.[20]

A helpful way to appreciate *Slavery Illustrated* is to read it within the context of Bourne's earlier 1813 *Marriage Indissoluble and Divorce Unscriptural,* an anti-Shaker essay published around the time he had been writing *Book and Slavery.* Slavery and marriage had been two important issues on Bourne's mind at the time. America's rising competitive capitalist ethos, which dispersed familial community networks, began to place greater importance on regulating the individual moral self.[21] Widely distributed popular literature warned against materialism, the trappings of wealth, and the competitiveness that threatened the bonds of family affection; conduct manuals emphasized the cultivation of character through self-control—especially sexual restraint and temperance—as a way to safeguard piety and economic efficiency. Marriage (of the middle-class sort) provided social and religious stability in a nonstable environment. Bourne recognized the detrimental effects of the market on the family unit and relied on traditional Christian views of marriage as the best means to preserve society and culture. Yet he shunned the novel practices of newer religious groups like the Shakers, a community (similar to the Oneidas and the Mormons) that reacted against America's increasing dependence on mammon and its threat to communities and individual piety. Practices that destabilized matrimony led inevitably to the collapse of morality, true religion, and society as a whole. Arguing against the Shaker commitment to "Virgin purity" as an important way to reach a sustained intimacy with the divine, Bourne believed that marriage, "the sole cement of society," kept at bay uncontrolled passions. Shaker life—and that of other nontraditional sects in America—inflamed sinful appetites: "the various bodily exercises which are permitted in the Shaker's meetings, must directly inflame the animal passions to the very highest degree; and this cannot promote a perfect abstinence from the sexual intercourse."[22] The "dictates of nature, the claims of morality, and the interests of religion" for Bourne, overwhelmed the "joyless arguments of philosophical celibacy." Marriage grounded individuals in society and established the complementary identities of husband and wife. Such an institution was "much more favorable to devotion and piety, than a single state."[23] *Marriage Indissoluble* served as a blueprint for Bourne's later writings against slavery and Catholicism.

But marriage and the family did more than just maintain morality. Bourne resisted the tendency in American evangelicalism to reduce religion to mere practical piety. There existed a world beyond the physical, and believers needed to be mindful of the overlap of these two realms. The affections of the truly converted, he wrote in an 1812 sermon, were "no longer cemented with the earth . . . they are principally transferred to unseen realities."[24] Marriage and the establishment of the family were earthly representations of the divine. Bourne did not separate such earthly institutions from their correspondence to an "other-worldly" engagement with the messiah, his body, and the new heavens and new earth. The "connubial union," he called marriage, was of "divine appointment . . . confirmed in heaven"; it prefigured "the connection between Christ and his church" and existed "under the sole jurisdiction of Heaven" for the "commencement to Paradise."[25] The individual who entered a union, despite unforeseen difficulties, anticipated and provided more than just a model of "the future world of blessedness" that characterized "mankind during the Millennium":

> To pierce beyond the veil which conceals Paradise from his vision, and by faith to realize the enrapturing meeting on the borders of the celestial Canaan with the family which he loved. . . . His marriage contract was arranged, and his matrimonial duties are performed with a distinct reference to future retribution, and the experience of the reward which the Son of Man shall bestow upon his servants when the voice of the Archangel and the trump of God shall have assembled the dormant dust, and revivified the body to never-ending existence.[26]

Since marriage was a sacred institution, it was important for those forming one to be sincere Christians themselves. The "great danger" of an unequal yoke between a believer and an unbeliever destabilized the covenant and provided a powerful "preventative to the 'progress of religion'": "a diversity of sentiment, feeling and action upon the subject of religion is generally attended with the utmost inconvenience, perplexity and pain."[27] A Christian woman, for example, married to a man who is not "a fellow heir of the grace of life" would be disastrous to personal piety; she would be reduced a "painful alternative, either to displease her most intimate relation, or to disobey her Master who is in heaven."[28] This, once again, corresponded to the otherworldly nature of marriage. Christ was joined with a community, the church, which gained its identity from an association with him. The savior could not be coupled to those whose religious sentiments were directed elsewhere.

As a means to advance religion in preparation for millennial bliss, the married couple had specific responsibilities. At this point, Bourne's theological understanding of marriage and the family accorded with nineteenth-century gender constructions. A stable marriage depended on the mutual and separate obligations of husband and wife: namely, service to one another. The husband was to love, honor, keep, and protect his wife; in contrast, the wife was to obey, serve, love, honor, and keep her husband. The former was the head, who ruled in accordance with "wise superintendence" and an "esteem for the condition of her worth" through undivided and "unrivalled affection." The "subjection" of the latter entailed "chaste conversation coupled with fear" with a God-honoring "meek and quiet spirit." The relations of authority had to be understood theologically as a "union between Christ and his church."[29] The husband was an earthly picture of Christ, and the wife an earthly picture of the church. In the same way that Christ submitted to the Father, so the wife was to submit to her husband. The two did not have an existence apart from one another, for they were equal in spirit—"all are one in Christ"—as Christ and the Father were equal. Christ was head over the church, not as an overbearing or arbitrary tyrant, but as a servant willing to die for his people.

The combined duty of the husband and the wife was only a means to an end. Marriage was instituted to "propagate and nurse offspring, to promote the mutual happiness of the couple intermarrying, and to form minds for the great duties and extensive destinations of life." The family opened vistas to the divine. Children could not be properly "nurtured without this institution." As God's vicegerents on earth, parents were required to prepare children for the duties of the state and "to imbue them with the holy sentiments of the Christian religion with reference to future existence."[30] And in the same way that a ruptured marriage negated the picture of salvation, children of a divorced home, which included those separated from their parents, as in the case of slave traders and, for anti-Catholics, Jesuit traffickers, would not be able to learn about true spirituality as represented in the heavenly family.

The sins of divorce and adultery shattered the marriage covenant, severed family bonds, destroyed personal piety, and stamped out the knowledge of true faith. Regulating marriage depended on following the moral commands found in the Old and New Testaments. Bourne proposed that ministers and legislators who enforced the transcendent moral codes of the Mosaic law (but not the judicial administration in relation to its violations) and the teachings of Christ would reduce the number of divorces and, therefore, bring the church closer to the millennium: "Prophecy incontrovertibly testifies, that during one thousand years upon earth, purity, virtue, religion, and happiness shall be universally diffused: but dissolution of marriage and supplication for divorce are totally subversive to the ordinances of Christianity, and consequently cannot during that period be possible . . . an examination of the millennial prospect before us demonstrates the extinction of all obstructions to marriage. . . . There will be no divorce during the millennium."[31] Although lawmakers could work to maintain marital stability, the best preventive against separation was "the general diffusion and influence of Christianity" as presented through the Bible, "the source of all virtue and knowledge."[32]

Ideas related to marriage were used to counter the national sin of slavery. By the time Bourne published *Slavery Illustrated,* however, southerners had been defending slavery as a benign institution that not only provided for the welfare of African Americans but also presented a stable hierarchical society that protected marriage and the family. Such an image contrasted with a cannibalistic North, a region under the tyranny of industry and capitalism that destroyed hierarchy and proper respect and, worse, dissolved the family unit.[33] The North perverted social relations. Southerners presented their world as the epitome of divinely directed social order, a region, though hierarchical, that preserved marriage, faith, and the gender identity of each individual, slave and free. Abolitionists faced an uphill rhetorical battle as they engaged with such twisted yet, for many, convincing arguments. As Kristin Hoganson has argued, radical abolitionists turned such gendered rhetoric against the South. Slavery not only kept black men and women from becoming true fathers and mothers, but also "desexed *all* slaves and their owners."[34] Abolitionists presented the southern region as inherently antagonistic toward domesticity, family harmony, and sexual restraint, which was the moral foundation of social order and individual sanctity (and sanity, according to sex reformers).[35]

Slavery Illustrated began as an essay titled "The Effects of Slavery on the Slave and the Slaveholders." The essay had been submitted for a prize offered by the New England Anti-Slavery Society and later delivered to various audiences in Boston, Providence, and New York. In terms of its content, *Slavery Illustrated* (along with the original essay) was an elaboration of what he had said about slavery, marriage, female "purity," and the family in *The Book and Slavery Irreconcilable* (and later *Picture of Slavery*). It countered the South's false sense of "honour [and] refined feelings of propriety, independence, and enlarged views of reciprocal obligation," revealing the "daily exhibitions" of slavery in the United States, a nation "boasting of its liberty, its benevolence, and its *Christianity,*" and the consequences of such practices on the family and its members.[36] In doing so, Bourne chipped away at the South's inflated sense of "self."

False religion stood behind the degradation of marriage and the family. The author not only contributed to constructing the South as an irreligious, erotic, and antidomestic realm, but he also related the region to "the most important theme of the whole [slavery] controversy": the violation of the law of God and the gospel of redemption. In this light, human bondage collapsed the affinity between faith and practice, the "ecclesiastical questions with all the grand moral points" and the heavenly picture of Christ, the church, and the millennium.[37] The heretical nature of slavery produced the most "desolating effects" on domesticity and on the character of northern and southern women, slave and free.[38] The plantation system spoiled individual purity and thus could not coexist alongside "marriage, female chastity, and domestic relationships." It transformed men and women "into fornicators and adulterers" and fettered "every woman as a creature for defilement without redress or possibility of escape whenever her vile tyrants choose to trample upon the seventh commandment." In short, the southern region was one large "brothel, in which multiform incest, polygamy, adultery, and other uncleanness are constantly perpetuated."[39]

As the title suggests, Bourne was concerned about the impact slavery had on women and marriage. The consequences on the two stemmed ultimately from false religion, which perpetuated slavery and decimated the family. One of the first consequences slavery had on the family was that it inflamed white southern children with "*haughty self conceit.*" From an early age, children came to understand the "palpable distinction existing" between the races. Educated by their fathers to see themselves as higher than black servants, these children underwent a "systematic process to corrupt the heart." Slavery attached "a permanent influence on their moral character during the entire course of their mortal existence."[40] The children of slaveowners were taught the inextricable relationship between difference and power. Second, the institution instilled a *marble-hearted insensibility,* transforming man-stealers "into monsters" and "ruthless barbarians." Those who disregarded the "necessities and anguish" of slaves could not retain a natural sensibility toward other humans, a sensibility that originated in the "hymeneal union." Husbands and wives could not show tenderness to one another, and children lived in an environment deprived of parental affections. Third, slavery caused husbands and fathers to "become sensual" and thus to "lose that instinctive pudicity [*sic*] which God, for the wisest and holiest purposes, has implanted in the hearts of mankind."[41] This was exhibited in the "promiscuous uncleanness" on the plantation whereby a white man gave in to his lust, raped innocent female slaves, and thus terminated "all domestic endearments and relative tenderness."[42] Slaveowners violated "all their conjugal vows without any remorse" and canceled "all the domestic relations of the coloured men, women, and children."[43] The final consequence was that the southern system rendered man-stealers "*irascible and turbulent*" and thus destroyed "*every correct view of equity,*" filling "*the adherent and practitioner of the system with all injustice and knavery.*"[44] The system reversed proper gender relations, toppled the reciprocal duties of husband and wife, and thus bred "effeminacy and indolence." But the ultimate and most deadly effect of slavery—since the breakup of the family came from the violation of God's law (the seventh commandment)—was that it was the "*prolific source of all infidelity and irreligion.*"[45]

An aspect of the South's representation as a sexually deviant and antidomestic region was that it failed to provide true patriarchal protection. This is what truly harmed the nature of women, according to Bourne. The earthly authority of husbands and fathers was analogous to the ultimate patriarchal authority of the godhead. As he wrote in *Picture and Slavery,* female purity was "the subject of [God's] constant care." Attempts at disrupting it with impunity invoked God's "tremendous retribution."[46] This was particularly absent in the case of female slaves: "despoiled of all protection; exposed to every indignity;

obliged to submit to the brutal demand of any lawless white man; coerced to degradation by heart rending tortures; doomed to sacrifice the tenderest affections; scourged to conceal their instinctive sensibilities; and robbed of a husband's love, a father's guardianship, a son's aid, and a brother's endearment; they are merely human tools to pander to the sensuality, and to gratify the unclean desires of their inhuman task-masters."[47] Preachers and state legislators ignored the cries of the female slave: "No one can hear her groans but he that searcheth the heart."[48] Living under the ubiquitous shadow of spiritual and physical rape, she "agonized with constant solicitations voluntary to abandon herself to her tyrant driver." This was not the case for white women, Bourne believed, for they could "fly to a father, or a brother, or a friend, or to the civil magistrate, to shield her from pollution." Indeed, a white woman could defend herself to the point of killing "her brutal assailant," at which time "the law would exculpate her, and she would be honored for her resistance."[49]

Not even white women could provide solace for their female slaves. Their "relative dependence" on their husbands "and the execrable civil laws" precluded them from "interposing their shield for the protection of their sex."[50] There was a kind of bondage that white women themselves were under. Bourne's opposition to unequal religious marriages that he wrote about in 1813 applied to northern Christian women marrying southern slaveholders (non-Christians by the very fact of being slaveowners), a point emphasized by a number of leading female abolitionists. Since man-stealers forfeited their manhood, casting off their independence to become "the devil's dogs," no true or proper woman could marry them. He directed his attention to northern women who underwent a "strange metamorphosis" when they traveled into the South to marry a slaveowner. Domesticity rapidly faded the more a young lady moved into the South, reinforcing the image of an antidomestic southern region that contrasted with the cradle of middle-class cultural identity in the North. In this discussion, Bourne revealed a picture of a change of religious morality over space. Christian women, unaware of the "trials through which they will have to pass, and the self-denial which they will have to exercise," moved from domestic and divine bliss into a demonic gothic realm of "anxiety and trepidation":

> [The northern lady] passes the southern boundary of William Penn's domain, and almost instantly the novel scenes produce a compound reverie tinged with Yankee notions. The smooth and sage turnpike is exchanged

> for rolling logs, and shapeless moving rocks, and sinking bridges. . . . The green pastures are transformed into old fields of gullies and sand. The stone walls adorned with lovely hedges have vanished, and in their place is a zig-zag fence of ugly rails. The decently dressed, manly-looking farmers, have metamorphosed into ill-clothed and downcast slaves; and the place of the rosy-faced tidy female domestic is supplied by a half-naked wretched-looking victim of toil and misery. Thus the daughter of the pilgrims travels onward, imbibing more knowledge of evil as she makes progress; and brooding over her forelorn condition with intenser emotion, as she realizes that every minute places her at a greater distance from all that she has ever known of good.[51]

Spiritual darkness advanced with every step made in the direction of the South, a recurring theme in abolitionist popular literature. All southern women, regardless of race, were under the yoke of tyranny. When a northern woman sealed her marital fate, she came to the realization that "for independence she has procured bondage; for the peace of God unceasing perturbation; for opportunities of doing good, the necessity of sanctioning evil." The young wife, "in law and by custom," became the "most favored slave of the planters' 'gang.'" The consequences of slavery on white women were similar to those on female slaves: a loss of patriarchal protection. A white southern woman "pungently realizes not only that she is powerless, but that she has no earthly friend and comforter." "Her husband . . . is the cause of her most distressful agonies."[52] Consequently (and what was worse), the wife could not participate in domestic life or reach the status of a "true" woman: "They become tame and spiritless, and of little more domestic utility than household statues; or they submit to the chief mistress manager to superintend, direct and provide for the rest of the harem and its appendages."[53] All women were enfettered under slavery. Bourne's argument here coincided with those advanced by the Anti-Slavery Convention of American Women.[54]

The importance of a marriage between two people of the same religion was connected to a specific courting ritual, which Bourne also discussed in *Marriage Indissoluble* and later incorporated into his argument in *Slavery Illustrated.* When it came to the premarital engagement, Bourne echoed nineteenth-century ideas concerning romantic love in his articulation of the sacredness of the covenantal union. "By the early 19th century," argues Anya

Jabour in *Marriage in the Early Republic,* popular literature excited Americans' "enthusiasm for the ardent affections of the heart, making the early American Republic a period of particular promise for egalitarian, loving relations between men and women within marriage."[55] Historian Karen Lystra writes that romantic love was characteristic of individual moral improvement by self-reservation and a complete divulgence of one's person to another. In America's fast-paced market context, young people were encouraged to guard their hearts from the deception of the confidence man and the painted lady. A romantic engagement, a divulging of one's inner feelings to another, was risky business. The sincere "ideal self," Lystra continues, "was meant to be completely revealed to one person only. Individuals were taught to reserve their truest or best or most worthy expressions for a single beloved."[56] A marriage contracted solely for the purposes of satisfying immediate lusts, which often induced men and women to marry, Bourne wrote, was "detestable in the sight of God, destructive of personal and social comfort, and injurious to morality and religion."[57] An honest union was cemented "with the desire of the heart."[58] The courting ritual, like the marriage covenant, also served as metaphor for spiritual conversion, anticipating a heavenly consummation. The essence of tender love was a mixture of kindly emotions, affectionate sympathy, and evangelical devotion. Genuineness assured a person's union with the spiritual husband, Christ. "Being in love," Jabour states, "was analogized repeatedly as being reborn."[59] The betrothed had to form a union based on exclusive genuine love, the same kind of love that drew a person to communion with the savior. Courting for Bourne was an earthly activity wrapped up in a sacred aura. It was vital, therefore, for the couple initiating such a sacred vow to be religiously one in mind and heart.

For many nineteenth-century writers, men had a greater responsibility to carefully fix their affections on the object of their desire and endeavor to compel a woman, a being whose heart was by nature easily manipulated, into an engagement. Bourne warned that male seduction, "a most odious and criminal fraud," swindled innocent women out of their honor, an action "worse than rape."[60] "A female, when her affections are settled" in accordance with a man who lacks Christian sincerity, would therefore "submit to any deprivation." If a young man's motives in finding a wife were corrupt, the woman he seduced would, therefore, "submit to any deprivation rather than withdraw them."[61] The man was responsible for protecting the heart and the religious sentiments of his wife. A suitor's seduction in taking advantage of the "weaker vessel" rendered him "useless to society" and thus disqualified him from "the regions of the blessed [i.e., the new heavens and earth]."[62] Men who initiated an engagement under false pretenses (to either satisfy their own materialism or worldly lusts) despoiled their betrothed and forced her to live in a union devoid of friendship, sexual purity, and proper protection. More importantly, such men alienated their spouses from seeing God.

Bourne demonstrated how man-stealers, whose lack of communion with the divine meant not only a loss of "manhood" but also a crisis of "womanhood," perverted courting customs. Such men would trap young northern women and force them "to become the chief manager and governess of the slaveholder's harem."[63] A white woman, therefore, "drawn into licentiousness by wicked men," would either plunge into "the world pool of infatuation and inordinate indulgence with him" or fix "the bandage" to her eyes, concealing "the horrors of the slave plantation" and passing "her life in a state of virtual alienation from her natural prop."[64] She may even enact revenge for her "own debasement by ensnaring others into the same corruption and moral action." Whatever the ultimate transformation, Bourne concluded, young women would "doubtless bewail their lot [and] live in one constant shuddering tremor when they survey their own connivance at a system which has transformed several successive generations of colored women into victims of lust under their own eyes."[65]

The final chapters of *Slavery Illustrated* focus on the obligations and practical steps of churchgoing women to end slavery. The "slave-holding women of the South," especially those who professed Christianity, "have a peculiar class of duties to perform": "To disseminate the truth upon the subject of slavery; to protect decidedly against the existing evils; to combine their efforts, that they may more efficiently resist the continued predominance of the hideous iniquity which surrounds them."[66] Women needed to awake from their spiritual slumber to stop the machinations of sinful men. He supported the political efforts to disperse "anti-slavery papers and pamphlets" that the 1837–38 female antislavery society pushed for. Yet in his mind, the petitioning campaigns would in the long run be less effective than a unified and vocal protest: "[T]he grand witness of their detestation of slavery, and of their own personal purity would be given emphatically and irresistibly."[67] As Christ threw out the moneychangers from the temple, organized women could "hurl slavery from its proud and usurped predominance."[68] Equally, their sisters in the North had "the high duty of testifying against [southern] atrocities, and of endeavoring to abolish the system of slavery."[69] They had the primary spiritual responsibility to save their southern women, black and white, from the clutches of mental, spiritual, and physical bondage, "to divulge those awful corruptions which our sisters among the slave-holders dare not reveal."[70] But before they could rescue the South from eternal damnation, these women had to confront their own prejudice and break the spell that kept them in their "present debasement."

Bourne offered two ways in which to execute his plan: "Christian women must loudly denounce that code of laws and that unholy practice which nullifies the matrimonial covenant" and "must resolutely discard all communion with slave-holders as members of the church of God."[71] But second, and most importantly, the only effectual means of accomplishing this task was through a reformation of the church. He encouraged women "to withdraw from the churches to which they respectively belong, as the only public testimony that they can give of their obedience to the apostolic mandate (1 Corinthians 6:9–11) 'not to keep company with the fornicators.'"[72] These spiritual "Deborahs," he urged, "must be heard protesting . . . must be seen withdrawing from the houses of prayer when a slave-driver enters the pulpit, or in any way attempts to lead the devotions, or offers himself as an acceptable communicant at the Lord's Supper."[73] Even a small minority of northern women would create a "moral hail-storm and whirlwind within twenty-four hours, which would so affright their 'lords and masters,' that they would hide themselves 'in the dens and in the rocks of the mountains.'"[74] These feminine warriors, united with godly ministers, would demand repentance and a solemn vow of immediate cessation from sin, which their male counterparts would be unable to ignore. The consequences would be immediate.

In his support of women in abolition, Bourne held to a position that divided fellow abolitionists. The ideology of separate spheres and the spiritually saturated "cult of domesticity" compelled and justified women as leaders in moral and spiritual reform. As Cott once again reminds us, "Ministers addressed women as a sex and, at the same time, as an interest group in the polity that had special civil and social responsibilities and special powers to defend its interests."[75] But by the 1830s, the same ministers began "reining in" women.[76] For conservatives, women who became convinced of immediate and universal abolition compromised their influence when they played the public role given to men by God, blurring the divinely ordained distinctions between the sexes. Catherine Beecher, a leading advocate of the power of domesticity, believed that radicalism was "entirely without the sphere of female duty."[77] The increasing role of women in public, a reality that came dangerously close to "spiritual and moral anarchy," forced reformers to consider, Beth Salerno writes, "new understandings of female citizenship."[78] Pioneering feminist Angelina Grimké tapped into the contradiction of gender exclusion by appealing to the perennial work of women in reform. "Have not *women,*" she asked rhetorically, "stood up in all the dignity and strength of moral courage to be the leaders of the people, and to bear a faithful testimony for the truth whenever the providence of God has called them to do so?"[79] What grounds did men have for keeping women from positions of leadership in reform?

Bourne never expressed concern over women's efforts to expose the hypocrisy within the ranks of abolition, but whether he noticed it or not, the direction in which the more radical branch reshaped reform ideologically alienated him from the movement. Confronting traditional cultural beliefs required a reconsideration of traditional theological constructions. According to Anna Speicher, leaders of female antislavery societies and the early women's rights movement—Angelina and Sarah Grimké, Abby Kelley, Lucretia Mott, Lydia Maria Child—were bonded by their "commitment to discovering and acting upon religious truth" as "the fundamental organizing principle of their lives."[80] In contrast to Bourne, their commitment to reform was based on "noninstitutional but quite specific religious principles."[81] Although they jettisoned time-honored Calvinistic formulations—the inerrancy of scripture, the depravity of man, the deity of Christ, creeds of confessions, and traditional ecclesiastical hierarchy—their beliefs were not necessarily antitheological. First, their ecclesiology, so to speak, was not tied to any institutional denomination: it was abolitionism. After years of frustration with religious sectarianism, the Grimké sisters, for instance, found their "church" and their faith in reform. So too did Abby Kelley, who once confessed, "I can say from my heart of hearts, with you, abolitionism is Christianity applied to slavery: here is the rock upon which our cause rests, and 'the gates of hell shall not prevail against it.'"[82] Second, their radical theology was closer to the physical realm than was traditional theology. Individual conversion and the preparation of the coming of the kingdom were accomplished in society, not above it. Redemption was wedded to earthly practical reform. Once again, Kelley best represented the religious position of radical women when she asked rhetorically, "While Lazarus lies at the gate, who can sit at speculative study in his library or revel in the cultivation of his tastes[?]"[83]

Finally, the "woman question" demanded a modern reading of the Bible. In the same way that abolitionists showed that the Bible did not support racial slavery, radical women, the Grimkés especially, offered a hermeneutical analysis of certain passages that diffused sexual inequality. Dismantling the patriarchy undergirding views on gender was crucial in this new feminist hermeneutic. Angelina Grimké was unsatisfied with "the circumscribed limits with which corrupt custom and a perverted application of Scripture have encircled" female reformers.[84] The traditional discourse related to patriarchal headship came from a number of Old and New Testament texts: Genesis 3:16 ("[a woman's] desire shall be to thy husband, and he shall rule over thee), Ephesians 5:22–23 ("Wives, submit yourselves unto your own husbands, as unto the Lord"), and 1 Peter 3:7 ("Husbands, in the same way be considerate as you live with your wives, and treat them with respect as the weaker vessel"). Those who favored a more liberal reading pointed out passages that countered a patriarchal exegesis such as Joel 2:28–32 ("I will pour out my Spirit on all people. Your sons and daughters will prophesy") and Galatians 3:28 ("there is neither Jew nor Greek, slave nor free, male nor female, for *you are all one* in Christ Jesus"). In her reading of Genesis 1:26–27 ("So God created man in his own image, in the image of God created he him, male and female he created them"), Sarah Grimké suggested that "not one particle of difference [was] intimated as existing between them [men and women]." Appeals to unequal social or cultural distinctions could not be supported biblically. Eve was not created as a dependent servant, but as a partner to her husband. Grimké further argued that Paul's letter to the Ephesians was written to Christian wives who were to act in a godly submissive manner in order to convert their unbelieving spouses. In no way was the apostle setting up a universal law. Such newer readings led to a theological defense of women's rights. Bourne, however, did not anticipate this alternative egalitarian interpretation.

This emerging hermeneutic challenged sexual inequality and therefore severely weakened appeals to normative roles within the family hierarchy. Historian Michael Pierson has argued that by the end of the 1850s reformers "stopped using patriarchy as a standard of behavior against which to judge the reality of southern plantation life. The result was that many white abolitionists . . . translated their newfound distaste for patriarchy as a social model into a more sophisticated attack on the 'patriarchal institution' than that deployed by abolitionists in the 1830s and 1840s."[85] The casting off of patriarchy as a rhetorical weapon, inspired by a number of reformist campaigns (e.g., sex and marriage reform, women's rights, and antipolygamy), resulted in a critical re-evaluation of the concept of dependency. Slaves could never be truly independent because their existence came from being under a patriarchal head. The same was true for women; they lived in dependent submission to male authority. Racial and sexual dependency was the root of slavery in all its forms. Radical women formulated a "newfound" belief that "dependency"—the heart of patriarchy—crumbled self-autonomy and thus reduced women, children, and blacks to an unfree status. More than a decade after Bourne's death, therefore, the support given to proper patriarchy by traditional theological underpinnings had been significantly challenged.

Despite Garrison's praise for Bourne's *Slavery Illustrated,* it is difficult to gauge the book's impact on the radical developments of the antislavery movement and the rise of first-wave feminism. *Slavery Illustrated* came out around the time that similar works by radicals in the abolitionist movement were also being published, including Lydia Maria Child's *Anti-Slavery Catechism* (1836) and James Thome's *Address to the Females of Ohio* (1836). *Slavery Illustrated* echoed much of what Angelina Grimké wrote in *Appeal to the Christian Women of the South* along with her sister Sarah in her *Epistle to the Clergy of the Southern States,* both published in 1836. For Angelina, slavery was contrary not only to God's word but also to the Declaration of Independence. Like Bourne, Sarah confronted "tenfold weight of guilt" among ministers for their failure to end slavery. The book can be seen as giving aid to discussions on women in the movement, but not, like *Book and Slavery,* for being a prime mover for women's rights. As Margaret Fuller wrote in *Woman in the Nineteenth Century,* published the year of Bourne's death, "now the time has come when a clearer vision and better action are possible. When man and woman may regard one another as brother and sister, the pillars of the porch, the priests of one worship."[86] Three years later at Seneca Falls, radicals would confront the long history of abuses against women and expand the language of the Declaration of Independence to meet the reality of gender equality.

In their modified theology, early abolitionist feminists vehemently opposed gender inequality on biblical grounds. Thus, according to Robert Abzug, they created "an explicit, tightly reasoned, full-blown rejection of traditional Christian visions of gender," using "words, ideas, and images to subvert or refute the seemingly ageless wisdom that guided humankind in its ideals of male and female."[87] In a sense, radicals not only brought the heavenly realities down to earth, perhaps confusing the sacred and the secular, but also formulated a religious justification for the individual rights of women *as* women, not as beings restricted to a secondary part of a larger and more important sacred reality. Theological modifications were not what Bourne had in mind, however. He supported liberal social changes without undermining his conservative religious base. His inability or perhaps unwillingness to alter his own traditional religious beliefs kept him from a critical engagement with the logical extent of the "woman question." As he wrote in a later work, "Man is not formed for himself alone."[88] Men and women were not made for themselves, but for ultimate communion with God and his kingdom in the millennium. A taste of that communion was found in the bonds of marriage. Nonetheless, pious women were the spiritual warriors who led the charge against immorality and irreligion in the American republic. The identity and moral duty of women stood as bulwarks against the growth of economic, political, and religious slavery. Bourne supported the activism of women in the fight against slavery, but he never articulated a radical concept of equality as others did as the movement progressed.

Bourne's Protestant radicalism fit with an earlier form of women's public reformist activities. An argument could be made that while Bourne aided in raising consciousness over the rights of women, he was not conscious himself, not conscious enough, that is, to give full assent to women's rights. Bourne avoided addressing the radicalism of more aggressive reformers who drew a link between the plight of slaves with that of women. "The investigation of the rights of the slave," Angelina Grimké wrote, "has led me to a better understanding of my own."[89] Lydia Maria Child likewise noted that women "have been kept in subjection by physical force, and considered rather in the light of property, than as individuals."[90] "The real roots of nineteenth-century feminism," Ronald Walters suggests, "lie not simply in inequities between the sexes but also in social and cultural changes and in the consciousness-raising potential of abolitionism."[91] Walters suggests that these reformers "reinforced feminine stereotypes by displaying the moral impulses everyone expected of them, by doing little that was unladylike, and by deferring to masculine leadership, particularly of the clergy." Bourne's writings on the issue fit with the first two phases of women's publicness described by Lasser and Robertson, especially those influenced not only by the Revolution but also by the revivalism of the Second Great Awakening. These women, as Walters corroborates, "posed no direct challenge to the status quo."[92] Bourne may have been out of touch in regard to the radical developments of the first wave of the women's rights movement. Many abolitionists held conflicting, even contradictory, opinions regarding the role of women, but all with the goal of ending slavery. For Bourne, women were to play a role in practicing true faith for the purpose of protecting and propagating true liberty. Such an end, in Bourne's mind, would not only liberate individual members of society but also the nation.

CHAPTER 6

THE NATION, THE MILLENNIUM, AND BOURNE'S *American Text-book of Popery*

> Although the retrospective scrutiny of the past produces humiliation for the extreme depravity and debasement of our ancestors, yet it is conjoined with the anticipations of triumph, that the hell born Usurper, "The Man of Sin and the Son of Perdition," ere long shall be dislodged from his odious papal throne; and that he who is "exalted Prince and Savior" shall possess his rightful authority over all the tribes of mankind.
>
> —GEORGE BOURNE, *The American Text-book of Popery*

In the preface to the 1836 British edition of *Lorette,* Congregationalist minister and educator Henry Wilkes considered southern slaveholders as "hereditary Catholics."[1] Abolitionist "come-outer" William Brown wrote in 1849 that slaveholding religious leaders held in their hand "the power which the Vatican wielded six hundred years ago." "The truth is," he continued, "the spirit of popery" among anti-Catholic benevolent organizations that were either indifferent or outright opposed to immediacy was "not yet cast out of protestant [*sic*] churches," especially as the issue related to "the rights of conscience in matters of religious faith and practice."[2] In order to be purged of spiritual impurity and experience the jubilation of complete freedom, American churches had to cast out the remaining traces of false religion. This included both the southern theological apologists of slavery and the false teachers of Roman Catholicism. The ministerial class was divinely commissioned, Bourne believed, to be the guardian of pure and undefiled religion. Those, Bourne wrote, who "lifted up their voice against the monstrous superstitions of popery" would usher in a reformation. They would then "merit the praise of every succeeding age, for their undaunted appearance in times of the most imminent danger" on behalf of the "glorious principles of divine truth."[3]

In his *Bible Argument*, Bourne stated that Catholicism was the type of spiritual bondage that historically preceded southern slavery. More specifically, the theological hermeneutic that supported human bondage, "as a historical fact worthy of notice," he believed, "first originated among the members of that [Catholic] Church." Revelation 18:13 prophesied about how the mystical Roman beast became the first to traffic, along with other propertied items, "the souls of men," "an exact description of human slavery."[4] Bourne was not saying that southerners evolved linearly from Catholicism or that they followed consistently a detailed blueprint for racial enslavement laid out by the pope and his minions. Rather, the perversion of the Bible was the initial act by which humans, stripped of their reason and social identity, could easily be turned into items of property, and Catholicism, as prophesied in the book of Revelation, was the firstborn of such a practice.[5] Only when "Protestants correctly interpret the holy scriptures," Bourne advised, would the "blasphemous imposture," the pope, be destroyed. The same was true for southern slavery.

Destroying the historical model of slavery, the offspring of bad exegesis, guarded the scriptures and thus opened the way for greater political and religious freedom. Bourne believed, according to Fenton, that Protestantism was "the only means of securing religious liberty for all U.S. citizens."[6] Americans needed to heed the lessons of the sixteenth-century Protestant Reformation, which was the first step in the historical expansion of absolute freedom. Slavery and Catholicism were symptoms of historical amnesia. The resurgence of monarchical conservatism and the reinvigoration of the Catholic Church in post-Napoleonic Europe threatened liberal egalitarian freedom in the Western world, bringing a return to an enslaving medieval age. Bourne believed that a study of the origins of spiritual and physical slavery, best shown in the emergence of the Catholic Church, would awaken the conscience of citizens and stir them to fight the cancer of religious slavery plaguing the modern world.

In his last publication against popery, Bourne formulated a radical sacred history, the type that provided a prophetic glimpse and a hope-filled confidence of the coming millennial age when religious corruption, political factions, and all forms of slavery would cease.[7] More than simply discussing life on earth as pictures of heaven (e.g., marriage), Bourne was prophesying actual historical events. The true church advanced via three momentous revolutions, each of which was prophesied in the New Testament book of Revelation. The first spanned from Christ's ascension to Constantine and the second from Constantine to the Reformation. The final revolution, the most important in history, came at the end of the long Reformation: the millennium. In addition, each revolution, Bourne carefully pointed out, was inaugurated by the efforts of a few God-fearing reformers who labored toward theological and ecclesiastical change as the primary means to protect biblical religion, eliminate society's ills, and offer political stability. As he wrote in *Picture of Slavery,* "no Reformation in the Church of Christ ever began with its ministers in their collective capacity. The alarm was sounded probably by one or more separate and isolated individuals."[8] Although he recognized the damaging effects of Catholicism and, like others, extolled the republican principles set up by the Reformation, Bourne stressed that a mere reliance on biblical values was only part of the aim in stamping out false religion. The key was not necessarily through violence or the establishment of more Protestant educational institutions in the West or the barring of Catholics from political activity, especially at a time when Irish Catholics were increasingly becoming a part of an expanding democracy, but through the work of divinely ordained "fanatical"—a label Bourne came to adopt—preachers. The "hand of God" appointed and "co-operated" with such agitators who worked toward the immediate eradication of institutionalized sin, against a hostile mainstream, and for the advancement of the church toward millennial paradise.[9]

Along with providing an analysis of Bourne's eschatological history within the political context of the early antebellum period, the goal of this chapter is first for the reader to consider Bourne as an American Protestant reformer who saw himself as a God-appointed actor in the drama of sacred history, a history shaped by his readings of the Bible. Late twentieth-century historians have correctly discussed the impact of post-Revolutionary evangelical revivalism in America that provided a critical ideological base for radical and immediate abolitionism.[10] Revivalism certainly supported Bourne's more radical position, but the core of his views on emancipation looked back even earlier to the sixteenth-century Reformation. Second, Bourne's sacred history offered a picture of an exceptional American national identity nurtured by the religious freedoms endemic to historic Protestantism. He identified the young republic, which in the first quarter of the nineteenth century entered a critical period in its own nationalistic development, as the last bastion against religious and political tyranny. The nation's distinctiveness rested on a Protestant foundation, and citizens needed to rely on the leadership of ministers—not, in the end, on institutions or benevolent societies—responsible for protecting such a faith. Such ministers would prepare the way for the final revolution in ecclesiastical history.

From childhood, Bourne was reminded not only of the importance of the Reformation and its theological influence, but also his ancestral lineage in it. According to Lewis Tappan, he was "a descendant of martyrs and of Puritans."[11] His mother was of the lineage of John Rogers, a convert of William Tyndale, the famous English Bible translator. Rogers became the first Protestant executed for his religious beliefs during the reign of Mary Queen of Scots. Bourne's grandmother traced her roots to John Cotton, one of the first Puritan ministers in New England. His great-great grandfather, James Johnstown, was martyred in Glasgow in 1684 "while singing the 87th Psalm with heroic courage," for his "defense of the Covenant and work of Reformation."[12] Throughout his career, Bourne wrote from within a historically reformed mindset. He frequently appealed to the examples of sixteenth-century Protestant European evangelists like Luther, Calvin, Knox, Cranmer, and Zwingli. His admiration for such leaders, likewise, extended to men like George Whitefield and, as mentioned earlier, John Wesley, both of whom, but especially the latter, laid the foundation for revivalism—what Bourne called "the marrow of ecclesiastical history"—in America.[13] Bourne was drawn to such a great cloud of witnesses. Evangelical preachers in both Europe and America, "whose piety 'like a city set upon a hill, could not be hid'; whose example so luminously shone among men 'that others seeing their good works, glorified their Father who is in heaven'; whose zeal for the Redeemer animated them to surmount every difficulty [and] to propagate that heavenly doctrine," were not only unprecedented but also necessary to move history closer to the millennial age.[14] Such men were true liberators. In the face of great opposition, they emancipated the church and society from spiritual darkness. It was through the channels of antislavery and anti-Catholicism that Bourne sought to become a member of this divinely ordained cohort.

As mentioned in an earlier chapter, Bourne helped fashion "no-popery" literature, which fueled American nativism. It was the public school controversy in his home state of New York in the late 1830s and 1840s that stirred him up to commence one final battle against the "Man of Sin." With the collapse of state-funded church establishments, a movement Bourne fully supported,

Americans turned to voluntary organizations to inculcate the principles of Christianity in the creation of virtuous citizens.[15] Education became an important ally in promoting such civic morality. In the early nineteenth century, New York legislators took authority away from private educational establishments, founded largely by religious leaders and wealthy businessmen, in order to make schooling a public endeavor toward national citizenship. By 1825, the state had one of the first publicly funded school systems in the country.[16] Lawmakers, the overwhelming majority of whom were Protestant, gave more centralized authority to the state's superintendent for public education, drafted the core curriculum, which included daily participation in the reading of the King James Bible, and made decisions regarding the distribution of funds for schools. Not surprisingly, Protestant dominance over the control of financial distribution for "common" education and the use of the King James Bible fomented animosity.[17] Catholics refused to recognize the Protestant scriptures, which did not contain the apocrypha, and they pushed the issue of using state funds for their own schools. It was not hard for them to turn the language of Protestantism, especially that of the freedom of conscience and worship, against their opponents. Catholics appealed to their own freedoms in the area of religion. What is more, they objected to the prejudicial politics of American Protestants at the center of the school fiasco. But Bourne, like other anti-Catholics, ignored such arguments and even blamed Catholics for creating the hullabaloo. For Protestants the opposition to true religion was undeniable: New York papists opposed the true Bible. For Bourne, all attempts to defend the religious rights of Catholics were null and void since they rejected the very fountainhead of those rights. Eventually, because of the intransigence of nativistic leaders, Catholics, with the leadership of men like Bishop John Hughes, organized their own parochial schools.

Convinced that the "ominous controversy concerning the entire exclusion of the Holy Bible, and [hence] Christianity . . . from our Common Schools" had been started by papal leaders in New York, Bourne felt compelled to write "an authentic exposure of the nature and extent of that universal supremacy and jurisdiction" that characterized the Roman Catholic Church.[18] Picking up his polemical pen, Bourne wrote his last anti-Catholic work, *The American Text-book of Popery,* a revision of his 1838 *Illustrations of Popery.*[19] One New York senator, Erastus Brooks, after having read *Illustrations,* proclaimed in a speech that "no better [authority] on this subject [of anti-Catholicim]" could have come from any other writer.[20] Readers should also note the "American" in the title, suggesting the book's importance for citizens of the republic. *American Text-book* was posthumously published in 1846.

American Text-book can be divided into two parts. The first is a compendium of quotations from Catholic theologians, popes, and councils defending the peculiarities of Romish doctrine and practice: the universal bishopric of the Roman see, infallibility, Mariolatry, purgatory, the sacraments, the doctrine of justification, and the duty of Catholics to use violence against Christian heretics, all of which were born out of the papacy's institutional supremacy and skewed view of the Bible.[21] There is no substantial difference in argument between *Illustrations* and the *Text-book* with the exception of Bourne's reasons for revising the latter (the Bible and the common school controversy). One interesting exception, however, comes by way of a cartoon in the opening pages of *Illustrations.* Four ministers, two of whom are Luther and Calvin, adorned in Reformation clothing and holding a variety of texts, stand on a large rock inscribed with the word "TRUTH" at its base. Below them, various leaders of the Catholic Church with a number of ecclesiastical articles, signifying their station in the papal hierarchy, drown in a sea bearing the inscription "untruth." Although the imprint was not reproduced later, it nonetheless captures the spirit of both works: namely, that Protestantism literally stands on the firm foundation of gospel truth.

The bulk of *Illustrations* and *Text-book* (the second part) relies heavily on Bourne's ecclesiastical history, *Lectures on the Progress and Perfection of the Church of Christ,* written while he was a teacher in New Pleasant, New York, in 1823.[22] As the title suggests, *Lectures* is a basic delineation of the major moments in the history of the Christian Church through the lens of Revelation. Bourne placed greater emphasis on the evils of Catholicism in the later works. Other parts of the *Text-book* were revised after 1838, with the introduction finally written in 1844. As an intended educational work, the *Illustrations* and *Text-book,* with the great support of the *Lectures,* emphasized the dangers of ecclesiastical and political Catholicism in Europe and especially America. And just as Bourne's enmity toward slavery intensified between *The Book and Slavery Irreconcilable* and *Picture of Slavery in the United States of America,* separated by nearly twenty years, so too did his anti-Catholicism between the *Lectures* and *Lorette,* and even more so between *Lorette, Illustrations,* and the *Text-book.* All three latter works, written within a quarter century, shared a similar tone related to the advancement of the Christian church. Each began with an apology for studying the relationship between the Bible and history. The former awakened "in the soul of man that 'fear of the Lord'" that extirpated "irreligious principles" and implanted "sublime, consistent, reverential sentiments concerning the Godhead."[23] As a "coadjutor" to the Bible, ecclesiastical history confirmed the "influence of the verities which a perusal of the sacred oracles imprints on the heart."[24] As an external witness, religious history testified to the supernatural workings of the scriptures but also provided a window into all of human history, which comprised "the most interesting and splendid topics for contemplation in the annals of the globe."[25]

Throughout every age, human nature expressed an "inextinguishable hatred" of Christ and his gospel and was, therefore, "ever prone and willing to depart from Jehovah."[26] The importance of history rested on the fact that it showed the "variegated hues" of human depravity—"the secret movements of our hearts, and the almost mysterious contradictions which adhere to the human character"—in real time.[27] Despots tapped into their sinful nature and emerged from the ignorance, immorality, and stagnation that befell a society when it forgot the works of God, leading inevitably to the establishment of institutions that kept members of society in perpetual darkness. Tyranny began with rebellion against the true God. The Bible and history provided an understanding of human nature and its relationship to God, a necessary symbiosis between the creature and the creator, but it also showed the origins of tyranny and enslavement. Special revelation provided the blueprint for absolute freedom, and sacred history was the practical unfolding of such a plan in historical time.

Another instructional benefit of this kind of literature, as in the case of biography, was to teach readers about "extraordinary characters," who successfully "excite the passions, and invigorate the talents of men: they animate exertion, raise merit from obscurity, and unfold the energy of genius."[28] I have already taken note that Bourne's 1806 *History of Napoleon Bonaparte* reflected his interest in narratives that celebrated the religious and political achievements of great individuals. Like *Napoleon,* Bourne's *Life of the Rev. John Wesley* celebrated the heroic accomplishments and virtuous character of this religious figure.[29] The various biographies and those "grand exemplars," Bourne emphasized, who acted as guideposts in the stages of history, provided an "ample source of self-knowledge": "The successive characters which are depicted, [furnish] either a caution to alarm, or an example to imitate."[30] Indeed, a faithful examination of sacred history would draw inquirers closer to "those faithful and unflinching witnesses" who defended the scriptures, rejected heterodoxy, and opposed that blasphemous apostate of New Testament history, the pope. Their example offered a model of what individual humans could become. More importantly, however, their significance came in how they facilitated a radical advancement toward spiritual enlightenment and religious freedom.

The final educational advantage of a work like *Text-book* was to see the indisputable manifestation of the glory and triumph of God's person and work. As an evangelistic tool, history revealed "the control of that supreme invisible hand, which still regulates the machinery of the universe."[31] The periods of spiritual enslavement were further instructive, for they showed the vanity of the ungodly "to extirpate the Gospel of Christ, and the Church of God." History offered the tools necessary to overcome spiritual oppression, which rested on the final triumph of God. Although the "retrospective scrutiny of the past produces humiliation for the extreme depravity and debasement" of human nature, Bourne wrote, history "is conjoined with the anticipations of triumph" in the end.[32] Even the most reprobate of sinners could not help but see the hand of providence in advancing the contemporary age toward greater freedom.

Beyond the mere practical rewards for such a study, an inextricable hermeneutical bond linked the scriptures and celestial history. The Bible was necessary to understand the events of the latter, and Revelation was the believer's interpretive guide for understanding post–New Testament developments. A number of nineteenth-century theological polemics, debates, sermons, and pamphlets that related John's visions to the papacy supported conspiratorial fears about the eminent threat of Catholicism.[33] Bourne's history was one of a handful of texts—including Abel Stevens's *A Sermon on the Political Tendencies of Popery Considered in Respect to the Institutions of the United States* (1835), William Brown's "Religious Organizations and Slavery," in *Oberlin Quarterly Review,* and Joseph Martin's *Influence, Bearing, and Effects of Romanism on the Civil and Religious Liberties of Our Country* (1844)—that traced the origins of popery beyond the Middle Ages or the Reformation. Stevens's history identified three distinct epochs, from the Persian war against the Greeks, to the Reformation, and finally to the modern American temperance movement. Martin dated his history back to the Roman Empire, but he focused predominantly on the birth of papal authority in Boniface VIII's *Unam Sanctam* of 1302. William Brown delineated the origins of chattel slavery to the ancient Near East.

Bourne's *Lectures* deciphered the cryptic and at times nightmarish prophecies—defined by Bourne as "the unquestionable intuition of future contingencies, in which neither the anterior determination nor the preliminary disposition is discovered"—of the apocalypse as they unfolded in the experience of the church from the first to the nineteenth century.[34] Certainly by the 1840s, Bourne affirmed that "nearly the whole of the divine predictions recorded" in John's vision (the book of Revelation) was devoted to the Roman Catholic Church, an interpretation emphasized more acutely in *American Text-book* than in *Lectures.* Each chapter of *American Text-book* moved the reader closer to the end of history when that "hell born Usurper" would be "dislodged from his odious papal throne."[35] Revelation 1–6 first dealt with the spread of the gospel beyond the boundaries of Judea and Samaria—to the "seven churches of Asia" (1:4) in Sardis, Philadelphia, and Laodicea—and recounted the life of the church under the Roman Empire in the first and second centuries (chapters 2–5). The "white horse" with its royal crown discussed in chapter 6, who went out "conquering, and to conquer" (6:2), represented the "general dispersal of the gospel" by the faithful of the early church.[36] With the opening of the second seal in verse 4, the "red horse" emerged, identifying "the Roman Empire, from the accession of the Emperor Trajan to the close of the [second] century."[37] Verses 5–8 announced the breaking of the third seal (6:5). The rider of the "black horse" held a balance in his hand, the symbol of governmental justice. This referred to Severus Alexander, an emperor who did much to build the geopolitical infrastructure of Rome—later used for the Roman episcopacy—and who also, according to tradition, was just toward Christians.

The same chapter drew out a central tenet of Christian morality. Persecution perennially accompanied the church. Throughout much of his professional career as a writer, Bourne highlighted persecution in the developing life of a Christian. Indeed, as the Apostles Paul and James talked about in their letters (2 Corinthians 12:10; 2 Thessalonians 1:4–7; James 1:2–4), the advancement of Christ's body toward the end of history came through trials and tribulations. According to historian James West Davidson, the harassment of the church was part of the "logic" of its eschatology, measuring "progress toward the millennium in terms of the judgments necessary for redemption."[38] Not long after Alexander's rule, during the "turbulent reign of Maximin" and later under Aurelian in 275, did the church enter an intense period of abuse worse than the time of Nero or Claudius. John envisioned this as the opening of the fourth seal: "the era of the Martyrs." Christians faced "death and hell" through "sword, famine, pestilence, and ferocious beasts."[39] Under Diocletian in 303 (the fifth seal), believers were marshaled "in the train of Death" by the "pale livid green horse" (6:8), experiencing an occasion of oppression "longer [in] continuance, wider [in] extension, [and] more atrocious [in] barbarity than all the former persecutions combined."[40] As a precursor to the escapist practices of monastic life, those who lived under the threat of martyrdom hid themselves "in the den and in the rocks of the mountains."[41]

The imperial tormenters of the early centuries who "participated in the horrors of the era of Martyrs" were soon "subjugated" with the coming of the first revolution in the second decade of the fourth century.[42] "The seventh chapter of the Revelations," Bourne wrote, applied "to the period immediately subsequent to the elevation of Constantine to the undivided government of the Roman empire."[43] The opening of the sixth seal made known the rise and success of Constantine, who defeated the rival emperor Maxentius at Milvian Bridge in 312 after literally taking the Christian cross as his military standard. In gratitude to the true God for his victory, Constantine adopted the Christian faith, "the seal of the living God" (7:2), and passed an edict of toleration in 313. As a result, the church, for a time, "came out of great tribulation." "Pure and undefiled religion" extended to the "four corners of the earth" (7:1); all nations could freely come to Rome to worship the lamb "clothed with white robes, and palms in their hands" (7:9).

Yet the protection of Christianity in 313 and its official adoption in Theodosius in 394, wherein "the gospel became the authoritatively established religion in every part of the Roman Empire," had not eliminated the problem of historical and theological neglect.[44] After the Edict of Milan and regardless of the actions of Julian the Apostate to revive the Roman pantheon, the church abandoned its early heritage and began to mimic the pagan practices of the surrounding heathen societies, instituting, for instance, the observance of holy days, repudiating matrimony, practicing private confessions, and venerating chosen saints. Since converting to the true faith could garner social and political favor, many throughout the empire became Christians in name only, anticipating the shallow exterior of Jesuitical piety. In the absence of persecution, the church became lethargic and spiritually undisciplined.

The waywardness of the church and the manifestation of false doctrine were both given support by corrupt institutions. Believing that unorthodoxy was the product of a false but powerful church (recall his battles against the slave-supporting Presbyterians), Bourne was chiefly concerned with how Revelation outlined the evolution of the Roman episcopacy. Distinctions began to be made between the primitive offices of the church (i.e., bishops, elders, and presbyters) as a result of the early doctrinal struggles against the Montanists, the Eclectics, and the Manicheans. The hierarchy of the church was further structured after the battles against Pelagianism and Arianism. Over time, select ministers were given charge over larger sections of the empire and recognized as more authoritative than the lower ecclesiastical orders.[45] Eventually, five influential cities in Christendom—Jerusalem, Antioch, Alexandria, Rome, and Constantinople—vied for allegiances and doubled as regional and diplomatic centers before and after the fall of Rome. Each city developed its own unique identity and often developed opposing attitudes toward one another, especially in the case of Rome and Constantinople.

But the rise of Rome's bishopric came as a result of the violence—a vital tool of enslavement—that fractured Europe in the late fifth century. Rome weathered the storm of violence, consolidating its political and ecclesiastical power over all of Europe. In the eighth chapter of Revelation, John of Patmos prophesied about the external barbarian threats that led to the collapse of the empire. The "first angel" sounded its trumpet (8:7). A violent storm of "hail and fire mingled with blood" followed, referring to "the desolations committed by Alaric and Attila the scourge of God."[46] The second angel (8:8) symbolized Genseric, king of the Vandals, and his "success in Africa and conquest in Rome." Genseric (or Gaiseric) gained control of the Mediterranean when he turned "the third part of the sea" into blood (8:8–9). The marauding activities of the barbarians forced the bishop of Rome to act as a kind of political ambassador. Impressing his followers, Leo I reinforced his power when he was able to pacify Attila the Hun. Recognizing the dangers surrounding Rome, Leo used his political clout to strengthen his religious authority, and he passed the Petrine Doctrine in the same century, making him and later Roman bishops the mouthpiece of God for the entire church:

> For [Peter] was ordained before the rest in such a way that from his being called the Rock, from his being pronounced the Foundation . . . the Doorkeeper of the kingdom of heaven . . . we might know the nature of his association with Christ. And still to-day he more fully and effectually performs

> what is entrusted to him. . . . And so if anything is rightly done and rightly decreed by *us,* if anything is won from the mercy of GOD by our daily supplications, it is of his work and merits whose power lives and whose authority prevails in his See.[47]

The "third angel" and the great star of heaven announced the final "destruction of the imperial authority" at which time chaos reigned in Europe: "In Italy, Africa, Spain, Gaul, and Britain, the contests were fierce and uninterrupted between natives and their barbarian invaders, and all the calamities, like wormwood, embittered every condition of society, and shortened the lives of infinite numbers of the wretched inhabitants."[48] The bishop of Rome used the disorder in Europe to his advantage, positioning himself within the already established geopolitical layout of the Roman Empire.

The barbarian aggression was followed by the rise and success of "Mohammedanism," as predicted in Revelation 9:1–11. "The star that fell from heaven [v. 1]," Bourne determined, "applied to the apostate monk Sergius, who was the principal writer of the Koran."[49] The "locusts" described in verse 7 "signified the Saracen armies [and] in numbers they were almost incalculable; and they spread desolation through all the Roman Empire." The life expectancy of locusts mirrored the short duration of the Muslim conquest: "[A] locust lives precisely five months and for the same prophetical duration, were these [Muslims] permitted to torture the nations." And the heads of the locusts resembled that of horses, which, according to Bourne, symbolized the equestrian skills of the Muslim warriors. "The 'crowns' [9:7] denote their turbans and other badges of majesty, or the extension of their sway; their faces exhibited a manly beard while their hair was decorated after the fashion of women: their lion-teeth prefigured their enraged force: their iron breast-plates bespoke their energy in self-defense."[50] The chapter ends (9:13–21) with "the four angels," the Turkish caliphates, and their success "over the Eastern empire." He then discusses the five pillars of Islam as essential doctrines of merit, similar to the beliefs of Rome, that contradicted the Protestant concept of grace—especially in the area of justification, a continual theme for Bourne—and the concept of heaven as a most "offensively indecent and voluptuous" place.[51] In Revelation 10–15, John prophesied the constant harassment of the Islamic administrations against four of the five patriarchal cities. The collapse of Alexandria, Antioch, Jerusalem, and later Constantinople at the hands of Muslim forces talked about in Revelation 16–17 and the prevention of Islam from advancing further into northwestern Europe after 732 geographically isolated the Latin Church in the West. Although a considerable anti-Christian force in history, Islam was not as dangerous as Catholicism, for it did not invoke the designation "Christian": "Romanism is an artful contrivance to tyrannize over all mankind, under the mask, and with the hallowed and attractive title of the word."[52]

The principal means, according to Bourne, "both to increase and consolidate" papal authority began with the Crusades in 1096. Under the command and sway of the pope, who had convinced Christians that his words were the very words of God, "all Europe was torn from its foundation, and seemed ready to precipitate itself in one united body upon Asia."[53] This holy war revealed Rome's ability to deceive its followers through false doctrine, proving "the liability of the human mind to be crazed by a sudden fantastic excitement" and, worse, masking its ambitions for the control of all the "national affairs" of Europe.[54] Unrestrained, however, the pope could easily use the rhetoric of a holy war to persecute "the servants of Jesus" whenever they became "obnoxious" to "church and clergy."[55] No legislative authority existed to check papal power. Consequently, the Crusades, along with the preceding events of the fall of Rome and the conquests of Islam, marked the beginning of the "Dark Ages," a period in which Europe reached its nadir. Western civilization became "enchained in that gloomy . . . mental darkness and ecclesiastical vassalage" by Rome's premier bishop, who exploited the violence done throughout the Christian world, especially in the East and North Africa, in order to become the supreme head of the church.

The ascendancy of the pope and his enslavement of the Western world was only part of Bourne's dialectical history. Whenever members of Christ's body strayed from doctrine and practice, God would raise up extraordinary individuals—like Wesley (and Bourne himself)—to stand up for truth. The more powerful the church became, the more revolutionary an impact such people would have in the advancement of the church. In the early centuries, such ministers, apologists, and philosophers as Polycarp, Justin Martyr, Ireneaus, Origin, Athanasius, and Augustine fought to defend the faith against external and internal threats. These individuals, involved principally in theological disputation, were unable to stem the violence that strengthened Episcopal Rome. Yet during the long medieval period, providence prepared the way for prereformers to chip away at the clay feet of the papacy. Revelation 11:1–14 made known the miraculous coming of the "two witnesses clothed in sackcloth" (11:3) who would "commence their prophetical opposition to the Papal perversions of evangelical truth."[56] Bourne identified the witnesses as "individuals" (viz., Peter Waldo, John Wycliffe, and John Huss) and their respective "societies" (viz., the Waldensians, the Lollards, and the Moravians).[57] Chapters 12 and 13 of Revelation discussed the persecution of the woman's child by the dragon, which denoted the pains of late medieval Rome (the dragon) to silence these prereformers, the offspring of the true church (the woman).[58]

The activities of these "morning stars" were supported by three critical changes occurring in Europe in the fourteenth and fifteenth centuries. The first came with the removal of the papal see to Avignon in France, the so-called "Babylonian Captivity" (1309–1376), and the Great Schism of 1378–1417, when two popes, in Italy and France, competed for catholic supremacy. When the rift between Avignon and Rome could not be settled, a council in Pisa (1409) elected Alexander V, but the current popes refused to relinquish their authority. Then, in 1417, the Council of Constance elected a fourth pope, Martin V, "whose daring impiety, treachery, and wickedness," Bourne argued, "exceeded all the criminality of those even who were ejected for their insupportable turpitude."[59] The consequence of such an embarrassing moment in the life of the Roman Church functioned to confound the divine voice of the pope, for, as Bourne asked rhetorically, "which of these pretenders was the legitimate infallible?"[60] The second change commenced with the invention of the Gutenberg press around the fifteenth century. Compared only to the "miraculous tongues of the Apostles," print "revolutionized mankind" by rapidly spreading in multiple languages "the wonderful works of God."[61] The pope could not stop such a tool, when "in the plastic hands of fervid Christians."[62] The final condition was the discovery of North America. European exploration was not only stimulated by a revival of learning sweeping the continent, augmented by the press, but also moved populations away from the geographic center of Christianity. This allowed ordinary Christians to worship freely, far from the authoritarianism of a religious tyrant who trampled the conscience by determining what followers were to believe.

With the rise of the prereformers, the technological innovations in print and exploration, and the embarrassing papal divisions, sixteenth-century Europe had been softened in preparation for Christendom's second radical revolution. Revelation 14 prophesied the gallant labors of an obscure monk and university professor, Martin Luther. Inaugurating the glorious Protestant Reformation in 1517, Luther's "genius, learning, boldness, inflexibility and perseverance, by the *assistance of Heaven,*" surmounted and demolished "the intrenchments [*sic*]" that enclosed "all the embattled hosts of the Papacy, and established the magnificent Reformation upon a basis hitherto immovable."[63] Rebelling against repression and rejecting the enslaving doctrines of Rome, Germany's reformer, whose influence benefited from the lack of centralized authority in the Holy Roman Empire, became the church's premier post–New Testament emancipator. Rome, the tyrant, now had its historical counterpart, and individual Christians had *the* historical precedent to oppose not only popery, but all forms of civil and spiritual interference.

Along with Luther, standing at the helm of the Protestant movement, "divine providence manifested itself in raising up very illustrious witnesses to the truth"—Ulrich Zwingli, John Calvin, Gustavus Adolphus, and Thomas Cranmer—each of whom "saw and opposed the intolerable corruptions" of the church.[64] The church's second revolution created a great outpouring of ministers to indefatigably defend the message of the gospel and the standards of the church. These guardians of the faith, scattered throughout Europe, were "supernaturally assisted" and "elevated to imperishable honor": "Their virtues, genius, learning, undaunted fortitude, and perseverance, by the sanction of Heaven, surmounted all impediments [and] battered the Babylonian fortress."[65] Protestantism laid the foundation for the emancipation of civilization and ushered in the modern liberal era.

Breaking the chains of spiritual bondage required reformers to lay siege against the doctrine upon which "the whole system of Romanism" rested: papal infallibility. The rising authority of Rome during the barbarian, Islamic, and papal conquests positioned the pope as the chief speaker and grand protector of Christianity. To convince Europe's inhabitants of his religious authority and thus to safeguard his monopoly, the pope had to keep the true source of light and life, the Bible, out of the hands of Christians. By determining the meaning of the sacred text—and not allowing it to speak for itself as the reformers taught—the pope imprisoned Christians and made himself God. Revealed truth, however, was necessary to dissipate "the mists of idolatry [and] the fog of superstition," which consequently freed the mind from perpetual darkness. By itself, the Word would supernaturally crush earthly powers that impeded one's right to experience its miraculous power. An undisturbed conscience, given greater value by Luther's idea of "the priesthood of all believers," contradicted the arbitrary and thus totalitarian dictates of history's leading religious tyrant. Bourne was confident that his sacred history would "restore the appropriate biblical phraseology," the foundation of religious and political freedom, which "the primitive Reformers so aptly delineated."[66]

True religious freedom would shatter the two leading forms of spiritual slavery that plagued Western history. Given the analogical correlation between the twin evils, it was easy for Bourne to move from a discussion of "popery" to slavery, directing his fellow abolitionists to break the "popish infallibility" of the southern master class. The life and liberty of the oppressed, as he stated in *Picture of Slavery,* was "despoiled" and "prolonged at the caprice of a tyrant."[67] It was preposterous that "one man," whether priest or slaveowner, could "justifiably be so reduced to the command of another, as to have no will but that of his director." The authority of the master was supported through ignorance. As presented in both pro- and antislavery antebellum literature, slaveholders thought that religious education—or just literacy in general—would create unmanageable and even dangerous slaves who would undermine the slaveholders' power. Slaveholders knew the danger of allowing their slaves to read the scriptures for themselves.[68] Blacks, however, Bourne argued, had a right to a free and unmediated reading of the Bible, for "all the knowledge which they acquire by a white preacher's discourse is both deceptive and insulting."[69] By refusing the free offer of the gospel, priests and man-stealers, in accordance with "the most diabolical impiety," "usurped the place of spiritual-mindedness" and kept their "vassals" from the rights, duties, and blessings of true liberty.[70] The free, undisturbed reading of the Protestant Bible, made possible only by social and institutional structures that protected "private conscience," broke the chains of every form of spiritual and physical slavery.[71]

In lockstep, then, the reformers' engagement with Rome's central theological dogma led naturally to break the weak link in its hierarchical chain. Repositioning the Bible as the exclusive authority over faith and practice placed limits on earthly institutions. Revelation 17 discussed the symbolic "heads" and "horns" of the beast, the plurality of which suggested the extent of the pope's authority "as both ecclesiastical and secular."[72] Historical examples of imperious papists like Leo I, Gregory VII, and Innocent III, to name a few, showed the pope's exclusive authority over all matters of church and state: "to dethrone monarchs, grant kingdoms, translate Emperors and empires, and to excommunicate all civil potentates."[73] This kind of power could be used to absolve the most heinous sin and punish even the least opposition to the church. And as an incentive to obedience, the pope arbitrarily determined that his most loyal disciples would be "perfectly free from all civil and even episcopal jurisdiction," forcing people to bend to the will of capricious autocrats.[74] Since "the sway of the nations was virtually confided in the Romish Priesthood," any national leader who dared defy Christ's vicar would be "degraded from all power and dignity" and their subjects "absolved from the oath of fidelity and obedience."[75] "Like a two-edged sword," then, the pope secured his supremacy by mingling the spiritual with the corporeal, situating himself as "*one over all;* and in obedience of all to that same *one.*"[76] By shattering the absolutism of the church and thus removing its involvement in the affairs of state, Protestants revolutionized the West, especially in "those countries where [the] degradation and barbarism, portrayed in the annals of the middle ages" dominated, transforming "the character, relations, and conditions of mankind [against] the *natural enemy of progressive knowledge and freedom.*"[77]

After the sixteenth century, the "principles of government among the nations" became "extensively reformed," creating formidable defenses against popish aggression. And no other country in the Western world better exemplified the consequences of the Protestant Reformation on nation building than the United States. The early European inhabitants of North America praised the example of the early reformers and made the Bible "the sole legislative authority" over church and state government. It is worth repeating here that America, for Bourne, became the "only existing instance of a nation commencing their social contract with pure and undefiled religion; and animated to the erection of a political edifice from their inextinguishable attachment to religious freedom," a type of freedom bound up with the Reformation's legacy.[78] In the history of statecraft, Protestant America was exceptional, for it displayed to "the world a condition previously unknown in the history of mankind."[79]

The strength of the young republic rested on the Bible, the "handbook of republicanism on which American civil as well as religious liberties were founded."[80] "Revealed religion," Bourne wrote in his *Bible Argument,* exhibited "a preference for the republican form" of government, for it guaranteed "the natural equality, the individual responsibility, the reciprocal duties of the human family, and the paramount claims of the most high God to the services, and the obedience of all his creatures."[81] And the key to maintaining a stable and ultimately free society—as well as that of a religious denomination (as in the case of Methodism, Bourne wrote in 1807)—came through the "total severance between the ecclesiastical and temporal relations of the citizens" and the establishment of a "constitutional order," both of which had been created directly from Protestantism.[82] This institutional bifurcation liberated religion "from every fetter, disconnected [it] from terrestrial associations, and left [it] to exert its own authority and energy, independent of governmental sanction and support."[83] More importantly, it permitted the church to flourish, but also left "the rights of conscience untrammeled."[84] "In unison with the decisions of the sacred volume," a constitution worked to counter tyrannical tendencies and thus cultivated a free citizenry.[85] America's republican constitution and not the monarchical dictates of a king paralleled the Protestant ideal of the rule of scriptural law against the arbitrary statutes of an uncivilized and heretical class, whether Jesuit or Christian slaveholder, that created degraded and ignorant slaves.[86]

Furthermore, the continuance of a church-state separation required the use of a critical Protestant weapon: the press, what Bourne considered as the most "delightful feature of the present era." A free press, the papacy's "Pandora's box" and "the source of all evil," "loosened the chains of darkness."[87] The rapid spread of the Bible's message through numerous religious and missionary tract societies in the nineteenth century exposed error and superstition and permitted individuals and communities to understand what the scriptures taught, without the intrusion of obstructing interpreters. It also pierced the dark spaces in which masters fed their insatiable desire for dominance, a common theme of anti-Catholic and antislavery literature.[88] Young people were regularly "despoiled" and made of ill use to society in the dark "prisons" of the confessional, the cell, the plantation, and the slave house.[89] Bourne compared southern slave quarters to "the dungeons of the Popish inquisition."[90] Whenever Americans were "barred from witnessing certain proceedings," David Brion Davis observed years ago, they imagined a "'mystic power' conspiring to enslave them."[91] "In a virtuous republic," not to mention in a benevolent age that placed greater emphasis on private morality (i.e., self-control, sincerity, etc.) for the public good (the logic of republican virtue), "why should anyone fear publicity or desire to conceal activities, unless those activities were somehow contrary to the public interest?" In revealing the evils done in private, the press, Bourne accepted, "guarded the public," for "through it [the press] that which was hidden came to the light of the public," under the guidance of the Bible.[92] Catholicism concealed "*itself* in crooked and hidden places"; Protestantism, in contrast, "seeks the utmost publicity."[93]

Anti-Catholics, as well as abolitionists, would write in order to arouse public sympathy and thus to move readers against such institutions, by force if necessary. Bourne warned that "an energetic and sleepless strife" existed between Protestantism and popery; both were locked in an eternal struggle in which "one of the contending parties" would eventually be extinguished.[94] Americans needed to defend Protestantism. The anti-Catholic rhetoric of writers like Beecher, Smith, and Morse, for instance, did in fact incite violence. In 1830, a Carmelite convent in Baltimore was defenseless against Protestant violence that lasted three days. Four years later, a zealous mob, galvanized by a series of sermons by leading no-popery crusader Lyman Beecher and the scurrilous tales of a runaway nun, Rebecca Reed, burned down an Ursuline convent in Charleston, Massachusetts. In 1844, a riot broke out in a predominantly Catholic area of Philadelphia, sparked by a conflict over the use of public funds for Catholic education, and it ended with the destruction of a number of private homes and two churches. And by the mid-1850s, a time when the politically organized nativistic "Know-Nothing" party gained a modicum of national success, more than thirty Catholics had been killed in disturbances in St. Louis, Missouri, and Louisville, Kentucky.[95]

Although severely weakened by the impact of the Protestant Reformation and the pressures of domestic and international Protestantism, Rome was in no way defeated.[96] Bourne recognized that in the nineteenth-century context, "Popery," "in all its gloom and malevolence in its ancient domains," continued to harass Western civilization, spreading "its odious leaven among Protestants."[97] The latter chapters of Revelation delineated the beast's final push against the forces of righteousness. The conservatism coming out of post-Napoleonic Europe helped revive Catholic influence and stoked fears in America of an imminent papal takeover. A host of religious and political writers warned against the pope's plans to reinvigorate its missionary activities, especially, as many believed, in its attempt to establish an empire in the western Mississippi Valley.[98]

Although not interested in a global takeover, the Church, thanks to the work of Pius VII and the aid of Austria, did in fact benefit from the changes occurring in nineteenth-century Europe. As early as 1808, Pius orchestrated the establishment of a variety of parishes in the North, South, and West. The most "counterrevolutionary" arm of the church and perhaps the greatest threat to American society came from members of the Society of Jesus, the "agents of darkness," wrote Bourne, who wanted to "impede the progress of the Reformation."[99] Pius VII helped to revive the order, using it to set up satellite institutions—churches, schools, and nunneries—throughout Europe and North America. The pope, however, did not approve local autonomy. Churches in America, despite their rapid growth, were under the direct authority of Rome. Pius's successors expressed open hostility to political liberalism. Gregory XVI and later Pius IX publicly opposed the freedom of conscience, the liberty of the press, and the separation of church and state, the fundamental elements that prevented political tyranny.

As a product of the Reformation, the United States was the foremost citadel of freedom and civilization in the known world. According to Dale Light, Catholic authoritarianism "stood in direct contrast to the liberal imperatives that were becoming ever more prominent in American political culture."[100] Europe, on the other hand, was on the verge of another "dark age." The "reformed nations" across the Atlantic, influenced by the strength of nationalistic conservatism in its hostility to political liberalism, were slowly becoming "popish" themselves. They became "chargeable," Bourne believed, for "the criminal infatuation of wantonly rejecting the Gospel of Christ, that noblest boon" offered by providence. Willfully facilitating its "own direful overthrow," Europe was abandoning its history, discarding the intellectual, religious, political, and economic freedoms established by the Reformation: "the plain truths of the Gospel, and the holy principles that were inculcated in the first *protests* against the usurpations, and the deadly enactments and requirements of the court of Rome, have become almost obliterated."[101] Predating the famous historical aphorism of Harvard's George Santayana, Bourne held strongly to the belief that those who neglected their history were bound to repeat it.

The common-school controversy, especially in New York, represented at a micro-level the cosmic Manichean contest between the forces of light and darkness and furthermore contributed to defining a specific American nationalism interwoven with Protestantism.[102] The attack against liberal politics necessitated an attack on Christianity's sacred text. A papal decree in 1844 forbade Catholics from using unauthorized versions of the Bible.[103] A rejection of the Protestant scriptures in the school's curriculum reflected the antiliberal bigotry of a religiously tyrannical organization. It was, in essence, a rejection of the sole source of tolerance, religious freedom, republican liberty, economic success, and social tranquility, all the things up-and-coming citizens would learn in the public schools. Catholics, nativist evangelicals proposed, did not espouse such ideals, but continued as lovers of a dark medieval past, one that was incompatible with the progressive nature of American republicanism.[104] To allow Catholics to establish a beachhead in America's common schools would threaten the nation's political and educational goals. For Bourne, Catholic institutions would deprive students of "all that knowledge which alone can sweeten them for social usefulness" and of "their future relations as American citizens."[105] There was no way that the Roman Church was at all interested in education, for it "prohibit[s] all persons from the perusal of the Scriptures." Consequently, papists stood as "ruthless enemies of all learning."[106] A free nation allowed its citizens to read the scriptures for themselves and thus to experience not only the greater meaning of the created order but also the true nature of spiritual and physical independence.

That North America was the last sanctuary of true Christianity and, as many proposed, the future place of a cosmic battle with the "Man of Sin" made it all the more necessary for Protestants to remain vigilant.[107] In publishing *Illustrations* under its new title, *The American Text-book,* Bourne had the young nation at the forefront of his mind.[108] Nineteenth-century America did not live solely under the menace of a "foreign conspiracy," to use the words of Samuel Morse's popular no-popery pamphlet, but under an internal one and was susceptible of falling into its own dark age. Bourne worried that a "specious and pestilential delusion" was infecting American politics. The factionalism of America's second party system provided an inroad for Catholics. The maneuvers of northern Democrats to incorporate the Irish vote in the state and federal elections of the 1830s and 1840s and to protect Catholics from Protestant fanaticism raised the ire of the emerging Whig Party, which increasingly identified itself as the "American" party of progress and Protestantism. (There is no evidence that associates Bourne with the Whigs, but his own political principles and especially his hatred for Andrew Jackson certainly places him closer to them.) How could modern and progressive Americans make peace with a retrogressive institution that publicly repudiated modern Protestant liberalism? The very nature of a Romanist, Bourne reasoned, excluded him from participation in American politics: "*[E]very sincere Papist is disqualified,* de facto, *from holding any office under a Protestant government.*"[109]

Bourne further feared that even antislavery leaders were becoming less aggressive toward "Jesuitical" slavery. And indeed, a handful of abolitionists opposed the intolerance of their fellow reformers. Theodore Weld wrestled with the New Testament reality that "in Christ there is neither Jew nor Greek."[110] All were one in Christ, Protestants and Catholics alike. Tired of the support Protestant churches gave to slavery, James Birney called for "distinguished *Catholics* who are friendly to the [American Anti-Slavery] Society."[111] Parker Pillsbury came to appreciate Catholic authorities, especially Gregory XVI's bull against the slave trade. Wendell Phillips lamented the "Prejudice against Catholics among abolitionists."[112] In "The Outrage of Washington," printed in the *National Anti-Slavery Standard* in 1856, the Reverend W. H. Furness presented a picture of the divine nature of liberty that transcended the peculiarities and popish tendencies of both Protestantism and Catholicism:

> [Liberty] is the sign of the influence of that Spirit in the hearts of men. Not cathedrals and costly churches, not pompous ceremonials, not Sabbaths and feast days and fast days—Easter and Lent—not morning and evening prayers, not the ringing of church bells, not baptism and sacraments—not these are the indubitable signs of the presence and power of the Spirit of the Most High; but liberty, liberty to think and to speak what we think; personal, civic, religious liberty . . . this it is that bears witness to the Spirit of the Lord dwelling in individuals and in nations. This is the grand test of the prevalence and power of religion, pure and undefiled, . . . In fine, liberty is divine—the Spirit of the Lord.[113]

Yet, ironically, attempts made by abolitionists to sever ties with Protestant nativism did not eliminate "popery" as a conceptual and linguistic device against which freedom—of whatever kind—could be measured. Not even those radicals who rejected the religious intolerance among antebellum reformers were themselves completely free from the rhetoric of anti-Catholicism. When Irish political activist Daniel O'Connell urged Catholics not to join abolitionist organizations because of the "many wicked and calumniating enemies of Catholicity and [of the] Irish" among their ranks, William Lloyd Garrison reassured him that not all the advocates of freedom, including himself, were "bigoted against Catholicism."[114] Yet in the same breath, Garrison continued, "There are many of our self-styled 'Evangelical' clergy who are as bigoted, proscriptive, and self-inflated as the Pope himself."[115] Here Garrison used no-popery language to describe Protestants. It is interesting to note that the rhetoric of anti-Catholicism, whether applied specifically to Protestants or Catholics, continued to be used as a marker of religious and even political intolerance. American freedom remained—and perhaps still does—essentially anti-Catholic. "Popery," writes Maura Jane Farrelly, "was not exactly the same as 'Catholicism.'" In order to be "popish," one "merely had to adopt what was frequently referred to as a 'slavish' mentality—that is, one that admired and utilized the tactics of tyrants and/or willingly succumbed to those tactics."[116] Despite the troubling views of his fellow reformers, Bourne was undeterred. There was an urgency in his tone, especially at the end of the *Text-book:* "All pretended pacification between Protestants and Papists is a phantom," for the two—as with the Bible and slavery—are "utterly irreconcilable." The spiritual lethargy and the opposition of Protestants to God's divine work had to be dispelled "or the municipal institutions of the United States" would be jeopardized, "if not destroyed."[117] Those ministers who shirked their responsibilities to the gospel were accountable for the growth of irreligion that, in turn, strengthened political, economic, and religious slavery.

Regardless of the growth of Catholicism and given the increasing lethargy among Protestant reformers, Bourne was confident that the events in the nation anticipated the last and final revolution in sacred history: the millennium. In the same way that the medieval period anticipated the second revolution of the church of Christ, the easing of tensions against Catholicism and conservatism in the second ushered in the third. Life in early nineteenth-century America, far from being an "Era of Good Feelings," as Sean Wilentz and a host of other historians now suggest, was fraught with social and political divisions. Nationalism was a contested field, but this was not something that necessarily worried Bourne. The church was to anticipate periods of harsh persecution. Partisanship, he acknowledged, was a characteristic of an unredeemed world; since the fall "the world has been the theatre of contention."[118] In fact, a true schism for him was a division between those who followed the teachings of Christ and those who did not. The only factionalists in the United States were the advocates of slavery and papism. Nonetheless, "sectarian distinctions" would be "absorbed by 'the unity of the spirit in the bond of peace'" in the thousand-year reign.[119] This last revolution would not only resolve all political, social, and religious disunion, but it would lead to the "overthrow of all the

Anti-Christian systems as they are recorded in the Apocalypse."[120] "The glory of the Millennium was the unrestricted operation of the Gospel of Christ upon every individual, in his personal experience and social relations."[121] The final historical era would literally confine spiritual and physical tyranny to the past.

Consistent with the progress of sacred history, the third and final revolution would be ushered in by God-ordained ministers. Slavery would not die a supposedly natural death, nor would it end through governmental policy, but by the indefatigable efforts of divinely appointed ministers. Bourne predicted the rise of preachers "like Knox and Whitefield" who would lead a rebellion against slavery.[122] The *Liberator* identified Bourne as a member of those associated with the Protestant Reformation: "for energy of purpose, he resembles Luther . . . for courage John Knox—and for zeal, the indefatigable Whitefield. His warfare against the Man of Sin has been prosecuted with amazing vigor and singular ability, although he has had to struggle almost single handed and endure severe privations."[123] For this reason, he was able to understand more fully the spiritual dynamics between slavery and freedom. For many of his fellow reformers, Bourne was an important figure in sacred history. He exemplified the life of a religious revolutionary in defending the purity of the scriptures in the face of immense persecution, opposing the tyranny of unconverted church leaders, and working to bring the church closer to millennial freedom.

CONCLUSION

THE BOURNE LEGACY AND AMERICAN CULTURE

Ye Gospel preachers! Why are you so dumb
Upon this solemn theme, to which each ray
Of Revolution points? And has the world
Such fascination, such corrupting power,
And vile intimidation's force, as thus
To paralyze all energies divine?

—GEORGE BOURNE, *Philanthropist,* October 14, 1836

Thus did his spirit forecast the three great movements of the day.

—THEODORE BOURNE

Bourne believed strongly in the power of the gospel, both to transform the heart and move one to reform society. A short story reprinted in the *Christian Union* in 1872 by an officer in the Dutch Reformed Church adequately captures Bourne's ministerial effectiveness. Sometime between 1840 and 1845, Bourne had been a delegate at the General Synod of the Reformed Church, held in Albany, New York. A local Baptist minister, T. B. Welch, attended the proceedings as a guest and remembered years before hearing Bourne preach a sermon in Philadelphia "where there was an immense assembly present." Approaching Bourne, Welch asked whether the now-aged minister could recall the sermon. Pointing to his head, Bourne replied, "Yes, very well." Mr. Welch then asked if he would give the same homily at his church on the upcoming Sunday, which Bourne agreed to do. Welch "invited the great assembly to attend in the evening to hear the same sermon" that had led to his own conversion. "The church was thronged," the Baptist minister observed, with attendees desiring to listen to this seasoned expositor. After the sermon, Welch commented that when he originally heard that sermon "about twenty young men," including Welch, not only accepted Christianity, but were compelled, because of his example, to "become ministers of the Gospel of the blessed God." "[D]eeply moved" and apparently unaware of his persuasiveness, Bourne responded, "I never heard of it before. 'Bless the Lord, O my soul.'"[1] A modern Protestant reformer, Bourne had a profound impact on those to whom he preached. He also stood as an inspiring example of one who courageously acted upon the truths of the gospel.

The effectiveness of Bourne as a minister was not limited to his rhetorical skills, but to what he preached against and to his wider vision of freedom for both the church and the nation. Those who knew him recognized the power and consistency of his message. In the tumultuous year of 1861, an anonymous writer, responding to Tappan's biography of the Reverend Bourne in the *Independent,* offered another account of a confrontation that Bourne had had with a small group of southern slaveholding ministers. Convinced and convicted over what Bourne said at an antislavery society meeting in New York, the southerners inquired as to how the end of slavery could be accomplished quickly and peacefully. Without a moment's thought, Bourne offered a terse response that was reminiscent of his tone in *The Book and Slavery Irreconcilable:* "Quit stealing!" The author of the article then gave a concluding remark regarding Bourne's weighty ministerial authority: "If the early church had had more men of the stamp of George Bourne—men who would call things by their right names—who would have demanded that the decree of God, 'He that stealeth a man and selleth him, or if he be found in his hand, he shall surely be put to death,' should be enforced, then had this rebellion never broken out."[2] In other words, for Tappan, if only a few ministers preached the gospel without reservation and acted upon it without compromise in the first half of the nineteenth century, then perhaps the Civil War would never have occurred. In his brief biography, Bourne's son Theodore wrote that had "the energies of [Garrison and Bourne] been devoted to the work of insuring the passage of laws securing to the slaveowners one thousand millions of dollars in bonds, payable from proceeds of revenue and lands, it is possible that the terrible price paid for freedom of the slaves might have been saved."[3]

On November 20, 1845, Bourne died of what appears to be a heart attack, ending, Theodore Bourne wrote, "the life of the intrepid pioneer of antislavery."[4] Lewis Tappan offered the most eloquent commemoration of his fellow reformer and longtime friend: "Thus has fallen an intrepid advocate of human rights, with his harness on, in a vigorous old age, after the life of singular health, activity, and usefulness. His death is a severe loss to the Antislavery cause, the cause of Christianity, and the Republic of Letters."[5] In his 1858 letter to William Lloyd Garrison, Theodore Bourne had written that both his father and Garrison were responsible for the successful campaign against slavery "more than any other . . . that can be named."[6] But Theodore took a moment to single out the importance of his father's prophetic voice in forecasting "the three great movements" of the age: "the overthrow of slavery, the downfall of Popery and the Unity of the Church. *One prophecy is fulfilled. The other two remain to be fulfilled.*"[7]

Two movements in the first half of the nineteenth century, the battles against slavery and against Roman Catholicism, played a significant role in shaping popular ideas related to American identity.[8] George Bourne was at the forefront of these divisive debates, doing more than any other reformer to sustain the connection between what he considered the opponents of radical freedom. It was a united church that would banish the enemies of freedom. His traditional and relatively high view of ecclesiastical order forced Bourne to focus much of his diatribes against the leaders of the church, doing so without completely rejecting the institution itself, never becoming a "come-outer." In the conclusion to *Book and Slavery,* Bourne suggested that true reformation required faithfully courageous—at times fanatical—church leaders: "Had the Christian church always done its duty in relation to public vices of every description they would have been continually checked and destroyed, and the world kept in comparative peace and happiness."[9] In the context of the nineteenth century, the clergy and, as he included later, gospel-wielding women had the prime responsibility to battle the twin forces of enslavement. Both slavish enterprises contradicted the ideals inherent not only to authentic spirituality but also to the American nation, which had been fashioned from historical Protestantism.

As a minister acting in the tradition of historical Protestantism, Bourne's interest was to advance the religious meaning of freedom through the preaching of the Bible and the activism of ministerial leadership. True freedom would never be accomplished without the two. Ever since the publication of *The Book and Slavery Irreconcilable,* Bourne concerned himself with the shape of American religious and political freedom. The proper interpretation of the Bible became the cornerstone of liberal politics. This required theological consistency, which compelled Bourne to join Catholicism with slavery since both enslaved bodies and souls. Such consistency in antebellum America was sometimes difficult to find and maintain. Many moderate antislavery reformers viewed Catholicism as a greater evil than that of slavery. One commentator in the *New York Observer* in 1834 showed a greater fear over the potentially rapid expansion of the Jesuit population than the growing slave population in the South.[10] Other writers for the *Observer* concurred.[11] Protestant minister Joseph Berg considered the slave "free" in comparison with the man who voluntary "surrenders himself, bound hand and foot, to the sovereign will and pleasure of a popish priest."[12]

The opposite, however, was true for a few radical abolitionists. Even before the publication of *Lorette* and the establishment of the American Anti-Slavery Society, abolitionists like Garrison refused to support Bourne's ultra-Protestantism.[13] The editor of the *Genius of Universal Emancipation* praised Bourne's antislavery activities, but he drew the line when it came to his anti-Catholicism: "We have nothing to say about [Bourne's] religious sentiments; but his remarks, on the subject of slavery bear the impress of a strong and vigorous mind, and the clearest perception of reason and justice."[14] The Grimké sisters likewise viewed slavery as a much greater evil, which seemed to temper their view of Catholicism. "I believe," wrote Sarah, "that if all the horrors of the Inquisition and all the cruelty and oppression exercised by the Church of Rome, could be fully and fairly brought to view and compared with the details of slavery in the United States, the abominations of Catholicism would not surpass those of slavery, while the victims of the latter are ten fold more numerous."[15] As a result, proslavery Protestants, according to Sarah's sister Angelina, were hypocritical and "more criminal" because they deprived slaves of "the Sacred Volume by not allowing them time and opportunity to learn to read, and do not a great majority urge the very same reason for their conduct that the Catholics do for theirs."[16] The physical violence endemic to slavery seemed more of an urgent issue than the intricacies of doctrinal disputation, which were neither integral to America's market culture nor a reality built on a foundation of violence and terror. A number of abolitionists, influenced by the antitheological trends of popular evangelicalism, detached true piety from its connection with traditional confessional theology and ecclesiology. Such a distinction, however, did not fit Bourne's concept of reform. Disconnecting slavery from Catholicism, the physical from the spiritual, or politics from theology was an inconsistency that would not allow for the realization of true freedom.

Bourne's writings were presented within a biblical interpretive framework that opened issues related to the nature of freedom, the strength of the institutional church, the progress of sacred history, the authority of scripture, and the stability of the family as the cornerstone of a healthy nation. And the means toward an effective reformation rested on the undaunting fortitude of church leaders. Bourne saved his harshest criticism for those ministers who neglected their responsibilities to preach redemption to those in bondage. Members of the clergy, those who were committed to the traditions of the Protestant Reformation, as well as piously radical women, brought spiritual and physical revolution by confronting injustice through the public presentation of the gospel. Evangelical silence or a lack of biblical consistency would stop the progress of divine power in saving and redeeming not only those individuals in bondage but also a republic threatened by the specter of slavery.

Although he did not live to witness the bloody conflagration that began in 1861, Bourne, like so many other reformers, preached a message of impending judgment for those religious leaders who neglected to speak against the nation's sin of slavery and thereby soften its commitment to the true faith. For many reformers, the American nation was under the wrath and curse of God for the sin of slavery. More broadly, for Bourne, the entire nation faced a darker spiritual bondage that threatened the bonds of peace. As C. C. Goen argued years ago in *Broken Churches, Broken Nation,* particularly in his concluding chapter "A Failure of Leadership," the religious factions battling over slavery and other issues—that divided the Presbyterians, Methodists, and Baptists, the three major denominations in antebellum America—exacerbated political sectionalism and anticipated the Civil War. Such schisms acted as the "catalyst of the imminent national tragedy."[17] Although he rarely spoke in detail about the sectional crisis while alive, Bourne may have included Catholicism as an agent in such a tragedy. African American slaves, Catholics under the spell of the papacy, and the American nation would have been able to obtain peace and freedom if only church ministers held on to the legacy of revolutionary Protestantism, without compromising traditional faith, and recognized their divine calling to preach deliverance to the captives.

Evaluating the historical impact of a figure like George Bourne can be a significant challenge for contemporary scholars. We can modestly say that Bourne continued to have an influence on American reform in a more direct way through his posterity. His children, grandchildren, and even a great grandchild inherited an Emersonian-like "self-reliance" and a courageous disposition to confront abuses of power. George Melksham Bourne (b. 1806) followed in his father's footsteps as a writer; he was also an accomplished physician, becoming an advocate of personal health reform (e.g., temperance and vegetarianism) and an advocate of some of the early medical practices of his day, including the water cure. He was most famous for his book *The Home Doctor: A Guide to Health,* published in 1878 while he and his family were living in Utah. Rowland Hill Bourne (1812–1886), the younger twin of Christopher Stibbs Bourne (1812–1860), became a minister and prison reformer in New York, focusing much of his energy on rehabilitating convicts and attempting to make the prison system more humane.

George's youngest son, William Oland Bourne (1819–1901), a minister, editor, children's author, and hymnist, was a hospital chaplain for Union soldiers during the Civil War.[18] In his care for the wounded, he noticed that many of the soldiers lost their ability to write with their dominant hand. Concerned that the loss of the ability to write would severely limit their re-entry into society, especially for the purposes of social and economic rehabilitation, Bourne created the "Left-Arm Corp," which began as a competition for soldiers who had lost the use of their right hand. He was also the editor of *The Soldier's Friend.* William Oland Bourne, unlike his father, witnessed the devastating and inhumane horrors of war but was determined to show that the human will was far more resilient, rejecting the notion that physical restrictions limited an individual's freedom. His humanitarianism was a matter of showing the adaptability of humans in the most tragic of circumstances. His father provided the unction for him to be the pioneer of disability rights and of the self-determination of this community. Indeed, one of William's hymns, "Never Say I Can't, My Dear," captures a bit of his view on human determinacy:

> Never say, "I can't," my friend.
> Never say it,
>
> When such words as those I hear,
> From the lips of boy or girl

Oft they make me doubt and fear
Never say it[19]

Theodore Bourne (1822–1910) likewise continued his father's legacy as a writer, minister, and social reformer. He was ordained in the Presbyterian Church after being educated at Union Seminary in New York, became a pastor in a local congregation in Sleepy Hollow, and later took a position as professor of language at the Huguenot Institute in New York. Along with his involvement as an active member of the Society for the Prevention and Suppression of Crime, Theodore worked as the secretary of the African Colonization Society, a position held due to his commitment to Benjamin Coates's market-driven plan to establish a cotton colony in Africa that would compete with southern cotton. His commitment to national independence and self-reliance moved him in the direction of becoming a vocal opponent of American empire, challenging President William McKinley's war in the Philippines. Theodore was, like his father, bold enough to highlight the hypocrisy of leadership, asking rhetorically in a letter to Garrison's son William (1838–1909) as to why the party of Lincoln, the Republicans, had not united with "Anti-Imperialism," "maintaining American principles and precedents against their traitorous foes [Spain] [while] now masquerading under the guise of Republicans and upholders of the Flag?"[20] In a separate letter to Garrison around the same time, Theodore described President William McKinley's "war of aggression" in the Philippines as "hideous." Garrison shared Bourne's sentiments: "I share your belief fully regarding the obliquity and horror of the Philippine aggression."[21] Here, as is obvious, Theodore demonstrated his radicalism, like that of his father, to expose the hypocrisy of those in power, in this case the ruling party. Republicans had committed themselves to ending the horrors of enslavement, but they had forgotten their legacy, which led to the suppression of a distant people.

The opposition to the abuses of American power continued with the great grandson of George Bourne.[22] Theodore Bourne and his wife Emeline Johnson (1828–1908) gave birth to Charles Rogers Bourne in 1859. Charles's wife later gave birth to the one Bourne whose name is much more familiar in American history and culture. Progressive journalist and public intellectual Randolph Bourne (1886–1918) inherited from his great grandfather a sharp eye for pointing out the abuses of American power, particularly that of unfettered capitalism and the actions of a hyper-nationalistic federal government. In "War and the Intellectuals," Bourne confronted academics for supporting the propaganda machine created by the Wilson administration, which functioned to eliminate the rights of citizens. In his posthumous "War Is the Health of the State," Bourne made the argument that war making was inextricably tied to the state. War, in truth, *is* the state: "the organization of the herd to act offensively or defensively against another herd similarly organized." War also threatened popular democracy, creating the

> irresistible forces for uniformity, for passionate cooperation with the Government in coercing into obedience that minority groups and individuals which lack the larger herd sense. The machinery of government sets and enforces the drastic penalties: the minorities are either intimidated into silence, or brought slowly around by a subtle process of persuasion which may seem to them really to be converting them.[23]

Bourne lived at a critical moment in the history of American empire. The Wilson administration attempted to impress on the American mind the need to sacrifice civil liberties in order for the nation to survive. Many citizens began to support such efforts, creating a kind of nationalistic hegemony—a proto-fascist regime—that has largely remained from Bourne's day to the post-9/11 period. The power of the state is not strictly speaking a matter of a direct force upon a reluctant citizenry; it is supported by the governed. Bourne anticipated Antonio Gramsci's notion of hegemony:

> A people at war have become in the most literal sense obedient, respectful, trustful children again, full of that naïve faith in the all-wisdom and all-power of the adult who takes care of them, imposes his mild but necessary rule upon them and in whom they lose their responsibility and anxieties. In this recrudescence of the child, there is great comfort, and a certain influx of power.[24]

Such nationalism has been consistently challenged by those interested in not only protecting and extending civil rights but also in exposing the hypocrisy of those who undermine such freedoms. Yet dissent always faces considerable opposition from those in power, since those in power have access to forms of discipline. Again, Bourne's words apply in our day as they did in his:

> Any interference with that [national] unity turns the whole vast impulse towards crushing it. Dissent is speedily outlawed, and the Government, backed by significant classes and those who . . . identify themselves with them, proceeds against the outlaws. . . . The herd becomes divided into the hunters and the hunted, and war-enterprise becomes not only a technical game but a sport as well.[25]

By examining the work of the pioneer of both immediate abolition and anti-Catholicism, I have attempted to provide an understanding of how the two "isms" of abolitionism and anti-Catholicism were brought together in the nineteenth century. Bourne's hostility to Catholicism and slavery were of one piece, which may seem quite difficult for the contemporary mind to fathom. The connection must be understood in a social and political context where revolutionary ideas and the urgency to protect American freedoms was given aid by Protestant hegemony. Nineteenth-century reformers believed that the right of "private interpretation" (freedom of thought, speech, and conscience), freedom associated with the ideals of a revolutionary republic, arose organically from historical Protestantism and that in order to maintain such civil liberties the tenets of Protestantism needed to be protected from external and internal enemies. For Bourne, the strength of the nation and the purity of religion depended on total liberty, body and soul. And it was the radical minister who took on the role of society's watchman, since the preacher was the one who took consideration of the deepest part of humanity: the soul. The southern slaveowner, under the hypnotic sway of slave-loving ministers, enslaved the body; Catholics, under the mind control of popish priests and ultimately to the pope in Rome, enslaved the soul. What may be missed in the contemporary mind is the seriousness of such Protestantism. The soul is just as important as the body, and the corruption of one is the corruption of the other.

But what, beyond posterity, can we identify as the continuing legacy of George Bourne? It is always a challenge to trace a direct line from past to present, from a historical actor to his or her impact on the present. The challenge becomes much more acute when the past has little bearing not only on collective but also historical memory. Reflecting on the mind of Bourne may highlight the historical issues that the contemporary era has yet to fully deal with. In this final section of the conclusion, I wish to spend some time reflecting a bit on how American culture remains indebted to its past, specifically, how American culture has largely ignored the need to battle contemporary slavery, but also how it has failed to come to grips with the continued influence of America's religious intolerant past.

History is an activity of remembering. The moral obligation to remember comes in the way we create and learn from our heroes, like William Lloyd Garrison, Lydia Maria Child, Frederick Douglass, the countless unnamed others in the battle against chattel slavery. We are moved by their example, and we try to find ways to emulate them. Yet we must remember our heroes as they were: humans with prejudices, inconsistencies, and moral failings. We often ignore the faults of our heroes. When we do so, when we romanticize, sanitize, or lionize them, we elevate them to a status beyond the human condition. We celebrate the better nature of such angels but ignore their fallen sides. In this way, we—in a very real sense—*de*-humanize important figures of the past. We distance our humanity from theirs. The point is not to ignore or overtly dismiss such failings, but rather to provide a clearer picture of these individuals in order to get a better picture of the ironies of the human condition, *our* condition. What is more, by distancing ourselves from the past, by objectifying it, we fall into the trap of believing that our contemporary world is better or more righteous than those of years past. We learn from our mistakes and, thus, are no longer bound to repeat them, or so we think. It may be a bit of a challenge for the modern mind to reconcile how a commitment to the cause of abolitionism could be shaped by invective bigotry, defying the simplistic positioning of a reformer like Bourne along a modern political spectrum. Beyond his mere influence, Bourne can be understood as representing two ostensibly contradictory paths that have shaped a peculiar if not tacit assumption about American liberty, raising the issue as to whether a concept of liberty and its application can be radically free of discrimination.

The utility of recollection is that it offers not a rigid blueprint but a suggestive guide for living in the present. As historian David Blight has recently written, "Historians are often reticent in linking then and now, shy of instrumental parallels and analogies that often do not work." There is hardly a clear-cut answer as to how to use the past. Indeed, we should be careful not to make facile historical comparisons. "We have no choice," Blight continues. "[T]he path to understanding goes through *shaky parallels* and *dimly lit analogies*."[26] Many assume that history is a compilation of cold and calcified facts that we commit to memory, and that we have supposedly "learned" from history, believing that the contemporary world is better than the past. The ramifications of historical facts, including the way they are continually interpreted and how they structure our perspective on the world, are given very little thought. We often lose sight of the wider issues related to the ongoing ramifications, interpretations, and applications of those "facts."

History, as an ongoing activity, is never really finished; paradoxically, it is never truly past. We depend on history for life in the present, yet we do not use it in the same way. Race-based slavery, we may assume, has been "dealt with." It is now something learned in the classroom, learned in such a way as to celebrate the "emancipatory accomplishments" of the present. However, the "downfall of slavery," to borrow the words of Theodore Bourne to Garrison, was only partly realized. As Frederick Douglass correctly stated in 1865, slavery "has been fruitful in giving itself names . . . and it will call itself by yet another name." There seems to be something philosophically peculiar about slavery; it has an ontological presence that is universal, though manifested in a variety of forms in history. That is, it tends be both immanent and transcendent. Slavery, in distinct forms, comes and goes in history, but it always seems to reappear.

The question, then, is how might we draw on the slavery of the past to battle the slavery in the present. What kind of new abolitionism can we forge from the old? This, of course, presupposes the existence of slavery today. Slavery in the contemporary era is different from slavery of the nineteenth century.[27] Yet real differences in systems (e.g., race-based slavery and modern-day human trafficking) may still be tied to shared and enduring conditions that have and will continue to create systems of slavery. While race-based slavery ended in the nineteenth century, that which helped to create it has not. And here I am referring to modern neoliberal global capitalism. Slavery, past and present, and capitalism are joined in that they both rely on discipline, including degrees of latent and manifest violence, to organize massive laboring classes. The expansion of *capital* (hence *capitalism*) may not require the same kind of slavery found in the nineteenth century, but it certainly requires modes and degrees of physical, political, and even psychological discipline. Slaves lived within a system of discipline, terror, and violence. Those laboring within a capitalist system, to one degree or another, have faced—and continue to face—similar realities. The abolition of legalized slavery has not at all led to the end of the integral discipline needed to create a dependent (unfree) laboring class. This does not mean that everyone is in the same state of dependency or faces the same level of violence. A Chinese employee of a multinational corporation faces greater enslaving conditions (i.e., violence) than an American employee of the same company in the United States. Nonetheless, both are disciplined to produce the surplus capital required for such a corporation to maintain its power around the globe. While many of us celebrate the end of slavery, we fail to address the conditions that perpetuate systems of oppression, systems of "unfreedom."

This, by the way, is another shared tenet of slavery and capitalism, namely, that the two are opposed to democracy. The "free" in free market is restricted to a small elite; never has it extended to the vast majority of those producing value. (And let's not confuse the ability to purchase consumer items—items generated by market capitalism—with freedom. If they are the same, Chinese citizens are just as free in their country as Americans are in theirs.) Exploited factory labor, sex trafficking, the fight for low wages, the destruction of the environment by neoliberal-minded corporate elites, though distinct from the ideological underpinnings of antebellum slavery, have yet to draw upon the full and radical power of the abolitionist legacy. Americans, regardless of political allegiances (though some are more champions of the capitalist system then others) may offer lip service to abolitionism, but they stop short of recognizing new forms of slavery, shaped in large part by political power, military violence, and a hegemonic neoliberal ethos. A number of scholars have written on the existence of "twenty-million slaves alive today," according to Zoe Trodd, where "people are paid nothing, are economically exploited, and are under violent control."[28] Low-wage exploitive industrial jobs, prostitution, debt peonage "akin to feudalism," mining, and the sugar industry all depend on violence, which in turn has produced new forms of slavery in certain parts of the world (e.g., South Asia).[29]

Contemporary readers may be inspired by Bourne's hostility toward slavery (as well as that of other radical abolitionists) but not so his views on religious liberty. When considering an influential figure like Bourne, it is important to put aside our own ideological proclivities to see all sides of the individual. On the one hand, we can commend Bourne's battle against slavery, but we must not ignore how his religious prejudice shaped his views of liberty, a concept foreign to the modern mind. Both are inextricably tied to the mind of the man. What many in the current cultural context may consider contradictory was of one piece in the mind of this nineteenth-century reformer. It is interesting to note, however, that Bourne's sons did not continue his anti-Catholicism.

His posterity said little or nothing about his hostility to Catholicism. Again, what the sons of Bourne took from their father and grandfather was a commitment to a universal humanitarianism that went beyond the narrow confines of the nation. More importantly, they inherited the disposition to speak truth to power, to confront the sins of leadership at every level, from church to empire.

The "downfall of Popery," according to Theodore, had not been accomplished in his father's day, but a latent anti-Catholicism has remained as part of American identity, undoubtedly the partial influence of George Bourne. Arthur Schlesinger Sr. may have been correct when he said that anti-Catholicism remains "the deepest-held bias in the history of the American people."[30] Anti-Catholicism is America's "last acceptable prejudice," as Mark Massa and Philip Jenkins have testified in their respective studies on the issue.[31] Such a bias indicates a failure to deal with the past. In nineteenth-century America, terms like *Catholicism* and *popery* had been used in political ways, appropriated as an aspersion against individuals and institutions considered "unfree," "tyrannical," and hence "un-American." Anxiety over the supposedly despotic Catholic presence threatening American values was not isolated, for instance, to a brief literary period and political moment in the antebellum period. Indeed, hostility toward Catholicism was a salient presence in North America years before the American Revolution and, with a brief thaw during the American Revolution, continuing throughout the long nineteenth century. It also survived well into the next century, manifesting itself during the labor movement and the new immigration era as well as during the red hysteria after the Great War and the opposition to Catholic presidential candidate Al Smith in 1928. It was also recharged during the Cold War, where authors compared Catholicism with the creeping specter of communism, indicated in the minds of some by the election of John F. Kennedy in 1960. The numerous cultural productions—books, films, television shows—and the ongoing sexual controversies that have contributed to creating a negative image of the Roman church have sustained America's anti-Catholic bias.[32] Hostility "toward the Catholic Church," Maura Jane Farrelly concludes in her study of anti-Catholicism in America, "is still alive and well."[33]

When discussing the ongoing legacy of history, the scholar engages in a deep genealogical dig, connecting hereditary features of the past with the present. Similarities between the anti-Catholicism of the nineteenth century and that of the contemporary era are striking. Two distinct transhistorical features stand out. The first is what some intellectuals considered to be the political danger that Catholicism continued to pose to the freedoms of the American republic. The freedoms of America rested on the legacy of Protestantism. The anti-Catholicism described in Elizabeth Fenton's *Religious Liberties* "did not fade from public discussion of democracy and difference at the close of the nineteenth century . . . [but] persisted well into the twentieth century."[34] The postwar anti-Catholicism in Loraine Boettner's 1949 *Roman Catholicism,* a book that continues to be used among certain Reformed and Presbyterian groups, is grounded in and motivated by the neo-nativism of the postwar era. Boettner writes in the introduction: "Our American freedoms are being threatened today by two totalitarian systems, Communism and Roman Catholicism. And of the two in our country Romanism is growing faster than is Communism and is the more dangerous since it covers its real nature with a cloak of religion." The one "consuming purpose of the Vatican," Boettner continues, "is to convert the entire world, not to Christianity but to Roman Catholicism." The notion that Catholicism is "more dangerous" because of its inherent deception, covered "with a cloak of religion," and that it seeks to consume America could have been authored by Bourne and later nativists in the nineteenth century. Boettner also connects the religious practices of Protestantism to American constitutional rights. Catholicism is, he says, an "attack upon our Protestant heritage and those precious rights of freedom of religion, freedom of conscience, and freedom of speech." Boettner's study, however, failed to generate an anti-Catholicism akin to that found in the antebellum era. This is due in part to the anticommunist hysteria that characterized the political ethos of the Cold War.

Liberal journalist Paul Blanshard stated in his bestselling *American Freedom, Catholic Power,* published in 1949, that "Catholicism conditions its people to accept censorship, thought control, and ultimately dictatorship." For Blanshard, the evil of Catholicism lay not with the doctrines of the religion itself nor among its practitioners, but rather in its leadership:

> To what extent are the bishops of the hierarchy in the United States agents of the Pope as the sovereign of the Vatican State? Their elaborate oath of allegiance is taken to the Pope; their political, sociological and religious reports are commingled and sent to the same central headquarters. Their in-

> structions to oppose certain types of American legislation come to them in the same type of encyclicals that cover matters of mysticism and ritual. . . . And the money that they raise and send to the Vatican is used for both religious and political activism.[35]

Countries that lack a strong Protestant establishment are vulnerable to totalitarian dictatorship. Catholicism, for Blanshard, represented the highest "undemocratic system of alien control." The way to stem the tide of a Catholic national takeover depends on the strength of America's Protestant heritage. Otherwise, he says, "the result undoubtedly would be the rapid conquest of this country and the rest of the world by Russian Communism." Boettner and Blanshard combined the sacred and secular in a way similar to that of Bourne. Blanshard called for a "resistance movement" against the enemies of American democracy. Boettner called for resistance against the Catholic religion. Ironically, what brought evangelicals and Catholics together was a shared fear and hostility toward the very evil that Catholicism by its supposed nature protected: the authoritarianism of atheistic communism. Boettner and Blanshard warned that Romanism was a much greater evil than communism itself.[36]

Yet when dealing with heredity, intellectuals must be aware that both similarities (continuity) and differences (change) will always accompany the historical record. We should acknowledge that opposition to Catholicism has not been as intense today as it was in the nineteenth century. Among the handful of reasons offered for the thaw between Catholics and Protestants, Farrelly emphasizes the efforts of Catholic leaders to re-evaluate the church's concept of freedom, shifting from a strict individualism to the conditions necessary for freedom beginning in the 1930s and maturing by the mid-1960s. At Vatican II, leaders coupled the freedom of conscience with the "dignity of the human person," two items that Protestants had for more than a century assumed could never be affirmed by the papacy. By the 1960s, this newer understanding of freedom was married to a more pressing opposition to "godless communism," an association made by writers like Blanshard and Boettner. In this way, Catholic leaders came to adopt, Farrelly writes, "a Protestant understanding of religious freedom."[37] As Philip Jenkins writes, Pope John XXIII "worried that the world was being threatened by a 'temporal order which some have wished to reorganize excluding God.' Under such circumstances, any belief in God became preferable to Communism."[38] This new understanding remained attached to an older "corporate approach to freedom," Farrelly concludes, "that the Catholic Church has always insisted upon."[39]

With the collapse of the Berlin Wall and the fall of the Soviet Union, the fear of communism and thus of Catholicism waned quite a bit. This does not mean, however, that the contemporary era has made a clean break with anti-Catholicism. The Roman Church has faced hostility from some conservative fundamentalist groups in the late twentieth century, fringe organizations like Historic Advent. But much of the opposition has come from more socially liberal groups like ACT UP and WHAM that have used direct action to protest the church's support for conservative social causes. Once again, this anti-Catholicism has more to do with morality than doctrine. Catholic views on women, contraception, sexuality, AIDS, and social justice—regardless of John XXIII's liberal opinions on "religious freedom" and even Pope Francis's progressive support for socioeconomic justice, especially his concern over exploitive capitalism and climate change—make the church a prime target for the left's indignation, despite the many Protestant evangelical-fundamentalists who hold similar views on such issues.

What is even more significant in explaining the reason for the unprecedented alliance between Protestants and Catholics is the moral front created by both in the culture wars: the efforts to stem the tide of secularism, especially related to confronting the morality of abortion and traditional marriage, the creation of the National Association of Evangelicals alliance between Protestants and Catholics in 1993, and the desire, for the more intellectually minded, to recover the "public square." Part of the union between these erstwhile enemies stems from the nature of American evangelicalism itself, which has come to elevate a therapeutic, consumeristic, and moralistic civil religion over that of doctrinal commitments. Indeed, American evangelicalism, forged in the revivals of the Second Great Awakening, expresses its concern for society on moral issues, not on theological ones.

Of course, we may wonder how long the peace will last, given the more progressive views of Pope Francis, which conflict with the ideological commitments of conservative evangelicals. But any foreseeable severance of ties will not be the result of doctrinal differences; indeed, anti-Catholicism has rarely been fueled by doctrinal issues. And this is where American evangelicalism, especially in relation to reform, diverges from Bourne's outlook. The Catholic-Protestant alliance, which would have been unthinkable if not reprehensible for Bourne, depends on evangelicalism's relegation of confessional doctrine. Despite the ostensible peace among evangelicals, Catholics remain an "uncomfortable other," an "other" that American Protestant evangelicals have had an uneasy relationship with. Protestant evangelicalism is not at all free of prejudice. Part of the reason for saying this is because of the nature of cultural evangelicalism itself, particularly its hyper-democratization, which often spills over into antiauthoritarianism, anti-intellectualism, and anti-institutionalism. Hostility toward central leadership or hierarchical leadership that relegates individual choice is the default posture of American evangelicalism. Moreover, evangelicalism's antiauthoritarianism includes an uneasiness with institutions, even though these institutions are crucial to their religious ethos (e.g., the church).

Evangelicalism's hostility to forms of central authority is, ironically, different in practice. Over the past forty years, evangelicals have been quick to demonstrate a great hostility toward an overreaching state, but they have a strange penchant for following dictatorial leaders who brook no favor with dissent. This is one reason why evangelicals can, without moral qualms, overwhelmingly support neoliberal-minded authoritarians. To say it differently, while conservative evangelicals clamorously oppose the overextended authority of the political state, they have no problem with other forms of centralized authority, especially that found in the corporate world. "The attraction to business-driven authoritarianism," historian Molly Worthen has recently written, "stems from a very long tradition of pastor-overlords who anoint themselves with the power to make their own rules."[40] "American evangelicals," she continues, "have sometimes shown a strong preference for leaders who demand unquestioning obedience—and who, like Trump, consider disagreement a form of disloyalty."[41] This places evangelicals in a conflicted situation vis-à-vis institutional dictatorship. On the one hand, they oppose centralized authoritarianism, which for decades was epitomized by popery, yet at the same time they are supporters of it in different forms. Consequently, the current peace between Catholics and Protestants may equally rest on some of the contradictions within evangelicalism, including the inconsistencies regarding modes of authority, which evangelicals have yet to deal with. Thus, the peace between Catholics and Protestants will remain so long as the fight against the moral decay of society continues and evangelicalism's antiauthoritarianism remains more bark than bite.

There have been more subtle means outside the social and political arena that have maintained the image of Catholicism as a presence antithetical to freedom. One such way has come largely through cultural productions. The sexual controversies roiling the Roman Church have been accompanied by the anti-Catholic cultural marker of the sexual predator in search of innocent young people. In nineteenth-century convent exposés, priests were often depicted as sexual deviants on the prowl to irrevocably corrupt young women. Today, Catholic priests conjure similar images. Ken Russell's *The Devils* (1971) and Bruno Mattei's *The Other Hell* [*L'altro inferno*] (1981) depict the convent as a terrorizing house of scandalous orgies far from any semblance of Christianity. The abuse of pedophilic Catholic priests serves the underlying plotline in the popular cable television show *Ray Donovan* (2013–present) and in award-winning films like *Doubt* (2008) and, in a more salient manner, *Spotlight* (2015), the latter of which tells the true story of investigative journalists who, without the logic of ultra-Protestantism, uncover the dark underbelly of the Catholic Church in Boston.

The nun and convent too have had an aura of horror, violence, eroticism, and authoritarianism from the antebellum period to the present. Nuns and convents (the latter often conflated with either a whorehouse or an insane asylum) have been depicted in nightmarish ways in cable shows like *American Horror Story* (2011–present) as well as recent horror films like *The Conjuring 2* (2016) and *The Nun* (2018). According to Cassandra Yacovazzi, no other anti-Catholic image has been as powerful as that of the convent and the nun, both of which functioned as perversions of true womanhood, sexuality, and domestic tranquility. Depictions of "true womanhood" were imbricated with contests over the ideal American. Exposing nunneries was not so much an exercise in contrasting but of constructing: constructing a true identity by means of contrasting with "the other." The nun "as a modern villain," according to Yacovazzi, and the convent as the place to corrupt the innocent remained throughout much of the twentieth century.[42]

Yet modern depictions of nuns have not always retained the image of the nun as monster (the 2018 horror film *The Nun*) or overbearing authoritarian (*Blues Brothers* [1980], *Magdalene Sisters* [2002], and *Doubt* [2008] come to mind). They have also been presented in a softer and more benevolent light. Films like *The Bells of St. Mary's* (1945), *The Sound of Music* (1965), *The Singing Nun* (1966), *The Trouble with Angels* (1966), and *Sister Act* and *Sister Act 2: Back in the Habit* (1992–93) present nuns in a more favorable, caring, just, and even jovial light. Tim Robbins's 1995 film *Dead Man Walking,* starring Susan Sarandon and Sean Penn, depicts a nun as redeemer. Sister Helen Prejean, played by Sarandon, works to "set free" by way of confession a convicted murderer, played by Penn, just days before his scheduled execution. One item of note is that unlike in the anti-Catholicism of the nineteenth century, nuns are absent players in the current abuse scandals. The anti-Catholicism throughout the nineteenth century presented *both* nuns and priests as twin evils conspiring to destroy innocent women. This is a striking difference in how Catholicism is portrayed today. Yacovazzi intimates that the reason the nun is not currently presented as an enabler of male lusts, though there are a host of erotic films that exploit the image of the nun, has to do with the involvement of nuns in appropriating the social and cultural changes brought about by second-wave feminism.

Nonetheless, viewers often miss the subtle anti-Catholic thread even in the most benign depiction of nuns, especially in works like *The Sound of Music* or *Sister Act,* namely, that the convent and superior nuns have the potential to hold back essentially free-spirited, confident, or "worldly" women. The convent, for instance, held Julie Andrews's character Maria from "finding her dream," which she found in the bourgeois domestic bliss of becoming a wife and mother. Maria had been afraid to accept her love for Captain von Trapp. It was the mother superior, acting contrary to traditional depictions of the mother superior, who convinced Maria that she could fulfill her desires only if she left the convent. Whoopi Goldberg's character Deloris had to hide from the mob in a convent, yet she was able to express herself, however limitedly, within the confines of the nunnery. During her time there, Deloris showed her fellow nuns how to let loose a bit, to express themselves, to be free, and find their literal voice, much to the ire of the mother superior, who ultimately could not contain such ebullience. It took a free-spirited outsider like Deloris to awaken the sisters. Even the ostensibly happy, ignorant, or flighty nun or the benevolent activities in the convent interior remain as impediments to full self-realization, to individual freedom. Depictions of the nun and the convent have certainly softened in the past few decades, but even in such family-friendly films there remains a mystique of both enslavement and unfulfilled desires.

When thinking about the Catholic Church, Americans are often unaware that their views have already been subconsciously processed through a predetermined cultural lens, making the issue of "truth" significantly challenging. Depicting the Catholic as deviant, however unstable or contradictory, raises a thorny dilemma when dealing with the contemporary crisis: the degree to which the many sexual abuse cases against the church are believed because they are true or because of the cultural lens—a historically inherited lens—that presents Catholics as predisposed to predatorial behavior. Addressing this issue requires an examination of the interpretive lens used to reinforce cultural stereotypes. The veracity of Catholic sexual abuse can often be colored by a predetermined cultural lens that many of us have subconsciously inherited. Coming to grips with our own bias, of course, is a very sensitive thing, so I want to tread lightly here. A culture is formed by recurring habits and especially interpretations about such habits. For instance, when Person *A* acts in a particular way, good or bad, and when discussions about the act are repeated ad nauseam, regardless of whether such an act is repeated, then a distinct culture emerges in which another person with similar features as Person *A,* though a completely different individual, is also understood in a like manner. The same is true in the reverse. When a large group, for instance, lives in poverty, there is a danger of thinking that each of the individuals within that group is poor by nature; they lack an entrepreneurial "spirit" and perpetuate poverty *because* of the essence of the group. What is more, when an individual in poverty commits a criminal act, then we tend to think that others in a similar socioeconomic context are also predisposed by nature to committing crime. Eventually, in this example, culture moves beyond a tight association between poverty and crime to the actual criminalization of poverty.

It is difficult to deny the parallels between the scandals of the Catholic Church in the nineteenth century and those of today, despite changes in variables, including predations against young girls in the nineteenth century and against boys *and* girls in the twenty-first.[43] I have asked a handful of historians of nineteenth-century anti-Catholicism how they would assess the current sexual controversies roiling the church. One accomplished scholar in the field (a lapsed Catholic) told me that the difference between the past and the present is that the claims of abuse today have more truth attached to them than the claims made in the nineteenth century. This, I suspect, is true, but how much of such a viewpoint has been impacted by the cultural productions of the Catholic "other"? It is one thing to show continuation of anti-Catholic imagery, but it is quite another to show how such imagery has created an enduring interpretive paradigm. The images we have passively received for nearly a century and a half—or even much of American history—have colored our vision. Has contemporary America inherited a conceptual lens that predictates the image of the Catholic—whether priest, nun, or convent—in predatorial overtones? In other words, has American culture offered an unconscious assumption about Catholicism prior to examining Catholicism itself? Is the perception of Catholics predetermined by a stereotype or by reality? Many Catholics today, including priests, feel that the church is irrevocably stigmatized. Yet over the past decade, a number of writers, mainly journalists, have challenged the assumption that sexual abuse among religious groups is mainly a Catholic problem.[44] One writer showed that abuses committed by Catholic priests are "no more than other males."[45] Admittedly, it is impossible to disentangle a textual grid from a separate, objective, or "real" world outside of our minds. What we take as real is already situated in a linguistic context, never divorced from it.

Having said all this, however, it may sound like I am dismissing the thousands of innocent people who have suffered at the hands of truly predatory priests. Allow me, then, to articulate a couple of crucial caveats. First, in saying that our understanding of the world is always already within a cultural context, I am not jettisoning truth, saying that we arbitrarily create our own truth or that those who have suffered are deluded because of their cultural blindness. Someone can experience very real trauma regardless of the functioning of a cultural framework. Second, my statement on culture should not discourage anyone from pursuing and verifying the claims made against the Catholic Church. (Unlike the nineteenth century, the church today has acknowledged such abuse, though it is not doing the best job administering justice.) My comments are directed more toward those whose views have largely been shaped by anti-Catholic cultural rhetoric. Growing up in a Protestant denomination, I can remember reading Boettner's *Roman Catholicism* at a young age and recognizing its anti-Catholic overtones. Thankfully, such anti-Catholicism never took hold; in fact, it has had the opposite effect: studying anti-Catholicism has contributed to creating a greater appreciation for religious liberty. Outsiders are in danger of letting their cultural context determine their understanding of Catholicism. Not to sound overly moralistic, but the pursuit of truth demands a recognition of our own ignorance, biases, and faults, deficiencies that can be ameliorated in part through the recovery of the past.

Bourne demonstrates the complexities of antislavery and religious prejudice in American thought and life. His work also reminds us of our own shortcomings in relation to the legacy of the past. The contemporary mind needs to continue to meditate on the ramifications of the antislavery movement, addressing in particular new modes of enslavement in our deeply integrated and paradoxically divided global community. The contemporary mind should also consider the legacy of religious prejudice in relation to the various understandings of freedom and democracy. On this latter point, I suspect that the average American has yet to come to grips with the undercurrents of anti-Catholicism, unaware of its erratic—though powerful—recurrences. Many are unaware that a latent anti-Catholicism continues to undergird America's cultural identity. Indeed, some are predicting the return of a virulent anti-Catholicism in the near future (if it has not arrived already).[46] Very few, it seems, have noticed such vitiating undercurrents behind the cultural items mentioned above. The failure to notice such similarities is symptomatic of an ignorance of the past. Forgetting is what has made anti-Catholicism "acceptable." Protestant anti-Catholicism may be so ingrained that most people have taken it for granted. "Anti-Catholic sentiment," Jenkins writes, "may simply be too deeply entrenched to eliminate in a decade or a lifetime, but this does not mean that it should simply be ignored." What needs to be done, Jenkins concludes, is to "acknowledge its existence and to treat it as a form of prejudice quite as pernicious as any other."[47] Like those who viewed slavery as a necessary contrast to freedom, anti-Catholicism has been used as a negative contrast to the freedoms inherent in a Protestant political establishment, revealing how deliberative and representative democracy and religious freedom were, writes Fenton, "fraught with tension and uncertainty."[48] Notwithstanding Catholicism's effort to participate in "representative governance," a politically driven Protestantism could never recognize the possibility that non-Protestants could participate in a religiously plural society. Indeed, anti-Catholicism has provided a frame to launch attacks against any religion that threaten civil freedoms. The conceptual mold of anti-Catholicism can easily be applied to other religious groups. "There is a thread," Farrelly writes in *Anti-Catholicism in America, 1620–1860,* "that ties our contemporary debates about the place of Muslims in American society to the country's history of anti-Catholicism. That thread is the idea of 'freedom.'"[49] Dealing with contemporary religious prejudice may require an examination of where and how such prejudice developed. Perhaps Americans can learn from their egalitarian forebears, confronting material and cultural systems of oppression in order to become agents of agitation. George Bourne offers a way for those of us in the present to confront not only the complexities of the human condition—our own condition—but also the deep desire for liberty and tolerance.

NOTES

INTRODUCTION: THE PROTESTANT MIND OF GEORGE BOURNE

1. William Lloyd Garrison, *The Letters of William Lloyd Garrison: From Disunionism to the Brink of War, 1850–1860,* ed. Louis Ruchames, vol. 4 (Cambridge, MA: Harvard University Press, 1975), 597, no. 254. Theodore Bourne was also ordained in the Presbyterian Church. He later became a professor of language. Like his father, Theodore pursued avenues of social reform, becoming "founder and first secretary of the Society for the Prevention of Crime in New York" (Ibid.). He was involved in the African Civilization Society and corresponded often with Benjamin Coates and Henry Highland Garnet. For a recent edited volume of Benjamin Coates's letters and correspondences, see Emma J. Lapsansky-Werner and Margaret Hope Bacon, eds., *Back to Africa: Benjamin Coates and the Colonization Movement in America, 1848–1880* (University Park: Pennsylvania State University Press, 2005), letters 32, 38, 41, 48, 56. Coates frequently corresponded with Garnet and Theodore on cotton production in Liberia.

2. William Allen, *The Philanthropist: Or Repository for Hints and Suggestions,* VI (1816), 334–50; Donald Mathews, *Slavery and Methodism: A Chapter in American Morality, 1780–1845* (Princeton, NJ: Princeton University Press, 1965), 122; Lawrence Lesick, *The Lane Rebels: Evangelicalism and Antislavery in Antebellum America* (Metuchen, NJ: Scarecrow Press, 1980). Ex-slave Frederick Douglass likewise admired Bourne and at least on one occasion referred to his trial and quoted from his *Picture of Slavery.* See Frederick Douglass, *The Frederick Douglass Papers. Series One: Speeches, Debates, and Interviews. Vol. 3: 1855–63* (New Haven, CT: Yale University Press, 1985), 24. It is also probable, according to Gerda Lerner, that Angelina Grimké, through her close association with the Reverend William McDowell, learned of Bourne's removal from the South for his uncompromising views against slavery. Gerda Lerner, *The Grimké Sisters from South Carolina: Pioneers for Women's Rights and Abolition,* rev. and exp. ed. (Chapel Hill: University of North Carolina Press, 2004), 50; William and Ellen Craft, *A Thousand Miles for Freedom: Or, The Escape of William and Ellen Craft From Slavery* (London: William Tweedie, 1860), 6–7.

3. Joshua Leavitt, *National Anti-Slavery Standard,* October 24, 1844, 3.

4. Lewis Tappan, "George Bourne," *The Independent,* October 31, 1861, 6.

5. Bourne Family Papers, Huntington Library, Munger Research Center, San Marino, California. Box 2(41), "Newspaper Clippings" (1818–1845).

6. John W. Christie and Dwight L. Dumond, *George Bourne and "The Book and Slavery Irreconcilable"* (Wilmington: Historical Society of Delaware, 1969), 1. See also *North American Magazine* 2, no. 10 (August 1833): 253. Samuel gave his son a cash advance for his travel to the United States. I want to thank Victoria Clark, a descendant of the Bourne family, for tracking down and

showing me an unpublished copy of Samuel Bourne's will. In it, he credits £400 to his son George for his trip to the United States. On at least two occasions in his editorial career, Bourne was unable to gather enough financial support for his newspapers. He was also late in paying his journal subscription bills.

7. Christie and Dumond suggest that Bourne's wife was never named. Donald Yacovone concurs in his brief biography of Bourne in *American National Biography.* Donald Yacovone "Bourne, George," *American National Biography Online* (February 2000), http://www.anb.org/articles/08/08-00158.html. Indeed, Mary hardly shows up in Bourne's writing. But in the obituary section of the *New York Evangelist* 22, no. 12 (March 20, 1851): 47, there is reference to a "Mary, wife of the late Rev. George Bourne" who died at the age of seventy-one. Furthermore, there is some disputed evidence about her specific origins. Christie and Dumond suggest Mary came from Bristol, England. At least two rumors circulated that Bourne first met Mary in Montreal (*Niles' Weekly Register 2, no. 24* (August 12, 1837): 370). There is also limited evidence that Mary, like George, was involved in benevolent activities. The couple had at least three children, William, Francis, and Theodore, all of whom had some involvement in social reform. Theodore, Bourne and Mary's youngest son, worked for a time with Henry Highland Garnet's and the African Civilization Society. Victoria Clark has identified about six children between George and Mary.

8. Stephen Zeigler, "Niles, Hezekiah," *American National Biography Online* (February 2000), http://www.anb.org/articles/16/16-01202.html.

9. George Bourne, *Validity of the Methodist Episcopacy* (Baltimore: George Dobbin and Murphy, for John Hagerty, 1807).

10. Christie and Dumond, *George Bourne and "The Book and Slavery Irreconcilable."* Christie and Dumond speculate that Bourne's illness and loss of hearing contributed to his irascible temper, an opinion that is difficult to back up with any hard evidence.

11. Kyle Roberts, *Evangelical Gotham: Religion and the Making of New York City, 1783–1860* (Chicago: University of Chicago Press, 2016), 3.

12. William Oland Bourne, "Newspaper Clippings" [1830–1918] Box 2(41), "Antislavery Leaders: The Pioneer of Abolition," *Boston Commonwealth,* July 25, 1885, Bourne Family Papers, the Huntington Library, San Marino, CA.

13. Theodore Bourne, letter to William Lloyd Garrison, July 25, 1870, https://www.digitalcommonwealth.org/search/commonwealth:6h442376h.

14. *New York Evangelist* 16, no. 48 (November 27, 1845): 191. Theodore Bourne, letter to William Lloyd Garrison, 1858. https://www.digitalcommonwealth.org/search/commonwealth:cv43qz808.

15. Don E. Fehrenbacher, *The Slaveholding Republic: An Account of the United States Government's Relations to Slavery* (New York: Oxford University Press, 2011), 262.

16. Matthew Mason, *Slavery and Politics in the Early Republic* (Chapel Hill: University of North Carolina Press, 2008), 133.

17. Ibid., 231; Manisha Sinha, *The Slave's Cause: A History of Abolition* (New Haven, CT: Yale University Press, 2016).

18. James Brewer Stewart, *Holy Warriors: The Abolitionists and American Slavery* (New York: Hill and Wang, 1997), 38. See also Anne Loveland, "Evangelicalism and 'Immediate Abolitionism' in American Antislavery Thought," *Journal of Southern History* 32, no. 2 (May 1966): 172–88, and David Brion Davis, "The Emergence of Immediatism in British and American Antislavery

Thought," *Mississippi Valley Historical Review* 49, no. 2 (Sept. 1962): 209–30. There are a host of secondary sources on abolitionism, including Gilbert Barnes, *The Antislavery Impulse, 1830–1844* (1933; rpr. New York: Harcourt Brace Jovanovich, 1964); Herbert Aptheker, *Abolitionism: A Revolutionary Movement* (Boston: Twayne Publishers, 1989); Whitney Cross, *The Burned-Over District* (Cambridge, MA: Harvard University Press, 1982); John Daly, *When Slavery Was Called Freedom: Evangelicalism, Proslavery, and the Causes of the Civil War* (Lexington: University Press of Kentucky, 2002); David Brion Davis, *The Problem of Slavery in the Age of Revolution, 1770–1823* (Oxford: Oxford University Press, 1999); James Essig, *The Bonds of Wickedness: Evangelicals against Slavery, 1770–1808* (Philadelphia: Temple University Press, 1982); Lawrence Friedman, *Gregarious Saints: Self and Community in American Abolitionism, 1830–1870* (New York: Cambridge University Press, 1982); Lesick, *The Lane Rebels;* John McKivigan, ed., *Abolitionism and American Religion: History of the American Abolitionist Movement* (New York: Garland Publication, 1999); Richard Newman, *The Transformation of American Abolitionism: Fighting Slavery in the Early Republic* (Chapel Hill: University of North Carolina Press, 2002); Michael Pierson, *Free Hearts and Free Homes: Gender and American Antislavery Politics* (Chapel Hill: University of North Carolina Press, 2003); P. J. Staudenraus, *The African Colonization Movement, 1816–1865* (New York: Columbia University Press, 1961); Anna Speicher, *The Religious World of Antislavery Women: Spirituality in the Lives of Five Abolitionist Lecturers* (Syracuse, NY: Syracuse University Press, 2000); John Stauffer, *The Black Hearts of Men: Radical Abolitionists and the Transformation of Race* (Cambridge, MA: Harvard University Press, 2001); Douglas Strong, *Perfectionist Politics: Abolitionism and the Religious Tensions of American Democracy* (Syracuse, NY: Syracuse University Press, 1999); Bertram Wyatt-Brown, *Lewis Tappan and the Evangelical War against Slavery* (Cleveland: Press of Case Western Reserve University, 1969); Jean Fagan Yellin and John C. Van Horne, eds., *The Abolitionist Sisterhood: Women's Political Culture in Antebellum America* (Ithaca, NY: Cornell University Press, 1994).

19. Nathan Hatch, *The Democratization of American Christianity* (New Haven, CT: Yale University Press, 1989), 71.

20. Bourne, *Lectures on the Progress and Perfection of the Church of Christ* (Mount Pleasant, NY: R. W. Knight, 1823), 7.

21. Bourne, *The Life of the Rev. John Wesley* (Baltimore: Dobbin and Murphy, 1807), 348.

22. Bourne, *Lectures on the Progress,* 235.

23. Ibid., 393.

24. By *conservative,* I mean the efforts to preserve and recover traditions for the purpose of applying them to the present.

25. Craig Calhoun, *The Roots of Radicalism: Tradition, the Public Sphere, and Early Nineteenth-Century Social Movements* (Chicago: University of Chicago Press, 2012), 12.

26. Ibid., 4.

27. Ibid., 12.

28. Ibid., 16. Jonathan Israel, *Radical Enlightenment: Philosophy and the Making of Modernity, 1650–1750* (Oxford: Oxford University Press, 2001), 6.

29. Theodore Bourne, "The Pioneer of Anti-Catholicism," *Methodist Quarterly Review* LXIV (January 1882): 71.

30. Davis, "The Emergence of Immediatism," 209–30. Quotation on page 223.

31. John McKivigan, *The War against Proslavery Religion: Abolitionism and the Northern Churches, 1830–1865* (Ithaca, NY: Cornell University Press, 1984), 93.

32. For discussions related to the problem of religion and slavery, see Davis, *The Problem of Slavery in the Age of Revolution;* David Brion Davis, *Inhuman Bondage: The Rise and Fall of Slavery in the New World* (New York: Oxford University Press, 2006); John McKivigan and Mitchell Snay, eds., *Religion and the Antebellum Debate over Slavery* (Athens: University of Georgia Press, 1998); and Strong, *Perfectionist Politics.*

33. Speicher, *The Religious World of Antislavery Women,* 89.

34. Davis, "The Emergence of Immediatism," 229.

35. Mark Noll, *History of Christianity in the United States and Canada* (Grand Rapids, MI: Eerdmans, 1992), 205–6.

36. Ray Allen Billington, *The Protestant Crusade, 1800–1860: A Study of the Origins of American Nativism* (Gloucester, MA: Peter Smith, 1963), 55–57, 96, 101, See also note 100 on page 115.

37. Samuel F. B. Morse, *Foreign Conspiracy against the Liberties of the United States* (New York: Leavitt, Lord, and Company, 1835), 8.

38. Bourne knew that slaveholders argued for a difference between spiritual and physical freedom. By preaching spiritual freedom for the slave, owners could then justify their enslavement of the body. The same dichotomy was used when discussing the place of women. Bourne nowhere supported such a distinction. Physical relationships on earth mirrored those in the heavenly realm. If absolute freedom was granted as a result of a spiritual transformation, then the physical had to imitate that reality.

39. Lewis Perry, *Radical Abolitionism: Anarchy and the Government of God in Antislavery Thought* (Ithaca, NY: Cornell University Press, 1973); Stewart, *Holy Warriors;* Dwight L. Dumond, *Antislavery: The Crusade for Freedom in America* (New York: Norton, 1961); Stanley Harrold, *The Abolitionists and the South, 1831–1861* (Lexington: University of Kentucky Press, 1995); McKivigan, *The War against Proslavery Religion;* Ronald Walters, *The Antislavery Appeal: American Abolitionism after 1830* (Baltimore: Johns Hopkins University Press, 1976); Aptheker, *Abolitionism.*

40. Ruth Bloch and Nathan Hatch have shown how anti-Catholicism shaped American politics in the colonial, revolutionary, and early republican periods. Ruth Bloch, *Visionary Republic: Millennial Themes in America Thought, 1756–1800* (Cambridge: Cambridge University Press, 1985); and Nathan Hatch, *The Sacred Cause of Liberty: Republican Thought and the Millennium in Revolutionary New England* (New Haven, CT: Yale University Press, 1977). Jenny Franchot, in a similar fashion, has shown the impact of anti-Catholic captivity narratives in the cultural consciousness of the nation in the antebellum period. Jenny Franchot, *Roads to Rome: The Antebellum Protestant Encounter with Catholicism* (Berkeley: University of California Press, 1994). Susan Griffin has written an excellent work on the influence of transatlantic anti-Catholic literature in both the United States and England. Susan Griffin, *Anti-Catholicism and Nineteenth-Century Literature* (Cambridge: Cambridge University Press, 2004).

41. Jay Dolan, *The Immigrant Church: New York's Irish and German Catholics, 1815–1865* (Baltimore: Johns Hopkins University Press, 1975); Jay Dolan, *The American Catholic Experience: A History From Colonial Times to the Present* (Garden City, NY: Doubleday, 1985); Chester Gillis, *Roman Catholicism in America* (New York: Columbia University Press, 1999); Joseph Varacalli, *The Catholic Experience in America* (Westport, CT: Greenwood Press, 2006).

42. William Warner, *At Peace with All Their Neighbors: Catholics and Catholicism in the National Capital, 1787–1860* (Washington, DC: Georgetown University Press, 1994); Dale Light, *Rome and the New Republic: Conflict and Community in Philadelphia Catholicism between the Revolution and the Civil War* (Notre Dame, IN: University of Notre Dame Press, 1996); Jason Duncan, *Citizens or Papists? The Politics of Anti-Catholicism in New York, 1685–1821* (New York: Fordham University Press, 2005).

43. Leslie Tentler, "On the Margins: The State of American Catholic History," *American Quarterly* 45 (March 1993): 104–27. Quotation on page 106.

44. Ibid., 105.

45. Elizabeth Fenton, *Religious Liberties: Anti-Catholicism and Liberal Democracy in Nineteenth-Century U.S. Literature and Culture* (New York: Oxford University Press, 2011), 1.

46. Ibid., 18.

47. Maura Jane Farrelly, *Anti-Catholicism in America, 1620–1860* (Cambridge: Cambridge University Press, 2017), 2.

48. Hugh Davis, *Joshua Leavitt: Evangelical Abolitionist* (Baton Rouge: Louisiana State University Press, 1990), 79.

49. Wyatt-Brown, *Lewis Tappan and the Evangelical War against Slavery*, 47–48. Wyatt-Brown implicates Bourne in influencing Tappan's anti-Catholicism, but this still does not help us understand such intolerance.

50. John McGreevy, *Catholicism and American Freedom: A History* (New York: W. W. Norton, 2003), 14.

51. Robert Abzug, *Cosmos Crumbling: American Reform and the Religious Imagination* (New York: Oxford University Press, 1994), xiii.

52. Ibid., 12, 63.

53. Dickson Bruce Jr., *Earnestly Contending: Religious Freedom and Pluralism in Antebellum America* (Charlottesville: University of Virginia Press, 2013), 1, 8.

54. Ibid., 172. Emphasis mine.

55. Ibid., 25.

56. Barnes, *The Antislavery Impulse.*

57. Merton Dillon, "Gilbert H. Barnes and Dwight L. Dumond: An Appraisal," *Reviews in American History* 21, no. 3 (September 1993): 539–52.

58. Ronald G. Walters, "The Erotic South: Civilization and Sexuality in American Abolitionism," *American Quarterly* 25, no. 2 (May 1973): 187.

59. Bourne, *The Life of the Rev. John Wesley*, 1.

60. Mark Noll, *The Civil War as a Theological Crisis* (Chapel Hill: University of North Carolina Press, 2006), 6.

61. Molly Oshatz, *Slavery as Sin: The Fight against Slavery and the Rise of Liberal Protestantism* (New York: Oxford University Press, 2011).

62. George Bourne, *A Condensed Anti-Slavery Bible Argument, by a Citizen of Virginia* (New York: S. W. Benedict, 1845), 6.

63. There are a host of studies that focus on the impact of reform on the status of women in the Early Republic and antebellum periods. Nancy Hewitt, *Women's Activism and Social Change: Rochester New York, 1822–1872* (Ithaca, NY: Cornell University Press, 1984); Lori Ginzberg, *Women*

and the Work of Benevolence: Morality, Politics, and Class in the 19th-Century United States (New Haven, CT: Yale University Press, 1990); Christine Stansell, *City of Women: Sex and Class in New York, 1789–1860* (New York: Knopf, 1986); Nancy Cott, *The Bonds of Womanhood: "Woman's Sphere" in New England, 1780–1835* (New Haven, CT: Yale University Press, 1977). For the pioneering historiographical discussion of the cult of domesticity, read Barbara Welter's "The Cult of True Womanhood, 1820–1860," *American Quarterly* XVIII (1966): 151–74. Another important work on domesticity and reform is Kathryn Kish Sklar's *Catharine Beecher: A Study in American Domesticity* (New Haven, CT: Yale University Press, 1973).

64. Mary Kelley, "Beyond the Boundaries," *Journal of the Early Republic* 12, no. 1 (Spring 2001): 76. See also Kelley's *Private Women, Public Stage: Literary Domesticity in Nineteenth-Century America* (New York: Oxford University Press, 1984), 100–101. It is in *Private Women, Public Stage* that Kelley indirectly challenges Welter's thesis. Another work that explores the complexities of Welter's domesticity is Monika Elbert's *Separate Spheres No More: Gender Convergence in American Literature, 1830–1930* (Tuscaloosa: University of Alabama Press, 2000). Elbert and others do not reject the idea of "separate spheres," but they acknowledge that, in Elbert's words, "ultimately, issues of gender seem not as divisive or pressing as those of race or class" (2).

65. Kelley, "Beyond the Boundaries," 77.

66. Ibid., 78. See also Julie Roy Jeffrey, *The Great Silent Army of Abolitionism: Ordinary Women in the Antislavery Movement* (Chapel Hill: University of North Carolina Press, 1998).

67. Ginzberg, *Women and the Work of Benevolence,* 8. Kelley, "Beyond the Boundaries," 78.

68. Speicher, *The Religious World of Antislavery Women,* 3.

69. Carol Lasser and Stacey Robertson, *Antebellum Women: Private, Public, Partisan* (Lanham, MD: Rowman & Littlefield, 2010), xvi.

70. Ibid., xii.

71. Ibid., xvii.

72. Ibid., xviii.

73. Child quote in Teresa Ann Murphy, *Citizenship and the Origins of Women's History in the United States* (Philadelphia: University of Pennsylvania Press, 2013), 72. See also Sara M. Evans and Harry C. Boyte, *Free Spaces: The Sources of Democratic Change in America* (Chicago: University of Chicago Press, 1992), 79.

74. Lasser and Robertson, *Antebellum Women,* xix.

75. Ibid., xvii.

76. Mark Noll, *America's God: From Jonathan Edwards to Abraham Lincoln* (New York: Oxford University Press, 2002), 73.

77. Michael Durey, *Transatlantic Radicals and the Early Republic* (Lawrence: University Press of Kansas, 1997), 1. Although such friends of liberty were those who tried "to change the world and to change it for the better," they, for the most part, repudiate traditional religious orthodoxy. Bourne acknowledged the new political world that the Revolution brought, but never put aside historical Christianity.

78. Here is a small sampling of the many times Bourne connected republican constitutional thinking with biblical religion: *Picture of Slavery in the United States of America (*Middleton, CT: E. Hunt, 1834), 25, 154; *Condensed Antislavery Bible Argument,* 74; *The American Text-book of Popery: Being an Authentic Compend of the Bulls, Canons, Decretals of the Roman Hierarchy (*Philadelphia: Griffith and Simon, 1846), 436; *Lectures on the Progress,* 96.

79. Durey, *Transatlantic Radicals,* 8.

80. Elizabeth Fenton, "Religious Liberties: Anti-Catholicism and Liberal Democracy in U.S. Literature and Culture, 1774–1789" (PhD diss., Rice University, 2006), 1.

81. Author unknown, *The Liberator,* March 3, 1832, 2.

82. Friedman, *Gregarious Saints,* 86.

83. Bourne, *Picture of Slavery,* 48.

84. Ibid., 220.

85. George Bourne, "Address to the Presbyterian Church Enforcing the Duty of Excluding all Slaveholders from the 'Communion of Saints'" (New York: n.p., 1833), 2.

1. BOURNE, BIOGRAPHY, AND AMERICAN IDENTITY

1. Unknown author, "Newspaper Clippings, 1830–1918," box 2(41), no. 2 of "First Pages of the Early History of Anti-Slavery in America," Bourne Family Papers, Huntington Library, San Marino, CA.

2. Theodore Bourne, "Rev. George Bourne: The Pioneer of Antislavery," *Methodist Quarterly Review* LXIV (January 1882): 72.

3. Nicole Eustace and Frederika Teute, *Warring for America: Cultural Contests in the Era of 1812* (Chapel Hill: University of North Carolina Press, 2017).

4. Jeremy Popkin, *You are all free: The Haitian Revolution and the Abolition of Slavery* (Cambridge: Cambridge University Press, 2010); John Kaminski, *Citizen Paine: Thomas Paine's Thoughts on Man, Government, Society, and Religion* (Lanham, MD: Rowman & Littlefield, 2002); Eric Foner, *Thomas Paine and Revolutionary America* (New York: Oxford University Press, 2005); William Hogeland, *The Whiskey Rebellion: George Washington, Alexander Hamilton, and the Frontier Rebels Who Challenged America's New Found Sovereignty* (New York: Simon & Schuster, 2015).

5. Seth Cotlar, *Tom Paine's America: The Rise and Fall of Transatlantic Radicalism in the Early Republic* (Charlottesville: University of Virginia Press, 2017), 12.

6. Gordon Wood, *Empire of Liberty: A History of the Early Republic, 1789–1815* (New York: Oxford University Press, 2011), 176.

7. Philipp Ziesche, *Cosmopolitan Patriots: Americans in Paris in the Age of Revolution* (Charlottesville: University of Virginia Press, 2010), 12.

8. François Furstenberg, *When the United States Spoke French: Five Refugees Who Shaped a Nation* (New York: Penguin, 2014), 28.

9. Ziesche, *Cosmopolitan Patriots,* 8.

10. Eustace and Teute, *Warring* for *America,* preface.

11. George Bourne, *The History of Napoleon Bonaparte: Emperor of the French, and King of Italy* (Baltimore: Warner and Hanna, 1806).

12. George Bourne, *The Life of the Rev. John Wesley* (Baltimore: Dobbin and Murphy, 1807).

13. Ibid., 11.

14. Scott Casper, *Constructing American Lives: Biography and Culture in Nineteenth-Century America* (Chapel Hill: University of North Carolina Press, 1999), 2.

15. Ibid., 6.

16. George Bourne, *Lectures on the Progress and Perfection of the Church of Christ* (Mount Pleasant, NY: R. W. Knight, 1823), 1.

17. Ibid., 19.

18. Bourne, *Napoleon,* 128.

19. Matthew Rainbow Hale, "For the Love of Glory: Napoleonic Imperatives and the Early American Republic," in Eustace and Teute, *Warring for America,* part 2, chap. 6.

20. Walter Scott, *The Life of Napoleon Bonaparte, Emperor of the French. With a Preliminary View of the French Revolution.* 9 vols. (Edinburgh: Ballantyne and Co. for Longman, Rees, Orme, Brown, & Green, London; and Cadell & Co., Edinburgh, 1827).

21. G. W. F. Hegel, *Hegel: The Letters,* trans. Clark Butler and Christiane Seiler (Bloomington: Indiana University Press, 1985); G. W. F. Hegel, *Outlines of the Philosophy of Right* (New York: Oxford University Press, 2008), x; Terry Pinkard, *Hegel: A Biography* (Edinburgh: Cambridge University Press, 2000), 228.

22. Howard M. Jones, *American and French Culture, 1750–1848,* trans. Teresa Wright (Chapel Hill: University of North Carolina Press, 1927), 556. See also Philip Dwyer, *Napoleon: The Path to Power, 1769–1799* (London: Bloomsbury, 2008); Philip Dwyer, *Citizen Emperor: Napoleon in Power, 1799–1815* (London: Bloomsbury, 2013); Alan Schom, *Napoleon Bonaparte: A Life* (London: HarperCollins, 1997); Andrew Roberts, *Napoleon: A Life* (New York: Penguin, 2015). Paul Johnson, *Napoleon: A Life* (London: Orion, 2003).

23. Samuel Austin, "A Sermon Preached in Worcester Massachusetts on the Occasion of the Special Fast, July 23, 1812" (Worcester, MA, 1812).

24. William Ellery Channing, "A Sermon Preached in Boston, April 5, 1810, The Day of the Public Fast" (Boston: J. Elliot, 1810).

25. Hale, "For the Love of Glory," part 2, chap 6.

26. Ibid.

27. Ibid.

28. John W. Christie and Dwight L. Dumond, *George Bourne and "The Book and Slavery Irreconcilable"* (Wilmington: Historical Society of Delaware, 1969), 7.

29. Bourne, *Napoleon,* 127.

30. Ibid., appendix, 1.

31. Janet Polasky, *Revolutions without Borders: The Call to Liberty in the Atlantic World* (New Haven, CT: Yale University Press, 2015), 4, 10.

32. Ibid., 3.

33. Wood, *Empire,* 177.

34. Ziesche, *Cosmopolitan Patriots,* 4.

35. Furstenberg, *When the United States Spoke French,* 28.

36. Cotlar, *Tom Paine's America,* 54.

37. Ziesche, *Cosmopolitan Patriots,* 6, 8.

38. Bourne, *Napoleon,* 10.

39. Ibid., 373.

40. Ibid., 10.

41. Ibid., 125.

42. Ibid., 127.

43. Ibid., 137.
44. Ibid., 367.
45. Ibid., 198.
46. Ibid., 230.
47. Ibid., 302.
48. Jean Trulard, *Napoleon: The Myth of the Savior* (London: Routledge, 1985).
49. Bourne, *Napoleon,* 130.
50. Stendhal [Marie-Henri Beyle], *A Life of Napoleon* (London: Rodale Press, 1956), 184.
51. Bourne, *Napoleon,* 133.
52. Hale, "For the Love of Glory, part 2, chap. 6.
53. Ibid., 233.
54. Ibid., 210.
55. Ibid., 214.
56. Bourne, *Lectures on the Progress,* 411.
57. Wood, *Empire,* 200.
58. Bourne, *Napoleon,* 165.
59. Ibid., 277.
60. Ibid., "Addenda," 15.
61. Wood, *Empire,* 476.
62. Bruce quote in Elizabeth Fenton, *Religious Liberties: Anti-Catholicism and Liberal Democracy in Nineteenth-Century U.S. Literature and Culture* (New York: Oxford University Press, 2011), 70.
63. David Bebbington, *Evangelicalism in Modern Britain: A History from the 1730s to 1980s* (London: Routledge, 1989); Mark A. Noll, David Bebbington, and George Rawlyk, eds., *Evangelicalism: Comparative Studies of Popular Protestantism in North America, the British Isles, and Beyond, 1700–1990* (New York: Oxford University Press, 1994); Mark A. Noll, *The Rise of Evangelicalism: The Age of Edwards, Whitefield, and the Wesleys* (Downers Grove, IL: InterVarsity Press, 2010).
64. Nathan O. Hatch, *The Democratization of American Christianity* (New Haven, CT: Yale University Press, 1989), 222.
65. Eustace and Teute, *Warring for America,* preface.
66. Bourne, *Lectures on the Progress,* 269.
67. Cotlar, *Tom Paine's America,* 33.
68. Bourne, *Lectures on the Progress,* 414.
69. Ibid., 422.
70. Wood, *Empire,* 597.
71. Bourne, *Wesley,* 321.
72. Ibid., 335.
73. Ibid., 336.
74. Nathan O. Hatch and John Wigger, *Methodism and the Shaping of American Culture* (Nashville, TN: Abingdon Press, 2001), 14.
75. Wood, *Empire,* 607.
76. Ibid.
77. Hatch, *The Democratization of American Christianity,* 6.

78. Wood, *Empire,* 596.

79. John Wigger, *Taking Heaven by Storm: Methodism and the Rise of Popular Christianity in America* (New York: Oxford University Press, 1998), 159.

80. Ibid., 105–6.

81. Hatch and Wigger, *Methodism,* 13.

82. Jefferson quote in Mark Noll, *America's God* (New York: Oxford University Press, 2002), 204.

83. Russell Richey, Kenneth Rowe, and Jean Miller Schmidt, *American Methodism: A Compact History* (Nashville, TN: Abingdon Press, 2012), 2.

84. Wigger, *Taking Heaven,* 7.

85. Gordon Wood, *The Radicalism of the American Revolution* (New York: Vintage Books, 1991); Edmund Morgan, *The Genuine Article: A Historian Looks at Early America* (New York: W. W. Norton, 2005), 238.

86. Wigger, *Taking Heaven,* 5.

87. Cotlar, *Tom Paine's America,* 15.

88. Frances Fitzgerald, *The Evangelicals: The Struggle to Shape America* (New York: Simon & Schuster, 2017), 6.

89. Dee Andrews, *The Methodists and Revolutionary America, 1760–1800: The Shaping of an Evangelical Culture* (Princeton, NJ: Princeton University Press, 2000), 5.

90. Ibid.

91. Bourne Family Papers (BFP); Munger Research Center, Huntington Library, "Social Duty" G.B.; 1 (30s) [before 1845].

92. Casper, *Constructing American Lives,* 6.

93. Bourne, *Lectures on the Progress,* 1.

94. Ibid., 19.

95. Ibid., 7.

96. Bourne, *Wesley,* vii.

97. Ibid., viii.

98. Ibid., 71.

99. Ibid., 284.

100. Ibid., 37.

101. Ibid., 120.

102. Ibid.

103. Ibid., 221.

104. Ibid.

105. Ibid., 70, 279.

106. Geordan Hammond, *Wesley in America: Restoring Primitive Christianity* (New York: Oxford University Press, 2016), 8.

107. Bourne, *Wesley,* 101.

108. Ibid., 102.

109. Bourne, *Lectures on the Progress,* 136.

110. Bourne, *Wesley,* 35.

111. Hammond, *Wesley in America,* vii. Noll, The *Rise of Evangelicalism,* 83.

112. Bourne, *Wesley,* 74.

113. Ibid., 121.

114. Ibid.

115. Benedict Anderson, *Imagined Communities: Reflections on the Origin and Spread of Nationalism* (London: Verso, 1991).

116. David Waldsreicher, *In the Midst of Perpetual Fetes: The Making of an American Nationalism, 1776–1820* (Chapel Hill: University of North Carolina Press, 1997).

117. Ziesche, *Cosmopolitan Patriots,* 9.

118. Eustace and Teute, *Warring for America;* Joyce Appleby, *Inheriting the Revolution: The First Generation of Americans* (Cambridge, MA: Belknap Press, 2000).

119. Christie and Dumond, *George Bourne and "The Book and Slavery Irreconcilable,"* 2.

120. Bourne, *Wesley,* 283.

121. George Bourne, *Picture of Slavery in the United States of America* (Middleton, CT: E. Hunt, 1834), 19.

122. Christie and Dumond, *George Bourne and "The Book and Slavery Irreconcilable,"* 5.

123. Ibid., 15.

2. THE CHURCH, IMMEDIACY, AND THE TRIALS OF BOURNE

1. Andrew Murray, *Presbyterians and the Negro* (Philadelphia: Presbyterian Historical Society, 1966), 23.

2. David Brion Davis, *The Problem of Slavery in the Age of Revolution, 1770–1823* (Oxford: Oxford University Press, 1999), timeline.

3. George Bourne, *Picture of Slavery in the United States of America* (Middleton, CT: E. Hunt, 1834), 154; *Liberator,* November 24, 1832.

4. Dumond quote in Herbert Aptheker, *Abolitionism: A Revolutionary Movement* (Boston: Twayne Publishers, 1989), 1.

5. Ibid., 2.

6. Dwight Dumond, *Antislavery: The Crusade for Freedom in America* (Ann Arbor: University of Michigan Press, 1961), 93.

7. Joseph S. Moore, *Founding Sins: How a Group of Antislavery Radicals Fought to Put Christ into the Constitution* (New York: Oxford University Press, 2016).

8. John McKivigan, *The War against Proslavery Religion: Abolitionism and the Northern Churches, 1830–1865* (Ithaca, NY: Cornell University Press, 1984), 29.

9. Molly Oshatz, *Slavery and Sin: The Fight against Slavery and the Rise of Liberal Protestantism* (New York: Oxford University Press, 2011), 7.

10. James B. Stewart, *Holy Warriors: The Abolitionists and American Slavery* (New York: Hill and Wang, 1997), 33.

11. Gary Nash, *Race and Revolution* (Lanham, MD: Madison House Publishers, 1990).

12. David Brion Davis, *The Problem of Slavery in the Age of Emancipation* (New York: Alfred A. Knopf, 2014), 176.

13. David Waldsreicher, *In the Midst of Perpetual Fetes: The Making of American Nationalism, 1776–1820* (Chapel Hill: University of North Carolina Press, 1997). 297.

14. Sean Wilentz, *The Rise of American Democracy: Jefferson to Lincoln* (New York: W. W. Norton, 2005).

15. Thomas Jefferson, *Notes on the State of Virginia,* ed. with introduction by William Peden (Chapel Hill: University of North Carolina Press, 1996), 138; P. J. Staudenraus, *The African Colonization Movement, 1816–1865* (New York: Columbia University Press, 1961), 1.

16. Archibald Alexander, *A History of Colonization on the Western Coast of Africa* (New York: Negro Universities Press, 1969), 83.

17. Staudenraus, *African Colonization,* 3.

18. Ibid., 62.

19. Manisha Sinha, *The Slave's Cause: A History of Abolition* (New Haven, CT: Yale University Press, 2016), 103.

20. Letter from Theodore Bourne, 48 Warren St., NY, to William Lloyd Garrison (1863). https://www.digitalcommonwealth.org/search/commonwealth:6h441s560. Theodore identifies his father's involvement in the "anti-slavery cause" from "1806 to the day of his death."

21. Christopher Phillips, *Freedom's Port: The African American Community of Baltimore, 1790–1860* (Urbana: University of Illinois Press, 1997), 235.

22. *Baltimore American,* November 30, 1816.

23. *Letter from General Harper, of Maryland, to Elias B. Caldwell, Esquire, Secretary of the American Society for Colonizing the Free People of Color, in the United States with Their Own Consent* (Baltimore, 1817), 6–7; 8–9; 10–11; T. Stephen Whitman, *Challenging Slavery in the Chesapeake: Black and White Resistance to Human Bondage, 1775–1865* (Baltimore: Maryland Historical Society, 2007), 108.

24. Angelina Grimké also owned a copy of Scott's *Commentary* and knew it very well.

25. Bourne's letter in John W. Christie and Dwight L. Dumond, *George Bourne and "The Book and Slavery Irreconcilable"* (Wilmington: Historical Society of Delaware, 1969), 39. It's unclear as to whether Bourne owned the slave, rented him, or hired him for a time. Perhaps Bourne regretted not confronting the issue of slavery in this particular instance.

26. Theodore Weld, *American Slavery as It Is: Testimony of a Thousand Witnesses* (New York: Arno, 1839), 52.

27. Dickson D. Bruce, *Rhetoric of Conservatism: The Virginia Convention of 1829–30 and the Conservative Tradition in the South* (San Marino, CA: Huntington Library, 1982).

28. *Acts and Proceedings of the General Assembly of the Presbyterian Church in the United States of America, 1794* (Philadelphia: Aitken and Son, 1794), 15 (hereafter *Acts*).

29. Extracts from the *Minutes of the General Assembly of the Presbyterian Church in the United States of America,* 1817 (Philadelphia: Thomas and William Bradford, 1817), 28 (hereafter *Extracts*).

30. Samuel Stanhope Smith, *A Comprehensive View of the Reading and Most Important Elements of Natural and Revealed Religion* (New Brunswick, NJ: Deare and Myer, 1816), 3.

31. It is unclear when Bourne actually developed his antislavery views. Theodore suggests they were formulated when George attended Homerton College outside of London. Christie and Dumond correctly expose this error. In the letters written to A. B. Davidson, Bourne intimates that he at one time owned a slave, but quickly repented of his sin: "That I did wrong in *hiring* a slave I *contritely* admit. I have repented; I have *made restitution;* and now I endeavor to counteract the

influence of my former example. 'Go and do likewise'" (Bourne's letter in Christie and Dumond, *George Bourne and "The Book and Slavery Irreconcilable,"* 39).

32. *Minutes of the General Assembly of the Presbyterian Church in the United States of America From Its Organization, 1789–1820* (Philadelphia: Presbyterian Board of Publications, 1847). See also *The Constitution of the Presbyterian Church in the United States of America, Containing the Confession of Faith, The Catechisms, and the Directory for the Worship of God: Together with the Plan of Government and Discipline as Amended and Ratified by the General Assembly at Their Sessions in May 1805* (Philadelphia, 1806), 277–78.

33. Bourne's quote in Howard McKnight Wilson, *Lexington Presbytery Heritage: The Presbytery of Lexington and its Churches in the Synod of Virginia, Presbyterian Church in the United States* (Verona, VA: McClure Press, 1971), 90. See also Murray, *Presbyterians and the Negro,* 22.

34. Quote in the Lexington Presbytery in Christie and Dumond, *George Bourne and "The Book and Slavery Irreconcilable,"* 90–91.

35. Christie and Dumond print the full letters sent by Bourne to Davidson. The letters from Davidson, however, are not provided. Nonetheless, looking at Bourne's letters, one can decipher aspects of what Davidson wrote. Quotes and comments regarding the letters are from Christie and Dumond, *George Bourne and "The Book and Slavery Irreconcilable,"* 37–45.

36. Ibid., 20–21.

37. Bourne's letter, ibid., 44.

38. Wilson, *Lexington Presbytery Heritage,* 91.

39. Murray, *Presbyterians and the Negro,* 23.

40. George Bourne, *The Book and Slavery Irreconcilable, with Animadversions Against Samuel Stanhope Smith* (Philadelphia: J. M. Sanderson & Co., 1816), 97.

41. Ibid., 89.

42. Ibid., 27.

43. Ibid., 155.

44. Around the time of Bourne's trial, the General Assembly considered but failed to resolve the issue of whether slavery was wrong in itself, but also whether those who held slaves were as individuals guilty of moral evil. On the first question, the majority decided in the affirmative, but in the case of the latter, the majority opinion was emphatically "no." See Andrew Murray's *Presbyterians and the Negro,* 18.

45. George Bourne, "Animadversion," in appendix to *Book and Slavery,* 4.

46. Ibid., 9.

47. Ibid., 11.

48. Bourne, *Book and Slavery,* 2.

49. Bourne, *Picture of Slavery,* 23,132.

50. Bourne, *Book and Slavery,* 20.

51. Bourne, *Picture of Slavery,* 131.

52. Bourne, *Book and Slavery,* 16–17

53. Ibid., 40.

54. Ibid., 25.

55. Bourne, *Picture of Slavery,* 42.

56. AASS *First Annual Report . . . 1834* (New York, 1834), 19; McKivigan, *The War against Proslavery Religion,* 14.

57. George Bourne, *A Condensed Anti-Slavery Bible Argument, by a Citizen of Virginia* (New York: S. W. Benedict, 1845), 47.

58. Mark Noll, *America's God: From Jonathan Edwards to Abraham Lincoln* (New York: Oxford University Press, 2002), 54, 58.

59. David Rice, *A Kentucky Protest against Slavery (New York: Samuel Wood, 1812),* 6–8.

60. Rice quote in Murray, *Presbyterians and the Negro,* 15–16.

61. Bourne, *Book and Slavery,* 11, 95.

62. Ibid., 25.

63. Bourne in *Liberator,* July 23, 1831.

64. Smith's quote in Arthur Dicken Thomas, *The Second Great Awakening and Slavery Reform in Virginia, 1785–1820* (ThD diss., Union Theological Seminary, Richmond, VA, 1981), 199–200.

65. Ibid., 9–10.

66. Bourne, *Book and Slavery,* 111.

67. *Liberator,* November 16, 1833.

68. Bourne, *Book and Slavery,* 1, 159.

69. Sinha, *The Slave's Cause,* 172.

70. Ibid., 173.

71. Oshatz, *Slavery and Sin,* 40.

72. Wilson, *Lexington Presbytery Heritage,* 92.

73. Bourne's quote in Christie and Dumond, *George Bourne and "The Book and Slavery Irreconcilable,"* 52.

74. Ibid., 45.

75. Ibid., 43.

76. Weld, *American Slavery as It Is,* 178–79.

77. *Minutes of the General Assembly of the Presbyterian Church in the United States of America From Its Organization, 1789–1820* (Philadelphia: Presbyterian Board of Publications, 1847), 627.

78. Ibid., 630.

79. Wilson, *Lexington Presbytery Heritage,* 92. The foremost charge was that Bourne, on his return trip from the 1815 General Assembly, purchased but failed to eventually pay for a horse which he purchased on the Sabbath. Bourne later revealed that the horse was worthless. Ironically, Bourne was prosecuted for mistreating an animal, while his ministerial colleagues remained free to mistreat their own human chattel.

80. *Extracts,* 20. A few ministers objected to the General Assembly's ruling, but they were silenced by the majority.

81. Wilentz, *The Rise of American Democracy,* 331.

82. Waldsreicher, *In the Midst of Perpetual Fetes,* 302.

83. Paul Goodman, *Of One Blood: Abolitionism and the Origins of Racial Equality* (Berkeley: University of California Press, 1998), 10. See also Nash, *Race and Revolution,* 49.

84. Emma Lapsansky and Margaret Hope Bacon, eds., *Back to Africa: Benjamin Coates and the Colonization Movement in America* (University Park: Pennsylvania State University Press, 2005).

85. Finley quote in Isaac Van Arsdale Brown, *Memoirs of the Reverend Robert Finley* (New Brunswick, NJ: Terhune and Letson, 1819), 77.

86. Ibid., 91.

87. "1818 Declaration," in *Extracts,* 28–29.

88. Ibid., 29–30.

89. Ibid., 31.

90. Ibid., 30.

91. Ibid., 31–32.

92. George Bourne, *Lectures on the Progress and Perfection of the Church of Christ* (Mt. Pleasant, NY: R. W. Knight, 1823), 355.

93. *Liberator,* September 14, 1838, 146.

94. Christie and Dumond, *George Bourne and "The Book and Slavery Irreconcilable,"* 63.

95. Quote from C. Bruce Saiger, "Abolitionism and the Presbyterian Schism of 1837–38," in *Abolitionism and American Religion: History of the American Abolitionist Movement,* ed. John McKivigan (New York: Garland Publication, 1999), 184.

96. Christie and Dumond, *George Bourne and "The Book and Slavery Irreconcilable,"* 60.

97. Bourne, *Picture of Slavery,* 191.

98. Ibid., 134. Although rejecting the plan of colonization on principle, Bourne did come around to the idea that even such an ungodly scheme could be discursively used to advance the gospel: "[Colonization] may then in some measure by instrumental to commute by the donation of the Gospel and its blessings, for the numberless and indescribable miseries which through the slave trade, the sons of Africa have suffered from the *civilized* nations of Europe and America." Quotation in *Lectures,* 420. Emphasis is Bourne's. His son Theodore became active in the colonization movement, working closely with leading activists like Henry Highland Garnet and Benjamin Coates. See Joel Schor, *Henry Highland Garnet: A Voice of Black Republicanism in the 19th Century* (Westport, CT: Greenwood Press, 1977), and the latest collection of Coates's letters in Lapsansky and Bacon, *Back to Africa.*

99. *Liberator,* April 23, 1831. See also Bourne, *Picture of Slavery,* 134.

100. *Liberator,* November 16, 1833.

101. William Lloyd Garrison, *Thoughts on African Colonization* (New York: Arno, 1969), 14.

102. James G. Birney, *Letters on Slavery* (New York: S. W. Benedict & Co, 1834), 20.

103. Bourne, *Book and Slavery,* 23.

104. Goodman, *Of One Blood,* 10.

105. Sinha, The *Slave's Cause,* 160.

106. Allen quote in Davis, *The Problem of Slavery in the Age of Emancipation,* 179.

107. Sinha, *The Slave's Cause,* 171.

108. Goodman, *Of One Blood,* 10.

109. Davis, *The Problem of Slavery in the Age of Emancipation,* 179.

110. Oliver Johnson, "Unwritten History: An Anti-Slavery Boanerges," *Boston Commonwealth,* June 6, 1885, Bourne Family Papers, Huntington Library (2016) 2(41), "Newspaper Clippings" [1830–1918].

111. William Oland Bourne, "Antislavery Leaders: The Pioneer of Antislavery," *Boston Com-*

monwealth, July 25, 1885, Bourne Family Papers, Huntington Library (2016) 2(41), "Newspaper Clippings" [1830–1918].

112. Bourne, *Picture of Slavery,* 1.

113. Printed in *Liberator,* August 25, 1832.

114. *Liberator,* March 17, 1832.

115. Lewis Tappan's article in *The Independent,* October 31, 1861, 6.

116. Margaret Abruzzo, *Polemical Pain: Slavery, Cruelty, and the Rise of Humanitarianism* (Baltimore: Johns Hopkins University Press, 2011), 138.

117. Bourne, *Picture of Slavery,* 7.

118. Martha Cutter, *The Illustrated Slave: Empathy, Graphic Narrative, and the Visual Culture of the Transatlantic Abolition Movement, 1800–1852* (Athens: University of Georgia Press, 2017), 94.

119. Eric Burin, *Slavery and the Peculiar Solution: A History of the American Colonization Society, 1816–1865* (Gainesville: University of Florida Press), 2005.

120. Ibid., 102.

121. Paxton's quote in Wilson, *Lexington Presbytery Heritage,* 93. See also Bourne, *Picture of Slavery.*

122. William Warren Sweet, *The Story of Religion in America,* 2nd ed. (New York: Harper & Brothers, 1950), 293–94. Sweet comments that John Christie revealed these facts in a paper presented before the American Society of Church History in Cleveland, Ohio, in December 1947.

123. Thomas, *The Second Great Awakening,* 203.

124. McKivigan, *Abolitionism and American Religion,* 412.

125. Baxter's quote in Christie and Dumond, *George Bourne and "The Book and Slavery Irreconcilable,"* 65; and Thomas, *The Second Great Awakening.*

126. Dumond, *The Antislavery Crusade in America,* 12–34.

127. Oshatz, *Slavery and Sin,* 40.

3. THE MATURATION OF BOURNE'S ANTISLAVERY BIBLE ARGUMENT

1. George Bourne, "Confession of Thomas Paine," *Christian Advocate,* September 25, 1879, 609. Bourne first wrote about his encounter in 1845; it was later republished in 1879 and confirmed by Theodore in 1882.

2. David Brion Davis, *The Problem of Slavery in the Age of Revolution, 1770–1823* (Oxford: Oxford University Press, 1999), 572.

3. Molly Oshatz, *Slavery as Sin: The Fight against Slavery and the Rise of Liberal Protestantism* (New York: Oxford University Press, 2011), 31.

4. Rankin quote in John McKivigan, *The War against Proslavery Religion: Abolitionism and the Northern Churches, 1830–1865* (Ithaca, NY: Cornell University Press), 31.

5. Lawrence Goodheart, *Abolitionist, Actuary, Atheist: Elizur Wright and the Reform Impulse* (Kent: Ohio State University Press, 1990), 128.

6. Mark Noll, *America's God: From Jonathan Edwards to Abraham Lincoln* (New York: Oxford University Press, 2002), 372. See also Mark Noll and Nathan Hatch, eds., *The Bible in America: Essays in Cultural History* (New York: Oxford University Press, 1982), 40–43.

7. David Paul Nord, *Faith in Reading: Religious Publishing and the Birth of Mass Media in America* (New York: Oxford University Press, 2004).

8. For studies related to the democratization of American Christianity and the explosion of faith in the post-Revolutionary era, see Nathan O. Hatch, *Democratization of American Christianity* (New Haven, CT: Yale University Press, 1989); and Jon Butler, *Awash in a Sea of Faith* (Cambridge, MA: Harvard University Press, 1990).

9. Mark Noll, *The Civil War as a Theological Crisis* (Chapel Hill: University of North Carolina Press, 2006), 161.

10. E. Brooks Holifield, *Theology in America: Christian Thought from the Age of the Puritans to the Civil War* (New Haven, CT: Yale University Press, 2003), 191.

11. Paul Conkin, *The Uneasy Center: Reformed Christianity in Antebellum America* (Chapel Hill: University of North Carolina Press, 1995), 270.

12. J. Albert Harrill, *Slaves in the New Testament: Literary, Social, and Moral Dimensions* (Minneapolis: Fortress Press, 2006), 166.

13. Holifield, *Theology in America,* 191.

14. Ibid., 194.

15. Ibid., 7–8. Weld's quote in *The Bible against Slavery* (New York: American Anti-Slavery Society, 1838), 18. Emphasis mine.

16. Ibid., 15.

17. Ibid., 61–62.

18. Ibid.

19. David Brion Davis, *Inhuman Bondage: The Rise and Fall of Slavery in the New World* (New York: Oxford University Press, 2006), 248.

20. George Bourne, *A Condensed Anti-Slavery Bible Argument, by a Citizen of Virginia* (New York: S. W. Benedict, 1845), 23–24.

21. Ibid., 22.

22. Ibid., 54.

23. Ibid., 63.

24. Ibid., 64. Bourne ignores the tenth commandment (coveting).

25. Ibid., 26

26. Ibid., 32.

27. Ibid., 33.

28. Ibid.

29. Straying a bit from his Bible argument, Bourne appealed to how such words were used in a figurative sense in his own day. "Buying" and "selling" were often used to describe recent immigrants who were said to sell their labor to pay for their journey, "venal politicians" who "sold" themselves to the people or sold out to powerful interests, historical figures like Benedict Arnold who sold himself to America's enemy, and moral reformers who redeemed (or purchased) the lost and dying.

30. Robert Abzug, *Passionate Liberator: Theodore Dwight Weld and the Dilemma of Reform* (New York: Oxford University Press, 1980), 162.

31. Bourne, *Bible Argument,* 52–53.

32. Ibid., 62.

33. Ibid., 72.

34. For an excellent study of Palmer's defense of the Hamitic curse, see Stephen Haynes, *Noah's Curse: The Biblical Justification of American Slavery* (New York: Oxford University Press, 2002).

35. Bourne, *Bible Argument,* 24–25.

36. Oshatz, *Slavery as Sin,* 5.

37. Citing, for instance, passages from Genesis 13:2, 24 and 35:30, 43, supporters of slavery declared that Abraham's servants must have been property, for they were listed along with other items of property (e.g., livestock). Yet, as Bourne countered, according to Genesis 12:5, Abraham's wife and nephew were also listed with his property. Was there no distinction between his wife and nephew and his slaves? This confounded in his mind the "relations of persons with those of things, merely because the latter happen to be mentioned in connection with the former."

38. Bourne, *Bible Argument,* 56–57.

39. Weld, *The Bible against Slavery,* 64–66.

40. Bourne, *Bible Argument,* 48.

41. Ibid., 45.

42. Ibid., 68. Elizabeth Fox-Genovese and Eugene Genovese, *The Mind of the Master Class: History and Faith in the Southern Slaveholders' Worldview* (New York: Cambridge University Press, 2005), 520.

43. Bourne, *Bible Argument,* 67.

44. Ibid., 69.

45. Ibid., 79.

46. Ibid., 81.

47. For other antislavery articles concerning Philemon, see George Cheever, *God against Slavery* (Cincinnati: American Reform Tract and Book Society, 1857), 143–44; and Albert Barnes, *An Inquiry into the Scriptural Views of Slavery* (Philadelphia: Perkins and Purves, 1846), 318–31.

48. Bourne, *Bible Argument,* 36.

49. Ibid., 36.

50. Holified, *Theology in America,* 30.

51. Lewis's quote in Noll, *The Civil War as a Theological Crisis,* 48.

52. William E. Cain, ed., *William Lloyd Garrison and the Fight to End Slavery: Selections from* The Liberator (Boston: Bedford Books of St. Martin's Press, 1995), 140–41.

53. Oshatz, *Slavery as Sin,* 44; Cain, *William Lloyd Garrison,* 141

54. Gerrit Smith, *Sermons and Speeches* (New York: Arno Press, 1861), 119.

55. Oshatz, *Slavery as Sin,* 45.

56. Bourne, *Book and Slavery,* 90–91.

57. Holifield, *Theology in America,* 494–504.

58. Fox-Genovese, *The Mind of the Master Class,* 473–527.

59. Oshatz, *Slavery as Sin,* 10.

60. Ibid., 11.

61. Ibid., 4.

62. Ibid., 115.

4. CATHOLIC SLAVERY AND PROTESTANT FREEDOM IN BOURNE'S *Lorette*

1. William Lloyd Garrison, *Letters of William Lloyd Garrison, 1836–1840,* vol. 2, ed. Louis Ruchames (Cambridge, MA: Belknap Press), August 14, 1841, 281; Garrison, *Letters,* vol. 5, 164.

2. Cheever and Webb quotes in John R. McGreevy, *Catholicism and American Freedom: A History* (New York: W. W. Norton, 2003), 57–59. *Ultramontanism* was an ideology that supported the central authority and power of the pope.

3. Swisshelm quote in Peter Walker, *Moral Choices: Memory, Desire, and Imagination in Nineteenth-Century American Abolition* (Baton Rouge: Louisiana State University Press, 1978), 164.

4. "Elijah Lovejoy as an Anti-Catholic," *Records of the American Catholic Historical Society* 62 (September 1951): 172–80.

5. Theodore Bourne, "George Bourne: The Pioneer of American Anti-Slavery," *Methodist Quarterly Methodist Quarterly Review* LXIV (January 1882); David Brion Davis, *The Problem of Slavery in the Age of Revolution, 1770–1823* (Oxford: Oxford University Press, 1999); Ray Allen Billington, *The Protestant Crusade, 1800–1860: A Study of the Origins of American Nativism* (Gloucester, MA: Peter Smith, 1963 [1938]); John W. Christie and Dwight L. Dumond, *George Bourne and "The Book and Slavery Irreconcilable"* (Wilmington: Historical Society of Delaware, 1969); Andrew Murray, *Presbyterianism and the Negro* (Philadelphia: Presbyterian Historical Society, 1966); Andrew Murray, review of Bourne's *Book and Slavery Irreconcilable,* in *American Presbyterians* 66 no. 4 (229–33); Daniel McInerney, *The Fortunate Heirs of Freedom: Abolition and Republican Thought* (Lincoln: University of Nebraska Press, 1994); Henry Mayer, *All on Fire: William Lloyd Garrison and the Abolition of Slavery* (New York: St. Martin's Press, 1998).

6. George Bourne in *The Liberator,* March 9, 1833.

7. George Bourne, *Picture of Slavery in the United States of America* (Middleton, CT: E. Hunt, 1834), 175.

8. For political anti-Catholic hysteria prior to the 1830s consider Nathan Hatch's *The Sacred Cause of Liberty: Republican Thought and the Millennium in Revolutionary New England* (New Haven, CT: Yale University Press, 1977); and Ruth Bloch's *Visionary Republic: Millennial Themes in American Thought, 1756–1800* (New York: Cambridge University Press, 1985).

9. George Bourne, *Lectures on the Progress and Perfection of the Church of Christ* (Mt. Pleasant, NY: R. W. Knight, 1823), 414; Billington, *The Protestant Crusade,* 42.

10. David Reynolds, *Faith in Fiction: The Emergence of Religious Literature in America* (Cambridge, MA: Harvard University Press, 1981), 181. Ray Allen Billington largely neglects *Lorette* in his encyclopedic study of the origins of American nativism. Frank Luther Mott, *Golden Multitudes: The Story of Bestsellers in America* (New York: MacMillan, 1947), 318. To become a bestseller, a book had to reach 1 percent of the total population in sales. A runner-up bestseller, like Bourne's *Lorette,* was just below that figure, but nonetheless maintained a wide readership. Susan Griffin, "Awful Disclosures: Women's Evidence in the Escaped Nuns Tales," *Publications of the Modern Language Association of America* 111, no. 1 (January 1996): 93–107.

11. Marie Anne Pagliarini, "The Pure American Woman and the Wicked Catholic Priest: An Analysis of Anti-Catholic Literature in Antebellum America," *Religion and American Culture: A Journal of Interpretation* 9, no. 1 (Winter 1999): 112.

12. Jenny Franchot, *Roads to Rome: The Antebellum Protestant Encounter with Catholicism* (Berkeley: University of California Press, 1994), xvii. The best essay that highlights the common themes shared by most escaped-nun tales is Pagliarini's "The Pure American Women and the Wicked Catholic Priest," 97–128.

13. Franchot, *Roads to Rome,* xix.

14. Richard Carwardine, *Evangelical Politics in Antebellum America* (New Haven, CT: Yale University Press, 1993), 81.

15. George Bourne, *Lorette: The History of Louise, Daughter of a Canadian Nun, Exhibiting the Interior of Female Convents* (New York: Charles Small, 1833), i.

16. One of the best recent works to analyze the fault lines of democracy during the Era of Good Feelings is Sean Wilentz, *The Rise of American Democracy: Jefferson to Lincoln* (New York: Norton, 2005). Chapter 6 is titled "The Era of Bad Feelings."

17. Jason K. Duncan, *Citizens or Papists?: The Politics of Anti-Catholicism in New York, 1685–1821* (New York: Fordham University Press, 2005), 23.

18. Mary Macauley Allodi and Rosemarie L. Tovell, *An Engraver's Pilgrimage: James Smillie in Quebec, 1821–1830* (Ontario: Royal Ontario Museum, 1989), 119.

19. Billington, *The Protestant Crusade;* Jay Dolan, *The Immigrant Church: New York's Irish and German Catholics, 1815–1865* (Baltimore: Johns Hopkins University Press, 1975); Jay Dolan, *The American Catholic Experience: A History from the Colonial Times to the Present* (Garden City, NY: Doubleday, 1985), chap. 4; Patrick Carey, *Catholics in America: A History* (Westport, CT: Praeger, 2004) chaps. 2 and 3.

20. Dale Light, *Rome and the New Republic: Conflict and Community in Philadelphia Catholicism between the Revolution and the Civil War* (Notre Dame, IN: University of Notre Dame Press, 1996), 101–3.

21. Billington, *Protestant Crusade,* 53.

22. Theodore Bourne, "Rev. George Bourne," 79.

23. *Religious Intelligencer,* December 26, 1829, 496.

24. Whitney Cross, *The Burned-Over District: The Social and Intellectual History of Enthusiastic Religion in New York* (Ithaca, NY: Cornell University Press, 1982), 231.

25. *Liberator,* March 17, 1832.

26. Ibid. Quotation from *Liberator,* March 17, 1832.

27. *North American Magazine,* July 1833, 193; *North American Magazine,* August 1833, 253; *United Catholic Miscellany,* May 8, 1830, 357; *United States Catholic Miscellany,* July 27, 1833, 31.

28. Lou Baldwin, "Pious Prejudice: Catholicism and the American Press over Three Centuries," in *Anti-Catholicism in American Culture,* ed. Robert Lockwood (Washington DC: Center for Media and Public Affairs, 2000), 60.

29. Billington, *Protestant Crusade.*

30. Alistair McGrath, *Reformation Thought: An Introduction* (Cambridge, MA: Blackwell Publishers, 1995), 220.

31. Alistair McGrath, "Calvin and the Christian Calling," *First Things* 94 (June/July 1999), para. 17. http://www.firstthings.com/ftissues/ft9906/articles/mcgrath.html.

32. McGrath, *Reformation Thought,* 220–22.

33. Ibid.

34. Jane Tompkins, *Sensational Designs: The Cultural Work of American Fiction, 1790–1860* (New York: Oxford University Press, 1985), 125.

35. Catherine Beecher and Harriet Beecher Stowe, *The American Woman's Home, or Principles of Domestic Science* (New York: J. B. Ford and Company, 1870), 19.

36. Ann Douglass, *Feminization of American Culture* (New York: Avon Books, 1978); Barbara Welter, *Dimity Convictions: The American Woman in the Nineteenth Century* (Athens: Ohio University Press, 1976); Cathy Davidson, *Revolution of the Word: The Rise of the Novel in America* (New York: Oxford University Press, 1986); Mary Kelley, *Private Women, Public Stage: Literary Domesticity in Nineteenth-Century America* (New York: Oxford University Press, 1984). Reynolds criticizes Ann Douglass for exaggerating the feminization of American culture. In *Faith and Fiction,* Reynolds argues that an equally valid argument can be made for a masculinization of American culture. One illustrative point is his analysis of the decline of Calvinism. For Douglass the decline of Calvinism gave way to a more sentimental, effeminate Protestantism. On the contrary, the revolt against Calvinism can be interpreted as an attempt to rebuild masculine Christianity. Calvinism, according to William Ellery Channing, emasculated men, making them slaves of the divine. The renewed man was one who courageously exercised his free will in society. For William Ware, those who were critical of Calvinism were strong and independent. Henry Ware believed that manly labor was necessary for salvation. See also David Reynolds, "The Feminization Controversy: Sexual Stereotypes and the Paradoxes of Piety in Nineteenth-Century America," *New England Quarterly* 53, no. 1 (March 1980): 96–106.

37. Ware's quote in Reynolds, *Faith and Fiction,* 100.

38. David Reynolds, "From Doctrine to Narrative: The Rise of Pulpit Storytelling in America," *American Quarterly* 32 no. 5 (December 1981): 484.

39. George Bourne, *Picture of Quebec and Its Vicinity* (Quebec: P. and W. Ruthven, 1831), 51.

40. Bourne, "George Bourne: The Pioneer of American Anti-Slavery," 14–16. Allodi and Tovell, *An Engraver's Pilgrimage,* 119. Initially, *Picture of Quebec* gained a meager profit. But after Smillie transferred publication to Bourne's eldest son, George Melksham, a New York news agent, profits soared. George Melksham Bourne owned and operated the Depository of Arts, Engravings and Fancy Store at 359 Broadway, New York. Smillie stayed in close contact with the Bourne family.

41. Bourne, *Picture of Quebec,* 47, 49.

42. Ibid., 47.

43. Ibid., 83.

44. Ibid., 83.

45. Ibid., 83.

46. Bourne, *Lorette,* xii, xiv.

47. Ibid., 84.

48. Ibid., 189.

49. George Bourne, *The American Text-book of Popery: Being an Authentic Compend of the Bulls, Canons, Decretals of the Roman Hierarchy* (Philadelphia: Griffith and Simon, 1846), 54.

50. Bourne, *Lorette,* 162.

51. Ibid., 164–65.

52. Bourne, *American Text-book,* 240.

53. Ibid., 240.

54. Ibid., 226.

55. Ibid., 237.

56. Ibid., 239.

57. Ibid., 240.

58. Bourne, *Lorette,* 167.

59. Ibid., 195.

60. Karen Halttunen, *Confidence Men and Painted Women: A Study of Middle-Class Culture in America, 1830–1870* (New Haven, CT: Yale University Press, 1982), 53.

61. Bourne, *Lorette,* 165.

62. The "born again" motif is well illustrated in Margaret Shepherd's *My Life in The Convent,* published in the late 1890s.

63. Ford Hendrickson, *The "Black Convent" Slave: The Climax of Nunnery Exposures, Awful Disclosures: The "Uncle Tom's Cabin" of Rome's "Convent Slavery"* (Toledo, OH: Protestant Missionary Publishing Company, 1914), 70.

64. John Calvin, *Institutes of the Christian Religion,* book I, chap. 1, sec. 1, ed. John McNeill, trans. Ford Lewis Battles (Philadelphia: Westminster Press, 1960).

65. Bourne, *American Text-book,* 349.

66. Bourne, *Lorette,* 186.

67. Ibid., 169, 133.

68. Ibid., 175.

69. Pagliarini, "The Pure American Woman," 104.

70. The absence of fatherly protection played a central role in Rebecca Reed's *Six Months in a Convent,* published a couple of years after *Lorette.* Reed, the daughter of a poor Protestant farmer from Charleston, Massachusetts, converted to Catholicism in 1831 at the age of nineteen and entered the Ursuline convent in the summer of the same year. She secretly left the institution in 1832, telling people of its rigid disciplines, harsh physical conditions, and the lack of affections from the superiors. Motivated by Reed's account, a working-class Protestant mob burned the Catholic establishment in 1834. In the spring of 1835, Reed published *Six Months* and sold five thousand copies in the first week, twenty-five thousand the first month, and fifty thousand the first year. Despite the popularity of the tale, which included a futile rebuttal by the mother superior, Sister Mary Edmond St. George, Reed fell into obscurity and died in 1838 of consumption. Unique to Reed's memoirs is the Ursuline mother superior as a usurper of male authority. The Catholic matriarch expected the girls to devote themselves to Christ and the Roman Church, "repeating the words of the Savior, 'He that loveth father or mother more than me is not worthy of me.'" The violence committed against the convent was largely directed toward an antimother who secured her power within a distorted domestic space.

71. Bourne, *American Text-book,* 370.

72. Hendrickson, *The "Black Convent,"* 8–9.

73. Bourne, *American Text-book,* 309.

74. Bourne, *Lectures on the Progress,* 174.

75. Bourne, *American Text-book,* 308.

76. Bourne, *Lorette,* 121; Hendrickson, *The "Black Convent,"* 23.

77. Elizabeth Fenton, *Religious Liberties: Anti-Catholicism and Liberal Democracy in Nineteenth-Century U.S. Literature and Culture* (New York: Oxford University Press, 2011), 71.

78. Bourne, *American Text-book,* 79.

79. Ibid., 430.

80. Ibid.

81. Bourne, *Lorette,* 115.

82. Ibid., 118.

83. Billington, *The Protestant Crusade,* 100.

84. Michael Williams, *Shadow of the Pope* (New York: Kessinger Publishing Company, 1932), 71.

85. Billington, *The Protestant Crusade,* 101, 115. Billington also discusses how each clergyman swindled Monk out of the book's profits: "Maria Monk and Slocum were jointly sued by Hoyt for a share of the profits. *New York Observer,* November 26, 1836. In a second suit brought by Maria Monk through Slocum as next friend against Harper Brothers and others, it was asserted that the copyright on the *Awful Disclosures* had been taken out by Bourne and used by him with the aid of Harper Brothers in such a way that Maria Monk received none of the profits. The court refused to grant her any relief. I *Endward's Chanc. Rep.* 109 (May 16, 1837), 115.

86. Bourne Family Papers, Huntington Library, 1(25), George Bourne, "Popery in Canada" [1830s].

87. Bourne Family Papers, Huntington Library, 1(37), Bourne, "Writings on Canadian Priests" (September 6, 1836).

88. Ibid.

89. Bourne, *Picture of Slavery,* 172. Emphasis is mine.

90. George Bourne, *Slavery Illustrated in its Effects on Women and Domestic Society* (Boston: Isaac Knapp, 1837), 34.

91. Bourne, *Lectures on the Progress,* 182.

92. Ibid., 184.

93. Bourne, *Picture of Slavery,* 175.

94. *New York Observer,* December 27, 1834.

95. Ibid.

96. Joseph Berg, *The Confessional; or, an Exposition of the Doctrine of Auricular Confession as Taught in the Standards of the Romish Church,* 3rd ed. (Philadelphia, 1841), 75.

97. Sarah Grimké, "An Epistle to the Clergy of the Southern States," (1836) in *American Catholics and Slavery: 1789–1866: An Anthology of Primary Documents,* ed. Kenneth Zanca (Lanham, MD: University Press of America, 1994).

98. Charles Wilbanks, ed., *Walking by Faith: The Diary of Angelina Grimké, 1828–1835* (Columbia: University of South Carolina Press, 2003), 55.

5. ABOLITION AND THE WOMAN QUESTION IN BOURNE'S *Slavery Illustrated in Its Effects on Woman and Domestic Society*

1. Letter from Garrison to Helen Eliza (1840). Associates of the Boston Public Library, Boston Public Library. http://archive.org/details/lettertomybelovedwoogarr.

2. George Bourne, *Picture of Slavery in the United States of America* (Middleton, CT: E. Hunt, 1834), 97.

3. Beth Salerno, *Sister Societies: Women's Antislavery Organizations in Antebellum America* (DeKalb: Northern Illinois University Press, 2005), 19–20.

4. William Lloyd Garrison, *The Letters of William Lloyd Garrison: From Disunion to the Brink of War,* vol. IV, ed. Louis Ruchames (Cambridge, MA: Belknap Press, 1975), 597.

5. Nancy Cott, *The Bonds of Womanhood: "Woman's Sphere" in New England, 1780–1835* (New Haven, CT: Yale University Press, 1997), 6.

6. Bourne, *Picture of Slavery,* 98. See also George Bourne, *Slavery Illustrated in its Effects on Woman and Domestic Society* (Boston: Isaac Knapp, 1837), 122.

7. Bourne, *Slavery Illustrated,* vii.

8. John McKivigan, ed., *The War against Proslavery Religion: Abolitionism and the Northern Churches, 1830–1865* (Ithaca, NY: Cornell University Press, 1984), 67.

9. George Bourne, *The Virtuous Woman, A Sermon, Delivered at Mount-Pleasant* (New York: Stephen Marshall, 1820), 5.

10. Ibid., 6.

11. Ronald Walters, *American Reformers, 1815–1860* (New York: Hill and Wang, 1997), 92.

12. Bourne, *Picture of Slavery,* 7.

13. Bourne, *Slavery Illustrated,* 91.

14. Ibid., 79.

15. Joseph M. Hawes and Elizabeth I. Nybakken, eds., *Family and Society in American History* (Urbana: University of Illinois Press, 2001), 6.

16. David Hackett, "Gender and Religion in American Culture, 1870–1930," *Religion and American Culture* 5, no. 2 (Summer 1995): 127–57.

17. Paul Johnson, *The Early American Republic, 1789–1829* (New York: Oxford, 2006), 115.

18. John Abbott, *The Mother at Home; or, The Principles of Maternal Duty Familiarly Illustrated,* revised and corrected by Daniel Walton (London: John Mason, 1834, repr. New York: Arno Press, 1972), 165–67.

19. Charles Sellers, *The Market Revolution: Jacksonian America, 1815–1846* (New York: Oxford University Press, 1991), 242; Barbara Epstein, *The Politics of Domesticity: Women, Evangelism, and Temperance in Nineteenth-Century America* (Middletown, CT: Wesleyan University Press, 1981), 70.

20. Karen Sanchez-Eppler, *Touching Liberty: Abolition, Feminism, and the Politics of the Body* (Berkeley: University of California Press, 1997), 42.

21. Chris Dixon, *Perfecting the Family: Antislavery Marriages in Nineteenth-Century America* (Amherst: University of Massachusetts Press, 1997), 9.

22. George Bourne, *Marriage Indissoluble and Divorce Unscriptural* (Harrisonburg, PA: Davidson and Bourne, 1813), 78.

23. Ibid.

24. George Bourne, *Sermon on the Majesty and Condescension of God: Delivered at the Opening of the Presbyterian Church in Port Republic on Christmas Day, 1812* (Staunton, VA: Isaac Collett, 1812), 31.

25. Bourne, *Marriage Indissoluble,* 10, 35.

26. Ibid., 40, 48.

27. Ibid., 28–29.

28. Ibid., 32.

29. Ibid., 38, 105.

30. Ibid., 23–25.

31. Ibid., 48–49.

32. Ibid., 68.

33. George Fitzhugh, *Cannibals All, or Slaves Without Masters* (Richmond, VA: A. Morris, 1857).

34. Kristen Hoganson, "Garrisonian Abolitionism and the Rhetoric of Gender, 1850–1860," *American Quarterly* 45, no. 4 (December 1993): 558–95.

35. Ronald Walters, "The Erotic South: Civilization and Sexuality in American Abolitionism," *American Quarterly* 25, no. 2 (May 1973): 177–201.

36. Bourne, *Picture of Slavery,* 104–22.

37. Bourne, *Slavery Illustrated,* 47.

38. Ibid., 39.

39. Ibid., 27–29.

40. Ibid., 16.

41. Bourne, *Picture of Slavery,* 87.

42. Ibid., 89.

43. Ibid., 121, 138.

44. Ibid., 98, 104.

45. Ibid., 131.

46. Ibid., 97.

47. Bourne, *Slavery Illustrated,* 26.

48. Ibid., 71.

49. Ibid., 46–47.

50. Ibid., 72.

51. Ibid., 78, 80.

52. Ibid., 80–81.

53. Ibid., 88.

54. Angelina Grimké, *Appeal to the Christian Women of the South* (New York: American Anti-Slavery Society, 1836).

55. Anya Jabour, *Marriage in the Early Republic: Elizabeth and William Wirt and the Companionate Ideal* (Baltimore: Johns Hopkins University Press, 1998), 2.

56. Karen Lystra, *Searching the Heart: Women, Men, and Romantic Love in Nineteenth Century America* (New York: Oxford University Press, 1989), 7.

57. Bourne, *Marriage Indissoluble,* 21.

58. Ibid., 17.

59. Lystra, *Searching the Heart,* 8.

60. Bourne, *Slavery Illustrated,* 55.

61. Bourne, *Marriage Indissoluble,* 20.

62. Ibid., 58.

63. Bourne, *Slavery Illustrated,* 94.

64. Ibid., 81.

65. Ibid., 71.

66. Ibid., 102. Grimké's objective in *Appeal to the Christian Women* was to arouse southern women, "as the wives and mothers, the daughters and sisters, of the South, to a sense of your duty as *women,* and as Christian women, on that great subject" (Grimké, *Appeal to the Christian Women,* 24).

67. Bourne, *Slavery Illustrated,* 104.

68. Ibid., 106.

69. Ibid., 122.

70. Ibid., 124.

71. Ibid., 123.

72. Ibid., 102.

73. Ibid., 125.

74. Ibid., 24.

75. Cott, *Bonds of Womanhood,* 148.

76. Sellers, *The Market Revolution,* 222.

77. Beecher's quotation in Jeanne Boydston, Mary Kelley, and Anne Margolis's *The Limits of Sisterhood: The Beecher Sisters on Women's Rights and Women's Spheres* (Chapel Hill: University of North Carolina Press, 1988), 127.

78. Salerno, *Sister Societies,* 24–25.

79. Ibid., 78. See also Robert Abzug, *Cosmos Crumbling: American Reform and the Religious Imagination* (New York: Oxford University Press, 1994), 189.

80. Anna Speicher, *The Religious World of Antislavery Women: Spirituality in the Lives of Five Abolitionist Lecturers* (Syracuse, NY: Syracuse University Press, 2000), 4.

81. Ibid., 9.

82. Kelley's quote in Speicher, *Religious World,* 63, 89.

83. Ibid., 89.

84. *Proceedings of the Anti-Slavery Convention of American Women,* held in the City of New York, May 9th, 10th, 11th, and 12th, 1837 (New York: William S. Dorr, 1837), 9.

85. Michael Pierson, "Slavery Cannot Be Covered Up with Broadcloth or a Bandanna": The Evolution of White Abolitionist Attacks on the "Patriarchal Institution." *Journal of the Early Republic* 23, no. 3 (Fall 2005): 383–415. Quote on page 387.

86. Timothy Patrick McCarthy and John Campbell McMillian, *Radical Reader* (New York: New Press, 2011), 171.

87. Abzug, *Cosmos Crumbling,* 184.

88. George Bourne, *The American Text-book of Popery: Being an Authentic Compend of the Bulls, Canons, Decretals of the Roman Hierarchy* (Philadelphia: Griffith and Simon, 1846), 318.

89. Ibid., 103.

90. Ibid., 108.

91. Walters, *American Reformers,* 104.

92. Ibid., 107.

6. THE NATION, THE MILLENNIUM, AND BOURNE'S *American Text-book of Popery*

1. Tracy Fessenden, *Culture and Redemption: Religion, the Secular, and American Literature* (Princeton, NJ: Princeton University Press, 2007), 117. The quotation is Fessenden's own brief comment on Wilkes's preface.

2. William Brown, "Religious Organizations and Slavery," *Oberlin Quarterly Review* (October 1849): 435. Emphasis mine.

3. George Bourne, *Lectures on the Progress and Perfection of the Church of Christ* (Mount Pleasant, NY: R. W. Knight, 1823), 375.

4. George Bourne, *A Condensed Anti-Slavery Bible Argument, by a Citizen of Virginia* (New York: S. W. Benedicts, 1845), 14.

5. Human nature, Bourne wrote in 1844, was "ever prone and willing to depart from Jehovah" (*The American Text-book of Popery: Being an Authentic Compend of the Bulls, Canons, Decretals of the Roman Hierarchy* [Philadelphia: Griffith and Simon, 1846], hereafter *Text-book*, 53). Throughout every age, societies express an "inextinguishable hatred" of Christ and his gospel (*Lectures on the Progress*, 4). Rebellion against the gospel is not something unique to slaveowners and Catholics, but endemic to all humanity. It's just that the depravity of the former is organized by religion.

6. Elizabeth Fenton, *Religious Liberties: Anti-Catholicism and Liberal Democracy in Nineteenth-Century U.S. Literature and Culture* (New York: Oxford University Press, 2011), 70.

7. Among the many newspapers that printed anti-Catholic and antislavery articles, Joshua Leavitt's *New York Evangelist* came closest to Bourne's own opinions regarding the two. Bourne was a colaborer in the area of reform with Leavitt, himself an anti-Catholic; he was also close friends with the financial backers (and nativists) of the *Evangelist*, Arthur and Lewis Tappan. Although aligned with Bourne's anti-Catholic abolitionism, the paper leaned more toward Finneyite revivalism, moving away from Bourne's traditional conservative theology.

8. George Bourne, *Picture of Slavery in the United States of America* (Middleton, CT: E. Hunt, 1834), 150.

9. George Bourne, *The Life of the Rev. John Wesley* (Baltimore: Dobbin and Murphy, 1807), 345.

10. Anne Loveland, "Evangelicalism and 'Immediate Abolitionism' in American Antislavery Thought," *Journal of Southern History* 32, no. 2 (May 1966): 172–88; David Brion Davis, "The Emergence of Immediatism in British and American Antislavery Thought," *Mississippi Valley Historical Review* 49, no. 2 (September 1962): 209–30.

11. Lewis Tappan, "George Bourne," *The Independent*, October 31, 1861, 6.

12. "Martyrs of Scotland," *The Independent*, January 21, 1863; John W. Christie and Dwight L. Dumond, *George Bourne and "The Book and Slavery Irreconcilable"* (Wilmington: Historical Society of Delaware, 1969), 1.

13. Hero worship was not uncommon in the Early Republic. Writers praised and in some cases deified extraordinary figures like Washington, Lafayette, Wesley, Whitefield, and Jackson, to name a few. Another of Bourne's heroes was Napoleon. He admired Napoleon not only for his military leadership, but as a creation of the French Revolution. For Bourne, however, these individuals were members of a divine club, used by God for the advancement of the kingdom.

14. Bourne, *The Life of the Rev. John Wesley,* 4.

15. Bourne, *Lectures on the Progress,* 362.

16. James Fraser, *Between Church and State: Religion and Public Education in a Multicultural America* (New York: St. Martins, 1999), 53.

17. Ibid., chap. 3; Patrick Carey, *Catholics in America: A History* (Westport, CT: Praeger, 2004), 21.

18. George Bourne, *Illustrations of Popery: The "Mystery of Iniquity" Unveiled* (New York: J. P. Callender, 1838); Bourne, *Text-book,* 1, 17.

19. The above quotation that states Bourne's reasons for writing *Illustrations of Popery* was actually reprinted in the *Text-book.* Although mentioning *Illustrations,* I will be citing the *Text-book* primarily.

20. Erastus Brooks, *Controversy Between Senator Brooks and John, Archbishop of New York: Growing Out of the Speech of Senator Brooks on the Church Property Bill* (New York: DeWitt and Davenport, 1855), 14.

21. The *Text-book* is similar to other no-popery monographs of the same period, especially John Dowling's *History of Romanism,* published a year after Bourne's.

22. Bourne, *Lectures on the Progress,* 10.

23. Ibid., 10; Bourne, *Text-book,* 10, 240.

24. Bourne, *Text-book,* 240.

25. Bourne, *Lectures on the Progress,* 1.

26. Ibid., 4; Bourne, *Text-book,* 53.

27. Bourne, *Lectures on the Progress,* 1. Bourne's view reflects the work of Richard Whately, Archbishop of Dublin, who argued that Romanism was essential to the institutionalization of human depravity. See Whately's *Essays: Errors of Romanism, Having Their Origin in Human Nature* (London: John W. Parker and Son, 1830): "Romanism is substantially the spirit of Human Nature" and is "the natural offspring of man's frail and corrupt character" (xxii–xiv).

28. George Bourne, *History of Napoleon Bonaparte: Emperor of the French and King of Italy* (Baltimore: Warner and Hanna, 1806), 1.

29. Bourne, *The Life of the Rev. John Wesley,* 2.

30. Bourne, *Text-book,* 11–12, 14.

31. Bourne, *Lectures on the Progress,* 17.

32. Ibid., 16, 83.

33. Such works include Samuel Smith's periodical *Downfall of Babylon;* John Dowling, *The History of Romanism: From the Earliest Corruption of Christianity to the Present Time* (New York: E. Walker, 1845); O. R. Butler, "'The Uncle Tom's Cabin of Nativism': Anti-Catholic Novels, Politics and Violence in the Antebellum United States," *Working With English: Medieval and Modern Language, Literature and Drama* 2, no. 1 (2006): 12–19. The front page of Samuel Smith's periodical *Downfall of Babylon* regularly opened with an exegetical essay that linked a portion of Revelation with the papacy.

34. Bourne, *Lectures on the Progress,* 147.

35. Bourne, *Text-book,* 16.

36. Bourne, *Lectures on the Progress,* 39.

37. Ibid., 41.

38. James West Davidson, *The Logic of Millennial Thought* (New Haven, CT: Yale University Press, 1977), 139.

39. Bourne, *Lectures on the Progress,* 72.

40. Ibid., 82.

41. Ibid., 72, 82. Bourne traces the origin of the word "nun" to third-century Egypt. "In Egypt . . . was formed the order of nuns. Nun is an ancient Egyptian word, and aptly expresses the character. It means a woman abjectly submissive to her superior in body, soul, and spirit, to the will of her superior" (*Text-book,* 79).

42. Bourne, *Lectures on the Progress,* 36.

43. Ibid., 88.

44. Bourne, *Text-book,* iii; Bourne, *Lectures on the Progress,* 94.

45. Bourne, *Lectures on the Progress,* 47.

46. Ibid., 100.

47. C. L. Feltoe, in *Sermons of Leo The Great,* in Library of Nicene and Post Nicene Fathers, 2nd Series, vol. XII (New York, 1895), 117, http://www.fordham.edu/halsall/source/leo1a.html.

48. Bourne, *Lectures on the Progress,* 101.

49. Ibid., 115.

50. Ibid., 116.

51. Ibid., 119.

52. Bourne, *Text-book,* 436.

53. Bourne, *Lectures on the Progress,* 208.

54. Bourne, *Text-book,* 132, 172.

55. Bourne, *Lectures on the Progress,* 213.

56. Ibid., 223.

57. Smith's *Downfall of Babylon* printed a series of articles on the importance of the Waldensians and Albigenses in the mid-1830s.

58. An acquaintance of Bourne, John McLeod, argued in *Protestantism, the Parent Guardian of Civil and Religious Liberty* (New York: Carter, 1843), something similar when he argued that the American ideals of liberty of conscience and freedom of speech could be found in the pre-Reformation activities of the Waldensians, Albigenses, and the Lollards.

59. Bourne, *Text-book,* 144.

60. Ibid.

61. Bourne, *Lectures on the Progress,* 236.

62. Ibid., 414.

63. Ibid., 139.

64. Bourne, *Text-book,* 104.

65. Bourne, *Lectures on the Progress,* 6; Bourne, *Text-book,* 52.

66. Bourne, *Text-book,* 438.

67. Bourne, *Picture of Slavery,* 16.

68. Bourne, *Lectures on the Progress,* 414.

69. Bourne, *Picture of Slavery,* 167.

70. Bourne, *Text-book,* 29; George Bourne, *The Book and Slavery Irreconcilable, with Animadversions against Samuel Stanhope Smith* (Philadelphia: J. M. Sanderson & Co., 1816), 106.

71. Bourne, *Text-book,* 176.

72. Ibid., 159.

73. Ibid., 99. Gregory divested Henry IV of his kingly authority in the eleventh century; Innocent placed an interdict upon the inhabitants of England in the thirteenth century, barring them from participating in the Eucharist.

74. Ibid., 135.

75. Ibid., 175, 311.

76. Ibid., 351, 355.

77. Ibid., 275, 282.

78. Bourne, *Lectures on the Progress,* 393.

79. Ibid., ix, 190.

80. Richard Carwardine, *Evangelical Politics in Antebellum America* (New Haven, CT: Yale University Press, 1993), 83.

81. Bourne, *A Condensed Anti-Slavery Bible Argument,* 74, 89–90; Bourne, *Book and Slavery,* 95.

82. Bourne, *Text-book,* 2.

83. Bourne, *Lectures on the Progress,* 190.

84. Ibid., iv; Bourne, *Text-book,* 166. Perhaps the best passage supporting the separation of church and state can be found in Matt. 22:21, Mark 12:17, and Luke 20:2, where Christ distinguished loyalties humans owed to both Caesar's kingdom and God's kingdom.

85. Bourne, *Picture of Slavery,* 38. The scriptures, according to the *New York Observer,* "are so interwoven with the institutions of our [American] land, that we must . . . amend our constitution, revise our statutes, and *destroy our memories* before we can abolish" the teachings of the Bible.

86. Bourne, *Book and Slavery,* 24, 44, 124.

87. Bourne, *Text-book,* 55, 348.

88. William Stevens Balch, *Romanism and Republicanism Incompatible* (New York: Dewitt & Davenport, 1852), 1: "Truth never shuns the light. It asks no shield. It needs no panoply." Lyman Beecher made a similar argument a few years earlier in his *Plea for the West.* Catholics, he was willing to admit, could indeed assimilate in American culture only if they submitted themselves to "the searching inspection of the public eye, and . . . pass the ordeal of an enlightened public sentiment." Lyman Beecher, *A Plea for the West* (Cincinnati: Truman and Smith, 1835), 83–84.

89. We need to be careful, however, not to erase the complexity of the private space, for in some accounts it was used to escape tyranny.

90. Beecher, *A Plea for the West,* 151. The *Protestant Vindicator* wrote in 1842: "NUNNERIES" had "uniformly been prisons to the inmates, and generally brothels for the priests." *Vindicator* quotation in Philip Hamburger, *Separation of Church and State* (Cambridge, MA: Harvard University Press, 2002), 215.

91. David Brion Davis, "Some Themes of Counter-Subversion: An Analysis of Anti-Masonic, Anti-Catholic, and Anti-Mormon Literature," *Mississippi Valley Historical Review* 47, no. 2 (Septembers 1960): 205–24. Quotes on page 211. For decades, the fear of the secret subversive—whether southern slaveholder, Mason, Mormon, or Catholic in the nineteenth-century or communist and now "terrorist" in the twentieth and twenty-first—has played a decisive role in structuring American identity.

92. Bourne, *Text-book,* 145. As she writes in her *Incidents in the Life of a Slave Girl,* Harriet Jacobs felt compelled to write publicly about her experience. In another important way, *Incidents*

shares similarities with anti-Catholic narratives: efforts by a slave girl to gain her freedom, to risk life to escape the clutches of a lustful owner, and her desire to be a true woman and mother.

93. Bourne, *Text-book,* 356.

94. Bourne, *Illustrations of Popery,* 438.

95. Ray Allen Billington, *The Protestant Crusade, 1800–1860: A Study of the Origins of American Nativism* (Gloucester, MA: Peter Smith, 1963 [1938]), 90.

96. Dale Light, *Rome and the New Republic: Conflict and Community in Philadelphia Catholicism between the Revolution and the Civil War* (Notre Dame, IN: University of Notre Dame Press, 1996), 105.

97. Bourne, *Lectures on the Progress,* 412.

98. *New York Observer,* August 14, 1824; Oct. 20, 1827; *Church Register,* June 6, 1829; *Episcopal Recorder,* June 25, 1831; *The Protestant,* January 9, 1830; *Christian Watchman,* April 6, 1832; *Observer,* July 12, 1834; August 14, 1830; July 16, 1831; *Massachusetts Yeoman,* April 17, 1830. *National Protestant* quote on page 370 of Ray Allen Billington's "Anti-Catholic Propaganda and the Home Missionary Movement, 1800–1860," *Mississippi Valley Historical Review* 22, no. 3 (December 1935): 361–84.

99. Bourne, *Text-book,* 272.

100. Light, *Rome and the New Republic,* 106.

101. Bourne, *Text-book,* 432–33.

102. Hamburger, *Separation of Church and State,* 202. Hamburger, along with Richard Carwardine and Tracy Fessenden, does well in opening up the issue of the changing meanings of the church and state relationship, showing in particular how the demand for severing the two institutions became in the 1830s a fundamental Protestant ideal. Fessenden likewise shows how the church-state debates do not suggest, as they do today, a battle between religion and irreligion or a contest between a sacred and secular order. Rather, unlike modern fundamentalists who view the battles between church and state as signifying an ominous portend of ungodly secularism, the separation between church and state has always been shaped within a Protestant interpretive framework.

103. Carwardine, *Evangelical Politics,* 83.

104. Along with the various Catholic newspapers, one publication that offers a Catholic rejoinder to such accusations comes from the debates between John Breckinridge and John Hughes, *A Discussion: Is the Catholic Religion Inimical to Civil or Religious Liberty? Is the Presbyterian Religion Inimical to Civil or Religious Liberty,* ed. John Hughes (New York: 1836). Perhaps the premier intellectual apologist for American Catholicism, John Hughes cogently showed how certain Protestant doctrines (e.g., Predestination) and practices (e.g., Calvin's condemnation of Servitus for his religious beliefs, not to mention the unwillingness of American Protestants to allow Catholics to worship freely) did in fact undermine the freedom of conscience, religion, and morality and were therefore harmful to the American nation. See also William Jason Wallace, "The Medieval Specter: Catholics, Evangelicals, and the Limits of Political Protestantism" (PhD diss., University of Virginia, 2005), ii.

105. Bourne, *Text-book,* v.

106. Ibid., 31, 240.

107. The battle would be waged in the Mississippi, many nativists predicted. *Observer,* October 15, 1835; December 31, 1835; *New York Observer,* August 14, 1824; Oct. 20, 1827; *Church Register,* June 6, 1829; *Episcopal Recorder,* June 25, 1831; *The Protestant,* January 9, 1830; *Christian Watchman,* April 6, 1832; *Observer,* July 12, 1834; August 14, 1830; July 16, 1831; *Massachusetts Yeoman,* April 17,

1830. *National Protestant* quote on page 370 of Ray Allen Billington's "Anti-Catholic Propaganda and the Home Missionary Movement, 1800–1860," *Mississippi Valley Historical Review* 22, no. 3 (December 1935): 361–84.

108. America was not the only country influenced by the liberalism of Protestantism. The French Revolution was born from the Reformation, but Bourne's intent was to show the uniqueness of American Protestant nationalism. Even after the French Revolution, France continued to struggle against the "popish" conservatism in the post-Napoleonic Europe.

109. Quotation from the *Protestant* in the United States Catholic Miscellany, vol. 9., 75, and cited by Peter Guilday, *The Life and Times of John England, First Bishop of Charleston* (1786–1842), 2 vols. (New York: American Press, 1970), II:221. Emphasis Bourne's.

110. Gilbert H. Barnes and Dwight L. Dumond, eds., *Letters of Theodore Dwight Weld, Angelina Grimké Weld, and Sarah Grimké, 1822–1844* (New York: D. Appleton-Century, 1934), 2:603.

111. Dumond, *Letters of James Birney* (New York: D. Appleton-Century, 1938), 22–23.

112. Phillips quote in John McGreevy, *Catholicism and American Freedom: A History* (New York: W. W. Norton, 2003), 50.

113. Rev. W. H. Furness, "The Outrage at Washington" (May 25, 1856), *National Anti-Slavery Standard,* March 31, 1856.

114. McGreevy, *Catholicism and American Freedom,* 56.

115. *Liberator,* August 25, 1832.

116. Maura Jane Farrelly, *Anti-Catholicism in America, 1620–1860* (Cambridge: Cambridge University Press, 2017), 82.

117. Bourne, *Text-book,* 436–37.

118. Bourne, *Lectures on the Progress,* 335.

119. Ibid., 377.

120. Bourne, *Text-book,* 426.

121. Ibid., 446.

122. Bourne, *Lectures on the Progress,* 433.

123. *Liberator,* March 3, 1832.

CONCLUSION: THE BOURNE LEGACY AND AMERICAN CULTURE

1. *Christian Union,* August 21, 1872, 6–7.

2. "W.E.W.," *The Independent,* November 14, 1861, 2.

3. Theodore Bourne, "Rev. George Bourne: The Pioneer of Antislavery," *Methodist Quarterly Review* (January 1882): 84.

4. Ibid., 90.

5. Tappan quote in Bourne, "Rev. George Bourne," 91.

6. Letter of Theodore Bourne to William Lloyd Garrison," 1858, https://www.digitalcommonwealth.org/search/commonwealth:6h442376h.

7. Theodore Bourne, "Who Lighted the Fires of Freedom?" Letter of Theodore Bourne to William Lloyd Garrison, 1858: https://www.digitalcommonwealth.org/search/commonwealth:cv43qz808.

8. At the time of its publication in 1852, Harriet Beecher Stowe's *Uncle Tom's Cabin* became

the most popular literary work in antebellum America, selling more than 300,000 copies in its first year, second only in sales to the Bible. What is not widely known, however, is that *Uncle Tom's Cabin* had displaced Maria Monk's erstwhile bestselling *Awful Disclosures of the Hotel Dieu Nunnery.* Indeed, *Awful Disclosures* was later dubbed the "Uncle Tom's Cabin of American nativism." O. R. Butler, "The Uncle Tom's Cabin of Nativism: Anti-Catholic Novels, Politics and Violence in the Antebellum United States," *Working with English: Medieval and Modern Language, Literature and Drama* 2, no. 1 (2006): 12–19.

9. George Bourne, *The Book and Slavery Irreconcilable, with Animadversions against Samuel Stanhope Smith* (Philadelphia: J. M. Sanderson & Co., 1816), 87.

10. *New York Observer,* December 27, 1834.

11. Ibid.

12. Joseph Berg, *The Confessional; or, an Exposition of the Doctrine of Auricular Confession as Taught in the Standards of the Romish Church,* 3rd ed. (Philadelphia, 1841), 75.

13. *Letters of William Lloyd Garrison,* vol. 6, 273.

14. *Genius of Universal Emancipation.* Reprinted in *The Liberator,* August 25, 1832.

15. Sarah Grimké, "An Epistle to the Clergy of the Southern States" (1836), in Kenneth Zanca ed., *American Catholics and Slavery: 1789–1866: An Anthology of Primary Documents* (Lanham, MD: University Press of America, 1994).

16. Charles Wilbanks, ed., *Walking by Faith: The Diary of Angelina Grimké, 1828–1835* (Columbia: University of South Carolina Press, 2003), 55.

17. C. C. Goen, *Broken Churches, Broken Nation: Denominational Schisms and the Coming of the American Civil War* (Macon, GA: Mercer University Press, 1985), 6.

18. "William Oland Bourne Papers," *https://blogs.loc.gov/loc/2016/06/new-online-william-oland-bourne-papers/.* W. O. Bourne was also the author of *History of the Public School Society of the City of New York* (1870) and a host of works of children's literature including *Little Silverstring: Tales and Poems for the Young* (1853); *Goldenlink: Tales and Poems for the Young* (1854).

19. William Oland Bourne, "Never Say I Can't, My Dear," https://hymnary.org/text/never_say_i_cant_my_dear.

20. "Letter from Theodore Bourne," c. 1898, https://www.digitalcommonwealth.org/search/commonwealth:cv43r940j.

21. Letter from Garrison's son to Theodore in 1899, "Photocopies re: Bourne family," Bourne Family Papers 2(42), Munger Research Center, Huntington Library, San Marino, CA.

22. Bruce Clayton, *Forgotten Prophet: The Life of Randolph Bourne* (Columbia: University of Missouri Press, 1984), 7; Bourne Family Papers, Munger Research Center, Huntington Library, San Marino, CA, https://oac.cdlib.org/findaid/ark:/13030/c8cv4pdq/entire_text/.

23. Randolph Bourne, *Untimely Papers,* ed. with foreword by James Oppenheim (New York: B. W. Huebsch, 1919), 145.

24. Ibid., 152.

25. Ibid., 171.

26. David Blight, "Preface: Solidarity of the Ages," in *Human Bondage and Abolition: New Histories of Past and Present Slaveries,* ed. Elizabeth Swanson and James Brewer Stewart (Cambridge: Cambridge University Press, 2018), xviii.

27. Elizabeth Swanson and James Brewer Stewart, *Human Bondage and Abolition: New Histories of Past and Present Slaveries* (Cambridge: Cambridge University Press, 2018).

28. Zoe Trodd, Kevin Bales, and Alex Kent Williamson, *Modern Slavery: A Beginners Guide* (Oxford: Oneworld Publications, 2011).

29. Sheldon Wolin, *Democracy Inc.: Managed Democracy and the Specter of Inverted Totalitarianism* (Princeton, NJ: Princeton University Press, 2008), 8.

30. Schlesinger quote in John Tracy Ellis, *American Catholicism* (Chicago: University of Chicago Press, 1969), 151.

31. Mark Massa, *Anti-Catholicism in America: The Last Acceptable Prejudice* (New York: Crossroads Publications, 2005); Philip Jenkins, *The New Anti-Catholicism: The Last Acceptable Prejudice* (New York: Oxford University Press, 2004).

32. Ellis, *American Catholicism,* 105.

33. Maura Jane Farrelly, *Anti-Catholicism in America, 1620–1860* (Cambridge: Cambridge University Press, 2017), 2.

34. Elizabeth Fenton, *Religious Liberties: Anti-Catholicism and Liberal Democracy in Nineteenth Century U.S. Literature and Culture* (New York: Oxford University Press, 2011), 143.

35. Paul Blanshard, *American Freedom and Catholic Power* (Boston: Beacon, 1951), 56–57.

36. Jenkins, *Anti-Catholicism,* 193.

37. Farrelly, *Anti-Catholicism in America,* epilogue.

38. Jenkins, *Anti-Catholicism,* 193.

39. Farrelly, *Anti-Catholicism in America,* epilogue.

40. Molly Worthen, "A Match Made in Heaven: Why Conservative Evangelicals Have Lined Up behind Trump," *The Atlantic,* May 2017.

41. Ibid. See also Molly Worthen's *Apostles of Reason: The Crisis of Authority in American Higher Education* (New York: Oxford University Press, 2013).

42. Cassandra Yacavozzi, *Escaped Nuns: True Womanhood and the Campaign against Convents in Antebellum America* (New York: Oxford, 2018), 143.

43. https://www.wgrz.com/article/news/local/catholic-priest-says-theres-a-stigma-against-clergy/71-d7498af3-f77e-4d4e-8e23-fa68bec14f4b.

44. Mark Clayton, "Sex Abuse Spans Spectrum of Churches," *Christian Science Monitor,* April 5, 2002, https://www.csmonitor.com/2002/0405/p01s01-ussc.html; Andrew Brown, "Catholic Child Abuse in Proportion," *The Guardian,* opinion, March 11, 2010, https://www.theguardian.com/commentisfree/andrewbrown/2010/mar/11/catholic-abuse-priests; Electa Draper, "Scandal Creates Contempt for Catholic Clergy," *Denver Post,* May 25, 2010, http://blogs.denverpost.com/hark/2010/05/25/scandal-creates-contempt-for-catholic-clergy/39/.

45. Pat Wingert, "Priests Commit No More Abuse Than Other Males," *Newsweek,* April 7, 2010, https://www.newsweek.com/priests-commit-no-more-abuse-other-males-70625.

46. Maureen Mullarky, "Why Anti-Catholicism Will Rise," *The Federalist,* March 1, 2016, http://thefederalist.com/2016/03/01/why-anti-catholicism-will-rise/. Although anti-Catholicism may be on the rise, it does not seem to be connected to a crisis of immigration. In other words, the rejuvenation of this underlying prejudice is not appearing in tandem with similar conditions found in the nineteenth century.

47. Jenkins, *Anti-Catholicism,* 215.

48. Ibid., 84.

49. Farrelly, *Anti-Catholicism in America.*

BIBLIOGRAPHY

WORKS BY GEORGE BOURNE

An Address to the Presbyterian Church, Enforcing the Duty of Excluding All Slaveholders from the "Communion of Saints." New York: n.p., 1833.

The American Text-book of Popery: Being an Authentic Compend of the Bulls, Canons, Decretals of the Roman Hierarchy. Philadelphia: Griffith and Simon, 1846.

The Book and Slavery Irreconcilable, with Animadversions against Samuel Stanhope Smith. Philadelphia: J. M. Sanderson & Co., 1816.

The Case of Baptis Irvin in a Matter of Contempt of Court. Baltimore: Printed for the reporter by S. Magill, 1808.

A Condensed Anti-Slavery Bible Argument, by a Citizen of Virginia. New York: S. W. Benedict, 1845.

The History of Napoleon Bonaparte: Emperor of the French, and King of Italy. Baltimore, Warner and Hanna, 1806.

Illustrations of Popery: The "Mystery of Iniquity" Unveiled. New York: J. P. Callender, 1838.

Lectures on the Progress and Perfection of the Church of Christ. Mount Pleasant, NY: R. W. Knight, 1823.

The Life of the Rev. John Wesley with Memoirs of the Wesley Family, to Which Are Subjoined, Dr. Whitehead's Funeral Sermons, and a Comprehensive History of American Methodism. Baltimore: Dobbin and Murphy, 1807.

Lorette: A History of Louise, Daughter of a Canadian Nun, Exhibiting the Interior of Female Convents. New York: Charles Small, 1833.

Man-stealing and Slavery by the Presbyterian and Methodist Churches: Together with an Address to All the Churches. New York: Garrison and Knapp, 1834.

Marriage Indissoluble and Divorce Unscriptural. Harrisonburg, VA: Davidson and Bourne, 1813.

Picture of Quebec and Its Vicinity. Quebec: P. and W. Ruthven, 1831.

Picture of Slavery in the United States of America. Middleton, CT: E. Hunt, 1834.

Sermon on the Majesty and Condescension of God: Delivered at the Opening of the Presbyterian Church in Port Republic on Christmas Day, 1812. Staunton, VA: Isaac Collett, 1812.

Slavery Illustrated in Its Effects on Woman and Domestic Society. Boston: Isaac Knapp, 1837.

The Spirit of the Public Journals, or Beauties of the American Newspapers. Baltimore: Dobbin and Murphy, 1805.

Validity of the Methodist Episcopacy. Baltimore: George Dobbin and Murphy, for John Hagerty, 1807.

The Virtuous Woman: A Sermon, Delivered at Mount-Pleasant. New York: Stephen Marshall, 1820.

PRIMARY SOURCES

Archival Sources

Bourne Family Papers, Huntington Library, Munger Research Center, San Marino, California

Early American Imprints series (UCI)

Historical Society of Pennsylvania, Gratz Collection

McCormick Theological Seminary (University of Chicago)

Presbyterian Historical Society (Philadelphia)

William L. Clemens Library (University of Michigan)

Periodicals

American Protestant Vindicator

Baltimore Evening Post

Boston Recorder

Christian Examiner

Christian Intelligencer

Christian Observer

Freedom's Journal

Liberator

Magazine of the Reformed Dutch Church

National Anti-slavery Standard

National Era

National Magazine

Native American

New York Evangelist

New York Observer

North Star
Pilot (Boston)
Protestant
Richmond Dispatch
Southern Standard
United States Catholic Intelligencer
United States Magazine

Books

Abbott, John. *The Mother at Home; or, the Principles of Maternal Duty Familiarly Illustrated.* Revised and corrected by Daniel Walton. London: John Mason, 1834. Reprint, New York: Arno Press, 1972.

Acts and Proceedings of the General Assembly of the Presbyterian Church in the United States of America, 1794. Philadelphia: Aitken and Son, 1794.

Allen, William. *The Philanthropist: Or Repository for Hints and Suggestions. London.* VI, 1816.

American Anti-Slavery Society [AASS]. *First Annual Report.* New York, 1834.

Austin, Samuel. "A Sermon Preached in Worcester Massachusetts on the Occasion of the Special Fast, July 23, 1812." Worcester, MA, July 23, 1812.

Balch, William Stevens. *Romanism and Republicanism Incompatible.* New York: Dewitt & Davenport, 1852.

Barnes, Albert. *An Inquiry Into the Scriptural Views of Slavery.* Philadelphia: Perkins and Purves, 1846.

Barrow, David. *Involuntary, Unmerited, Perpetual, Absolute, Hereditary Slavery, Examined; on the Principles of Nature, Reason, Justice, Policy and Scripture.* Lexington, KY, 1808.

Beecher, Catherine, and Harriet Beecher Stowe, *The American Woman's Home, or Principles of Domestic Science.* New York: J. B. Ford and Company, 1870.

Beecher, Edward. *The Papal Conspiracy Exposed, and Protestantism Defended, in the Light of Reason, History, and Scripture.* Boston, 1855.

Beecher, Lyman. *Autobiography and Correspondence.* Edited by Charles Beecher. 2 vols. New York: Harper, 1865.

———. *A Plea to the West.* Cincinnati: Truman and Smith, 1835.

Berg, Joseph F. *The Confessional; or, An Exposition of the Doctrine of Auricular Confession as Taught in the Standards of the Romish Church.* 3rd ed. Philadelphia, 1841.

———. *The Great Apostacy, Identical with Papal Rome: or, An Exposition of the Mystery of Iniquity, and the Marks and Doom of Antichrist.* Philadelphia, 1842.

Birney, James Gillespie. *The American Churches: The Bulwarks of American Slavery.* New York: Arno, 1969.

———. *Letters on Slavery.* New York: S. W. Benedict & Co, 1834.

Bourne, Theodore. "George Bourne, the Pioneer of American Antislavery." *Methodist Quarterly Review* LXIV (January 1882): 71–92.

Brooks, Erastus. *Controversy Between Senator Brooks and John, Archbishop of New York: Growing Out of the Speech of Senator Brooks on the Church Property Bill.* New York: DeWitt and Davenport, 1855.

Brown, Isaac Van Arsdale. *Memoirs of the Reverend Robert Finley.* New Brunswick, NJ: Terhune and Letson, 1819.

Brown, William. "Religious Organizations and Slavery." *Oberlin Quarterly Review* (October 1849): 435.

Calvin, John. *Institutes of the Christian Religion.* Edited by John McNeill. Translated by Ford Lewis Battles. Philadelphia: Westminster Press, 1960.

Channing, William Ellery. *Conversations in Rome: Between and Artist, a Catholic, and a Critic.* Boston: William Crosby and H. P. Nichols, 1847.

———. *A Sermon Preached in Boston, April 5, 1810, the Day of the Public Fast.* Boston: J. Elliot, 1810.

———. *Slavery.* 1835. Reprint, New York: Arno Press, 1969.

Cheever, George. *The Fire and Hammer of God's Word against the Sin of Slavery.* New York: American Abolitionist Society, 1858.

———. *God against Slavery.* Cincinnati: American Reform Tract and Book Society, 1857.

———. "The New York Tribune and the Bible in Schools." *Independent,* March 19, 1854.

———. *The Right of Our Bible in Our Public Schools.* New York, 1854.

———. *Wanderings of a Pilgrim in the Shadow of Mont Blanc.* New York, 1846.

Colton, Calvin. *Protestant Jesuitism. By a Protestant.* New York: Harper and Brothers, 1836.

The Constitution of the Presbyterian Church in the United States of America, Containing the Confession of Faith, The Catechisms, and the Directory for the Worship of God: Together with the Plan of Government and Discipline as Amended and Ratified by the General Assembly at Their Sessions in May 1805. Philadelphia, 1806.

Craft, William and Ellen. *A Thousand Miles for Freedom: Or, the Escape of William and Ellen Craft From Slavery.* London: William Tweedie, 1860.

Cramp, J. M. *A Textbook of Popery.* New York: D. Appleton, 1831.

Cross, Andrew B. *Priests' Prisons for Women.* Baltimore, 1854.

Douglass, Frederick. *Frederick Douglass Papers.* Vol. 1–5. New Haven, CT: Yale University Press, 1999.

Dowling, John. *The History of Romanism: From the Earliest Corruption of Christianity to the Present Time. New York: E. Walker, 1845.*

Dwight, Theodore. *Open Convents: or, Nunneries and Popish Seminaries Dangerous to the*

Morals, and Degrading to the Character of a Republican Community. New York: Van Nostrand and Dwight, 1836.

Elliot, Charles. *The Bible and Slavery.* Cincinnati: L. Swormstedt and A. Poe, 1857.

———. *Sinfulness of American Slavery.* Cincinnati: L. Swormstedt and A. Poe, 1851.

Farrand, William, ed., *General Assembly's Missionary Magazine, Evangelical Intelligencer for 1805.* Philadelphia: William Farrand, 1806.

Fitzhugh, George. *Cannibals All, or Slaves Without Masters.* Richmond, VA: A. Morris, 1857.

Foster, Eden. *The Rights of the Pulpit, and the Perils of Freedom: Two Discourses Preached in Lowell.* 1854.

Furman, Richard. *Conversion Essential to Salvation: A Sermon Preached at the First Presbyterian Church in S.C., before the Religious Tract Society, June 10, 1816.* Charleston, SC: J. Hoff, 1816.

Garrison, William Lloyd. *The Letters of William Lloyd Garrison: From Disunionism to the Brink of War, 1850–1860.* Edited by Louis Ruchames. vols. 1–6. Cambridge: Belknap Press, 1975.

———. *Thoughts on African Colonization.* New York: Arno, 1969.

Gavin, Anthony. *The Great Red Dragon: or, The Master-Key to Popery.* New York, 1856.

Grimké, Angelina. *Appeal to the Christian Women of the South.* New York: American Anti-Slavery Society, 1836.

Hegel, G. W. F. *Hegel: The Letters.* Translated by Clark Butler and Christiane Seiler. Bloomington: Indiana University Press, 1985.

———. *Outlines of the Philosophy of Right.* New York: Oxford University Press, 2008.

Henry, Stuart. *Unvanquished Puritan: A Portrait of Lyman Beecher.* Grand Rapids, MI: Eerdmans, 1973.

Hogan, William. *Popery! As It Was and as It Is: Auricular Confession.* Hartford, 1855.

Hughes John. *Complete Works of the Most Reverend John Hughes.* 2 vols. New York, 1865.

———. *"The Decline of Protestantism and Its Cause": A Lecture Delivered in St. Patrick's Cathedral, November 10, 1850.* New York: Edward Dunigan and Brother, 1860.

———, ed. *A Discussion: Is the Catholic Religion Inimical to Civil or Religious Liberty? Is the Presbyterian Religion Inimical to Civil or Religious Liberty?* New York: De Capo, 1970 [c. 1836].

Jay, William. *An Inquiry Into the Character and Tendency of the American Colonization and the American Anti-Slavery Societies.* New York: Negro Universities Press, 1969.

Jefferson, Thomas. *Notes on the State of Virginia.* Edited with introduction by William Peden. Chapel Hill: University of North Carolina Press, 1996.

Letter from General Harper, of Maryland, to Elias B. Caldwell, Esquire, Secretary of the American Society for Colonizing the Free People of Color, in the United States with Their Own Consent. Baltimore, 1817.

Luke, Jemima Thompson. *The Female Jesuit: The Spy in the Family.* New York: M. W. Dodd, 1851.

Mayhew, Jonathan. *Popish Idolatry: A Discourse.* Boston: R. and S. Draper, 1765.

McCarthy, Timothy Patrick, and John Campbell McMillian. *Radical Reader.* New York: New Press, 2011.

McLeod, John. *Protestantism, the Parent Guardian of Civil and Religious Liberty.* New York: Carter, 1843.

McNeile, Hugh. *Anti-Slavery and Anti-Popery: A Letter Addressed to Edward Copper, Esquire, and Thomas Berry Horsfall, Esquire.* London, 1838.

Minutes of the General Assembly of the Presbyterian Church in the United States of America From Its Organization, 1789–1820. Philadelphia: Presbyterian Board of Publications, 1847.

Minutes of the General Assembly of the Presbyterian Church in the United States of America, 1816, 1817, 1818. Philadelphia: Thomas and William Bradford, 1816, 1817, 1818.

Monk, Maria. *Awful Disclosures of the Hotel Dieu Nunnery.* New York: Published by Maria Monk, 1836.

Morse, Samuel F. B. *Foreign Conspiracy against the Liberties of the United States.* New York: Leavitt, Lord, and Company, 1835.

Murray, Nicholas. *"The Decline of Popery and Its Causes": An Address Delivered in the Broadway Tabernacle on January 15, 1851.* New York: Harper and Brothers, 1851.

———. *Romanism at Home. Letters to the Hon. Roger B. Taney, Chief Justice of the United States.* 6th ed. New York: Harper and Brothers, 1852.

Nevins, William. *Thoughts on Popery.* 1836. Reprint, New York: Arno Press, 1977.

Parker, Theodore. "A Sermon of the Dangers Which Threaten the Rights of Man in America" (July 2, 1854), in *Additional Speeches, Addresses, and Occasional Sermons,* vol. 2. Boston: Little, Brown and Company, 1855.

"The Philosophy of Conversion." *Catholic World* 4, no. 22 (1867).

Pope or President? Startling Disclosures of Romanism as Revealed by Its Own Writers. 1859. Reprint, New York: Arno Press, 1979.

"Popery and Our Common Schools." *National Magazine* 3 (July–December 1853).

"The Priest—the Wife—the Family." *United States Magazine* 17 (1846).

Proceedings of the Anti-Slavery Convention of American Women, held in the City of New York, May 9th, 10th, 11th, and 12th, 1837. New York: William S. Dorr, 1837.

Reese, David Meredith. *Humbugs of New-York: Being a Remonstrance against Popular Delusion; Whether in Science, Philosophy, or Religion.* New York: John S. Taylor, Brick Church Chapel; and Boston: Weeks, Jordan and Company, 1838.

Reynolds, Ignatius, ed. *The Works of the Right Reverend John England.* Baltimore: John Murphy and Company, 1849.

Ricci, Scipio de. *Female Convents. Secrets of Nunneries Disclosed.* New York, 1834.

Rice, David. *A Kentucky Protest against Slavery. New York: Samuel Wood, 1812.*

Robinson, Robert. *Slavery Inconsistent with the Spirit of Christianity.* Cambridge, 1788.

Schaff, Philip. *Principles of Protestantism.* Chambersburg, PA: "Publication Office" of the German Reformed Church, 1845.

Scott, Walter. *The Life of Napoleon Bonaparte, Emperor of the French. With a Preliminary View of the French Revolution.* 9 vols. Edinburgh: Ballantyne and Co. for Longman, Rees, Orme, Brown, & Green, London; and Cadell & Co., Edinburgh, 1827.

Smith, Gerrit. *Sermons and Speeches.* New York: Arno Press, 1969.

Smith, Samuel Stanhope. *A Comprehensive View of the Reading and Most Important Elements of Natural and Revealed Religion.* New Brunswick, NJ: Deare and Myer, 1816.

———. *An Essay on the Causes of the Variety of Complexion and Figure in the Human Species.* Edited by Winthrop Jordan. Cambridge: Belknap Press, 1965.

Sparry, C. *Papacy in the Nineteenth Century; or, Popery—What It Is, What It Aims at, and What It Is Doing.* New York: C. Sparry, 1846.

Stenhouse, Frances. *A Lady's Life Among the Mormons.* New York, 1872.

Stuart, Moses. *Conscience and Constitution.* Boston: Crocker and Brewster, 1850.

Warfield, Benjamin Breckinridge. *The Westminster Assembly and Its Work.* In *The Works of Benjamin Breckinridge Warfield,* vol. VI. Ada, MI: Baker, 1932.

Weld, Theodore D. *American Slavery as It Is: Testimony of a Thousand Witnesses.* New York: Arno, 1839.

———. *The Bible against Slavery.* New York: American Anti-Slavery Society, 1838.

Westminster Assembly of Divines. *The Confession of Faith, together with the Larger Catechism.* Boston: Kneeland for Henchman, 1723.

Whately, Richard. *Essays: Errors of Romanism, Having Their Origin in Human Nature.* London: John W. Parker and Son, 1830.

White, Joseph Blanco. *A Letter to Protestants Converted from Romanism.* Oxford: W. Baxter, 1827.

Wolff, George D. "The Mercersburg Movement: An Attempt to Find Ground on Which Protestantism and Catholicity Might Be United." *American Catholic Quarterly Review* 3 (1878).

SECONDARY SOURCES

Books

Abruzzo, Margaret. *Polemical Pain: Slavery, Cruelty, and the Rise of Humanitarianism.* Baltimore: Johns Hopkins University Press, 2011.

Abzug, Robert H. *Cosmos Crumbling: American Reform and the Religious Imagination.* New York: Oxford University Press, 1994.

———. *Passionate Liberator: Theodore Dwight Weld and the Dilemma of Reform.* New York: Oxford University Press, 1980.

Allodi, Mary Macauley, and Rosemarie L. Tovell. *An Engraver's Pilgrimage: James Smillie in Quebec, 1821–1830.* Ontario: Royal Ontario Museum, 1989.

Anbinder, Tyler. *Nativism and Slavery: The Northern Know-Nothings and the Politics of the 1850s.* New York: Oxford University Press, 1992.

Anderson, Benedict. *Imagined Communities: Reflections on the Origin and Spread of Nationalism.* London: Verso, 1991.

Andrews, Dee. *The Methodists and Revolutionary America, 1760–1800: The Shaping of an Evangelical Culture.* Princeton, NJ: Princeton University Press, 2000.

Appleby, Joyce. *Inheriting the Revolution: The First Generation of Americans.* Cambridge, MA: Belknap Press, 2000.

———. *Liberalism and Republicanism in the Historical Imagination.* Cambridge, MA: Harvard University Press, 1992.

Aptheker, Herbert. *Abolitionism: A Revolutionary Movement.* Boston: Twayne Publishers, 1989.

Baldwin, Lou. "Pious Prejudice: Catholicism and the American Press over Three Centuries." In *Anti-Catholicism in American Culture,* ed. Robert Lockwood. Washington DC: Center for Media and Public Affairs, 2000.

Bailyn, Bernard. *The Ideological Origins of the American Revolution.* Cambridge, MA: Belknap Press, 1967.

Barnes, Gilbert. *The Antislavery Impulse, 1830–1844.* 1933; rpr. New York: Harcourt Brace & World, 1964.

Barnes, Gilbert H., and Dwight L. Dumond, eds. *Letters of Theodore Dwight Weld, Angelina Grimké Weld, and Sarah Grimké, 1822–1844.* Vol. 2. New York: D. Appleton-Century, 1934.

Bebbington, David. *Evangelicalism in Modern Britain: A History from 1730s to the 1980s.* London: Routledge, 1989.

Bernstein, Susan David. *Confessional Subjects: Revelations of Gender and Power in Victorian Literature and Culture.* Chapel Hill: University of North Carolina Press, 1997.

Billington, Ray Allen. *The Origins of Nativism in the United States, 1800–1840.* New York: Arno Press, 1974.

———. *The Protestant Crusade, 1800–1860: A Study of the Origins of American Nativism.* Gloucester, MA: Peter Smith, 1963 [1938].

Blanshard, Paul. *American Freedom and Catholic Power.* Boston: Beacon, 1951.

Bloch, Ruth. *Visionary Republic: Millennial Themes in American Thought, 1756–1800.* Cambridge: Cambridge University Press, 1985.

Blue, Frederick. *No Taint of Compromise: Crusaders in Antislavery Politics.* Baton Rouge: Louisiana State University Press, 2005.

Bochen, Christine M. "Personal Narratives by Nineteenth-Century American Catholics: A Study in Conversion Literature." PhD dissertation, Catholic University of America, 1980.

Bourne, Randolph. *Untimely Papers.* Edited with foreword by James Oppenheim. New York: B. W. Huebsch, 1919.

Boyd, Lois, and R. Douglas Brackenridge. *Presbyterian Women in America: Two Centuries of a Quest for Status.* Westport, CT: Presbyterian Historical Society, Greenwood Press, 1983.

Boydston, Jeanne, Mary Kelley, and Ann Margolis. *The Limits of Sisterhood: The Beecher Sisters on Women's Rights and Women's Spheres.* Chapel Hill: University of North Carolina Press, 1988.

Brown, Jerry Wayne. *The Rise of Biblical Criticism in America, 1800–1870.* Middletown, CT: Wesleyan University Press, 1969.

Browne, Stephen Howard. *Angelina Grimké: Rhetoric, Identity, and the Radical Imagination.* East Lansing: Michigan State University Press, 1999.

Bruce, Dickson Jr. *Earnestly Contending: Religious Freedom and Pluralism in Antebellum America.* Charlottesville: University of Virginia Press, 2013.

———. *Rhetoric of Conservatism: The Virginia Convention of 1829–30 and the Conservative Tradition in the South.* San Marino, CA: Huntington Library, 1982.

Burin, Eric. *Slavery and the Peculiar Solution.* Gainesville: University of Florida Press, 2005.

Butler, Jon. *Awash in a Sea of Faith.* Cambridge, MA: Harvard University Press, 1990.

Cain, William E., ed. *William Lloyd Garrison and the Fight to End Slavery: Selections from* The Liberator. Boston: Bedford Books of St. Martin's Press, 1995.

Calhoun, Craig. *The Roots of Radicalism: Tradition, the Public Sphere, and Early Nineteenth-Century Social Movements.* Chicago: University of Chicago Press, 2012.

Carey, Patrick W. *Catholics in America: A History.* Westport, CT: Praeger, 2004.

Carwardine, Richard. *Evangelicals and Politics in Antebellum America.* New Haven, CT: Yale University Press, 1993.

Casper, Scott. *Constructing American Lives: Biography and Culture in Nineteenth-Century America.* Chapel Hill: University of North Carolina Press, 1999.

Christie, John W., and Dwight L. Dumond. *George Bourne and "The Book and Slavery Irreconcilable."* Wilmington: Historical Society of Delaware, 1969.

Claydon, Tony, and Ian McBride. *Protestantism and National Identity: Britain and Ireland, 1650–1850.* Cambridge: Cambridge University Press, 1998.

Clayton, Bruce. *Forgotten Prophet: The Life of Randolph Bourne.* Columbia: University of Missouri Press, 1984.

Colley, Linda. *Britons.* New Haven, CT: Yale University Press, 1992.

Conkin, Paul K. *The Uneasy Center: Reformed Christianity in Antebellum America.* Chapel Hill: University of North Carolina Press, 1995.

Cotlar, Seth. *Tom Paine's America: The Rise and Fall of Transatlantic Radicalism in the Early Republic.* Charlottesville: University of Virginia Press, 2017.

Cott, Nancy. *The Bonds of Womanhood: "Woman's Sphere" in New England, 1780–1835.* New Haven, CT: Yale University Press, 1977.

Cross, Whitney. *The Burned-Over District: The Social and Intellectual History of Enthusiastic Religion in New York.* Ithaca, NY: Cornell University Press, 1982.

Cutter, Martha. *The Illustrated Slave: Empathy, Graphic Narrative, and the Visual Culture of the Transatlantic Abolition Movement, 1800–1852.* Athens: University of Georgia Press, 2017.

Daly, John. *When Slavery was Called Freedom: Evangelicalism, Proslavery, and the Causes of the Civil War.* Lexington: University Press of Kentucky, 2002.

Davidson, Cathy. *Revolution of the Word: The Rise of the Novel in America.* New York: Oxford University Press, 1986.

Davidson, James West. *The Logic of Millennial Thought.* New Haven, CT: Yale University Press, 1977.

Davis, David Brion. *Inhuman Bondage: The Rise and Fall of Slavery in the New World.* New York: Oxford University Press, 2006.

———. *The Problem of Slavery in the Age of Emancipation. New York: Alfred A. Knopf, 2014.*

———. *The Problem of Slavery in the Age of Revolution, 1770–1823.* Oxford: Oxford University Press, 1999.

———. *The Slave Power Conspiracy and the Paranoid Style.* Baton Rouge: Louisiana State University Press, 1969.

Davis, Hugh. *Joshua Leavitt: Evangelical Abolitionist.* Baton Rouge: Louisiana State University Press, 1990.

DeCaro, Louis A. Jr. *"Fire from the Midst of You": A Religious Life of John Brown.* New York: New York University Press, 2002.

Dixon, Chris. *Perfecting the Family: Antislavery Marriages in Nineteenth-Century America.* Amherst: University of Massachusetts Press, 1997.

Dolan, Jay. *The American Catholic Experience: A History From Colonial Times to the Present.* Garden City, NY: Doubleday, 1985.

———. *The Immigrant Church: New York's Irish and German Catholics, 1815–1865.* Baltimore: Johns Hopkins University Press, 1975.

Douglass, Ann. *The Feminization of American Culture.* New York: Avon Books, 1978.

Dublin, Thomas. *Women at Work: The Transformation of Work and Community in Lowell, Mass., 1826–1860.* New York: Columbia University Press, 1993.

Dumond, Dwight L. *Antislavery: The Crusade for Freedom in America.* Ann Arbor: University of Michigan Press, 1961.

———. *Letters of James Birney.* New York: D. Appleton-Century, 1938.

Duncan, Jason. *Citizens or Papists? The Politics of Anti-Catholicism in New York, 1685–1821.* New York: Fordham University Press, 2005.

Dwyer, Philip. *Citizen Emperor: Napoleon in Power, 1799–1815.* London: Bloomsbury, 2013.

———. *Napoleon: The Path to Power, 1769–1799.* London: Bloomsbury, 2008.

Elbert, Monika. *Separate Spheres No More: Gender Convergence in American Literature, 1830–1930.* Tuscaloosa: University of Alabama Press, 2000.

Ellis, John Tracy. *American Catholicism.* Chicago: University of Chicago Press, 1969.

Epstein, Barbara L. *The Politics of Domesticity: Women, Evangelism, and Temperance in Nineteenth-Century America.* Middletown, CT: Wesleyan University Press, 1981.

Ericson, David. *The Debate Over Slavery: Antislavery and Proslavery Liberalism in Antebellum America.* New York: New York University Press, 2000.

Essig, James. *The Bonds of Wickedness: Evangelicals against Slavery, 1770–1808.* Philadelphia: Temple University Press, 1982.

Eustace, Nicole, and Frederika Teute. *Warring for America: Cultural Contests in the Era of 1812.* Chapel Hill: University of North Carolina Press, 2017.

Evans, Sara M., and Harry C. Boyte. *Free Spaces: The Sources of Democratic Change in America.* Chicago: University of Chicago Press, 1992.

Fanuzzi, Robert. *The Abolitionist's Public Sphere.* Minneapolis: University of Minnesota Press, 2003.

Farrelly, Maura Jane. *Anti-Catholicism in America, 1620–1860.* Cambridge: Cambridge University Press, 2017.

Fay, Terrence. *A History of Canadian Catholics.* Montreal: McGill-Queen's University Press, 2002.

Felder, Cain Hope, ed. *Stony the Road We Trod: African American Biblical Interpretation.* Minneapolis: Augsburg Press, 1991.

Fehrenbacher, Don E. *The Slaveholding Republic: An Account of the United States Government's Relations to Slavery.* New York: Oxford University Press, 2011.

Fenton, Elizabeth. *Religious Liberties: Anti-Catholicism and Liberal Democracy in Nineteenth-Century U.S. Literature and Culture.* New York: Oxford University Press, 2011.

Fessenden, Tracy. *Culture and Redemption: Religion, the Secular, and American Literature.* Princeton, NJ: Princeton University Press, 2007.

Fitzgerald, Frances. *The Evangelicals: The Struggle to Shape America.* New York: Simon & Schuster, 2017.

Foner, Eric. *Free Soil, Free Labor, Free Men: The Ideology of the Republican Party before the Civil War.* New York: Oxford University Press, 1995.

———. *Thomas Paine and Revolutionary America.* New York: Oxford University Press, 2005.

Fox-Genovese, Elizabeth, and Eugene Genovese. *The Mind of the Master Class: History and Faith in the Southern Slaveholders' Worldview.* New York: Cambridge University Press, 2005.

Franchot, Jenny. *Roads to Rome: The Antebellum Protestant Encounter with Catholicism.* Berkeley: University of California Press, 1994.

Fraser, James. *Between Church and State: Religion and Public Education in a Multicultural America.* New York: St. Martin's Press, 1999

Frei, Hans F. *The Eclipse of Biblical Narrative: A Study in Eighteenth and Nineteenth-Century Hermeneutics.* New Haven, CT: Yale University Press, 1974.

Friedman, Lawrence, *Gregarious Saints: Self and Community in American Abolitionism.* New York: Cambridge University Press, 1982.

Fuller, Louis. *Crusade Against Slavery, 1820–1860.* Algonac, MI: Reference Publications, 1986.

Furstenberg, François. *When the United States Spoke French: Five Refugees Who Shaped a Nation.* New York: Penguin, 2014.

Gallagher, Catherine, and Thomas Laqueur, eds. *The Making of the Modern Body: Sexuality and Society in the Nineteenth Century.* Berkeley: University of California Press, 1987.

Gilley, Sheridan, and W. J. Shiels, eds. *A History of Religion in Britain.* Cambridge, MA: Wiley-Blackwell, 1994.

Gillis, Chester. *Roman Catholicism in America.* New York: Columbia University Press, 1999.

Gilter, John. *Moses Stuart: The Father of Biblical Science.* Atlanta: Scholars Press, 1988.

Ginzberg, Lori. *Women and the Work of Benevolence: Morality, Politics, and Class in the 19th-Century United States.* New Haven, CT: Yale University Press, 1990.

Goen, C. C. *Broken Churches, Broken Nation: Denominational Schisms and the Coming of the American Civil War.* Macon, GA: Mercer University Press, 1985.

Goodheart, Lawrence. *Abolitionist, Actuary, Atheist: Elizur Wright and the Reform Impulse.* Kent: Ohio State University Press, 1990.

Goodman, Paul. *Of One Blood: Abolitionism and the Origins of Racial Equality.* Berkeley: University of California Press, 1998.

Griffin, Susan M. *Anti-Catholicism and Nineteenth-Century Literature.* Cambridge: Cambridge University Press, 2004.

Guilday, Peter. *The Life and Times of John England, First Bishop of Charleston (1786–1842),* 2 vols. New York: American Press, 1970.

Halttunen, Karen. *Confidence Men and Painted Women: A Study of Middle-Class Culture in America, 1830–1870.* New Haven, CT: Yale University Press, 1982.

Hamburger, Philip. *Separation of Church and State.* Cambridge, MA: Harvard University Press, 2002.

Hammond, Geordan. *Wesley in America: Restoring Primitive Christianity.* New York: Oxford University Press, 2016.

Hansen, Debra. *Strained Sisterhood: Gender and Class in the Boston Female Anti-Slavery Society.* Amherst: University of Massachusetts Press, 1993.

Harrill, J. Albert. *Slaves in the New Testament: Literary, Social, and Moral Dimensions.* Minneapolis, MN: Fortress Press, 2006.

Harrold, Stanley. *The Abolitionists and the South, 1831–1861.* Lexington: University of Kentucky Press, 1995.

Hatch, Nathan. *The Democratization of American Christianity.* New Haven, CT: Yale University Press, 1989.

———. *The Sacred Cause of Liberty: Republican Thought and the Millennium in Revolutionary New England.* New Haven, CT: Yale University Press, 1977.

Hatch, Nathan, and John Wigger. *Methodism and the Shaping of American Culture.* Nashville, TN: Abingdon Press, 2001.

Hawes, Joseph M., and Elizabeth I. Nybakken, eds. *Family and Society in American History.* Urbana: University of Illinois Press, 2001.

Haynes, Stephen R. *Noah's Curse: The Biblical Justification of American Slavery.* New York: Oxford University Press, 2002.

Helminski, Joseph John. "Rome in America: Anti-Catholicism and American Identity in Antebellum Literature." PhD dissertation, Wayne State University, 2001.

Hendrickson, Ford. *The Black Convent Slave: The Climax of Nunnery Exposures, Awful Disclosures: "Uncle Tom's Cabin" of Rome's "Convent Slavery."* Toledo, OH: Protestant Missionary Publishing Company, 1914.

Hennesey, James. *American Catholics: A History of the Roman Catholic Community in the United States.* New York: Oxford University Press, 1981.

Hewitt, Nancy. *Women's Activism and Social Change: Rochester New York, 1822–1872.* Ithaca, NY: Cornell University Press, 1984.

Hinks, Peter. *To Awaken My Afflicted Brethren: David Walker and the Problem of Antebellum Slave Resistance.* University Park: Penn State University Press, 1997.

Hoffert, Sylvia. *Jane Grey Swisshelm: An Unconventional Life, 1815–1884.* Chapel Hill: University of North Carolina Press, 2004.

Hofstadter, Richard. *The Paranoid Style in American Politics and Other Essays.* New York: Alfred A. Knopf, 1965.

Hogeland, William. *The Whiskey Rebellion: George Washington, Alexander Hamilton, and the Frontier Rebels Who Challenged America's New Found Sovereignty.* New York: Simon & Schuster, 2015.

Hole, Robert. *Pulpits, Politics, and Public Order in England, 1760–1832.* Cambridge: Cambridge University Press, 1989.

Holifield, E. Brooks. *Theology in America: Christian Thought from the Age of the Puritans to the Civil War.* New Haven, CT: Yale University Press, 2003.

Howard, Victor. *Conscience and Slavery: The Evangelistic Calvinist Domestic Missions, 1837–1861.* Kent, OH: Kent State University Press, 1990.

Howe, Daniel Walker. *The Political Culture of the American Whigs.* Chicago: University of Chicago Press, 1979.

Israel, Jonathan. *Radical Enlightenment: Philosophy and the Making of Modernity, 1650–1750.* Oxford: Oxford University Press, 2001.

Jabour, Anya. *Marriage in the Early Republic: Elizabeth and William Wirt and the Companionate Ideal.* Baltimore: Johns Hopkins University Press, 1998.

Jeffrey, Julie Roy. *The Great Silent Army of Abolitionism: Ordinary Women in the Antislavery Movement.* Chapel Hill: University of North Carolina Press, 1998.

Johnson, Paul. *Napoleon: A Life.* London: Orion, 2003.

Johnson, Paul E. *The Early American Republic, 1789–1829.* New York: Oxford, 2006.

Jones, Howard M. *American and French Culture, 1750–1848.* Translated by Teresa Wright. Chapel Hill: University of North Carolina Press, 1927.

Juster, Susan. *Disorderly Women: Sexual Politics and Evangelism in Revolutionary New England.* Ithaca, NY: Cornell University Press, 1994.

Kaminski, John P. *Citizen Paine: Thomas Paine's Thoughts on Man, Government, Society, and Religion.* Lanham, MD: Rowman & Littlefield, 2002.

Kelley, Mary. *Private Women, Public Stage: Literary Domesticity in Nineteenth-Century America.* New York: Oxford University Press, 1984.

Lambert, Frank. *Inventing the "Great Awakening."* Princeton, NJ: Princeton University Press, 1999.

Lapsansky-Werner, Emma J., and Margaret Hope Bacon, eds. *Back to Africa: Benjamin Coates and the Colonization Movement in America, 1848–1880.* University Park: Pennsylvania State University Press, 2005.

Lasser, Carol, and Stacey Robertson. *Antebellum Women: Private, Public, Partisan.* Lanham, MD: Rowman & Littlefield, 2010.

Lerner, Gerda. *The Grimké Sisters from South Carolina: Pioneers for Women's Rights and Abolition.* Revised and expanded edition. Chapel Hill: University of North Carolina Press, 2004.

Lesick, Lawrence Thomas. *The Lane Rebels: Evangelicalism and Antislavery in Antebellum America.* Metuchen, NJ: Scarecrow Press, 1980.

Levine, Robert. *Conspiracy and Romance: Studies in Brockden Brown, Cooper, Hawthorne, and Melville.* New York: Cambridge University Press, 1989.

Light, Dale. *Rome and the New Republic: Conflict and Community in Philadelphia Catholicism between the Revolution and the Civil War.* Notre Dame, IN: University of Notre Dame Press, 1996.

Lystra, Karen. *Searching the Heart: Women, Men, and Romantic Love in Nineteenth Century America.* New York: Oxford University Press, 1989.

Mason, Matthew. *Slavery and Politics in the Early Republic.* Chapel Hill: University of North Carolina Press, 2008.

Massa, Mark. *Anti-Catholicism in America: The Last Acceptable Prejudice.* New York: Crossroads Publications, 2005.

Mathews, Donald. *Slavery and Methodism: A Chapter in American Morality, 1780–1845.* Princeton, NJ: Princeton University Press, 1965.

Mayer, Henry. *All on Fire: William Lloyd Garrison and the Abolition of Slavery.* New York: St. Martin's Press, 1998.

McClay, Wilfred M., ed. *Figures in the Carpet: Finding the Human Person in the American Past.* Grand Rapids, MI: Eerdmans, 2007.

McGrath, Alistair. *Reformation Thought: An Introduction.* Cambridge, MA: Blackwell Publishers, 1995.

McGreevy, John. *Catholicism and American Freedom: A History.* New York: W. W. Norton, 2003.

McInerney, Daniel J. *The Fortunate Heirs of Freedom: Abolition and Republican Thought.* Lincoln: University of Nebraska Press, 1994.

McKivigan, John, ed. *Abolitionism and American Religion: History of the American Abolitionist Movement.* New York: Garland Publication, 1999.

———. *The War against Proslavery Religion: Abolitionism and the Northern Churches, 1830–1865.* Ithaca, NY: Cornell University Press, 1984.

McKivigan, John, and Mitchell Snay, eds. *Religion and the Antebellum Debate over Slavery.* Athens: University of Georgia Press, 1998.

Morgan, Edmund. *The Genuine Article: A Historian Looks at Early America.* New York: W. W. Norton, 2005.

Moore, Joseph. *Founding Sins: How a Group of Antislavery Radicals Fought to Put Christ into the Constitution.* New York: Oxford University Press, 2016.

Mott, Frank Luther. *Golden Multitudes: The Story of Bestsellers in America.* New York: MacMillan, 1947.

Murphy, Teresa Ann. *Citizenship and the Origins of Women's History in the United States.* Philadelphia: University of Pennsylvania Press, 2013.

Murray, Andrew. *Presbyterians and the Negro.* Philadelphia: Presbyterian Historical Society, 1966.

———. Review of Bourne's *Book and Slavery Irreconcilable.* In *American Presbyterians* 66, no. 4: 229–33.

Nash, Gary. *Race and Revolution.* Lanham, MD: Madison House, 1990.

Newman, Richard. *The Transformation of American Abolitionism: Fighting Slavery in the Early Republic.* Chapel Hill: University of North Carolina Press, 2002.

Noll, Mark. *America's God: From Jonathan Edwards to Abraham Lincoln.* New York: Oxford University Press, 2002.

———. *The Civil War as a Theological Crisis.* Chapel Hill: University of North Carolina Press, 2006.

———. *History of Christianity in the United States and Canada.* Grand Rapids, MI: Eerdmans, 1992.

———. *The Rise of Evangelicalism: The Age of Edwards, Whitefield, and the Wesleys.* Downers Grove, IL: InterVarsity Press, 2010.

Noll, Mark, David Bebbington, and George Rawlyk, eds. *Evangelicalism: Comparative Studies of Popular Protestantism in North America, the British Isles, and Beyond, 1700–1990.* New York: Oxford University Press, 1994.

Noll, Mark, and Nathan Hatch, eds. *The Bible in America: Essays in Cultural History.* New York: Oxford University Press, 1982.

Nord, David Paul. *Faith in Reading: Religious Publishing and the Birth of Mass Media in America.* New York: Oxford University Press, 2004.

Oshatz, Molly. *Slavery as Sin: The Fight against Slavery and the Rise of Liberal Protestantism.* New York: Oxford University Press, 2011.

Paul, Robert S. *The Assembly of the Lord: Politics and Religion in the Westminster Assembly and the 'Grand Debate.'* Edinburgh: T. & T. Clark, 1985.

Perry, Lewis. *Radical Abolitionism: Anarchy and the Government of God in Antislavery Thought.* Ithaca, NY: Cornell University Press, 1973.

Phillips, Christopher. *Freedom's Port: The African American Community of Baltimore, 1790–1860.* Urbana: University of Illinois Press, 1997.

Pierson, Michael. *Free Hearts and Free Homes: Gender and American Antislavery Politics.* Chapel Hill: University of North Carolina Press, 2003.

Pinkard, Terry. *Hegel: A Biography.* Edinburgh: Cambridge University Press, 2000.

Polasky, Jane. *Revolutions without Borders: The Call to Liberty in the Atlantic World.* New Haven, CT: Yale University Press, 2015.

Popkin, Jeremy. *You Are All Free: The Haitian Revolution and the Abolition of Slavery.* Cambridge: Cambridge University Press, 2010.

Reedy, Gerard, S.J. *The Bible and Reason: Anglicans and Scripture in Late Seventeenth-Century England.* Philadelphia: University of Pennsylvania Press, 1985.

Reynolds, David S. *Faith in Fiction: The Emergence of Religious Literature in America.* Cambridge, MA: Harvard University Press, 1981.

Rice, Alan J., and Martin Crawford, eds. Liberating Sojourn: Frederick Douglass and Transatlantic Reform. Athens: University of Georgia Press, 1999.

Richey, Russell, Kenneth Rowe, and Jean Miller Schmidt. *American Methodism: A Compact History.* Nashville, TN: Abingdon Press, 2012.

Ripley, C. Peter. *The Black Abolitionist Papers.* 5 vols. Chapel Hill: University of North Carolina Press, 1985.

Roberts, Andrew. *Napoleon: A Life.* New York: Penguin, 2015.

Roberts, Kyle. *Evangelical Gotham: Religion and the Making of New York City, 1783–1860.* Chicago: University of Chicago Press, 2016.

Rogers, Jack Bartlett. *Scripture in the Westminster Confession: A Problem of Interpretation for American Presbyterianism.* Grand Rapids, MI: Eerdmans, 1967.

Roy, Jody. *Rhetorical Campaigns of the 19th-Century Anti-Catholics and Catholics in America.* Lewiston, NY: Edwin Mellen Press, 2000.

Royle, Edward, and James Walvin. *English Radicals and Reformers, 1760–1848.* Brighton: Harvester, 1982.

Ryan, Mary. *Cradle of the Middle Class.* New York: Cambridge University Press, 1981.

Salerno, Beth. *Sister Societies: Women's Antislavery Organizations in Antebellum America.* DeKalb: Northern Illinois University Press, 2005.

Sanchez-Eppler, Karen. *Touching Liberty: Abolition, Feminism, and the Politics of the Body.* Berkeley: University of California Press, 1997.

Schom, Alan. *Napoleon Bonaparte: A Life.* London: HarperCollins, 1997.

Schor, Joel. *Henry Highland Garnet: A Voice of Black Republicanism in the 19th Century.* Westport, CT: Greenwood Press, 1977.

Sellers, Charles. *The Market Revolution: Jacksonian America, 1815–1846.* New York: Oxford University Press, 1991.

Shwarz, Philip J. *Slave Laws in Virginia.* Athens: University of Georgia Press, 1996.

Simon, Paul. *Freedom's Champion: Elijah Lovejoy.* Carbondale: Southern Illinois University Press, 1994.

Sinha, Manisha. *The Slave's Cause: A History of Abolition.* New Haven, CT: Yale University Press, 2016.

Skinner, Quentin. *Liberty before Liberalism.* Cambridge: Cambridge University Press, 1998.

Sklar, Kathryn Kish. *Catharine Beecher: A Study in American Domesticity.* New Haven, CT: Yale University Press, 1973.

Smith-Rosenberg, Carroll. *Disorderly Conduct: Visions of Gender in Victorian America.* New York: Oxford University Press, 1985.

Speicher, Anna. *The Religious World of Antislavery Women: Spirituality in the Lives of Five Abolitionist Lecturers.* Syracuse, NY: Syracuse University Press, 2000.

Staudenraus, P. J. *The African Colonization Movement, 1816–1865.* New York: Columbia University Press, 1961.

Stauffer, John. *The Black Hearts of Men: Radical Abolitionists and the Transformation of Race.* Cambridge, MA: Harvard University Press, 2001.

Stendhal [Marie-Henri Beyle]. *A Life of Napoleon.* London: Rodale Press, 1956.

Stewart, James B. *Holy Warriors: The Abolitionists and American Slavery.* New York: Hill and Wang, 1997.

Strong, Douglas. *Perfectionist Politics: Abolitionism and the Religious Tensions of American Democracy.* Syracuse, NY: Syracuse University Press, 1999.

Swanson, Elizabeth, and James Brewer Stewart, eds. *Human Bondage and Abolition: New Histories of Past and Present Slaveries.* Cambridge: Cambridge University Press, 2018.

Sweet, William Warren. *The Story of Religion in America.* 2nd ed. New York: Harper & Brothers, 1950.

Terry, Milton. *Biblical Hermeneutics: A Treatise on the Interpretation of the Old and New Testaments.* Republished, Grand Rapids, MI: Eerdmans, 1974.

Thomas, Arthur Dicken. *The Second Great Awakening and Slavery Reform in Virginia, 1785–1820.* ThD dissertation, Union Theological Seminary, Richmond, VA, 1981.

Tise, Larry. *Proslavery: A History of the Defense of Slavery in America, 1701–1840.* Athens: University of Georgia Press, 1987.

Tompkins, Jane. *Sensational Designs: The Cultural Work of American Fiction, 1790–1860.* New York: Oxford University Press, 1985.

Trodd, Zoe, Kevin Bales, and Alex Kent Williamson. *Modern Slavery: A Beginners Guide.* Oxford: Oneworld Publications, 2011.

Trulard, Jean. *Napoleon: The Myth of the Savior.* London: Routledge, 1985.

Tweed, Thomas A., ed. *Retelling U.S. Religious History.* Berkeley: University of California Press, 1997.

Varacalli, Joseph. *The Catholic Experience in America.* Westport, CT: Greenwood Press, 2006.

Waldsreicher, David. *In the Midst of Perpetual Fetes: The Making of an American Nationalism, 1776–1820.* Chapel Hill: University of North Carolina Press, 1997.

Walker, Peter F. *Moral Choices: Memory, Desire, and Imagination in Nineteenth-Century American Abolition.* Baton Rouge: Louisiana State University Press, 1978.

Walters, Ronald G. *American Reformers, 1815–1860.* New York: Hill and Wang, 1997.

———. *The Antislavery Appeal: American Abolitionism after 1830.* Baltimore: Johns Hopkins University Press, 1976.

Walvin, James. *Making the Black Atlantic.* London: Cassell, 2000.

Warner, William. *At Peace with All Their Neighbors: Catholics and Catholicism in the National Capital, 1787–1860.* Washington, DC: Georgetown University Press, 1994.

Welter, Barbara. *Dimity Convictions: The American Woman in the Nineteenth Century.* Athens: Ohio University Press, 1976.

Whitman, Stephen. *Challenging Slavery in the Chesapeake: Black and White Resistance to Human Bondage, 1775–1865.* Baltimore: Maryland Historical Society, 2007.

Worthen, Molly. *Apostles of Reason: The Crisis of Authority in American Higher Education.* New York: Oxford University Press, 2013.

Wigger, John. *Taking Heaven by Storm: Methodism and the Rise of Popular Christianity in America.* New York: Oxford University Press, 1998.

Wilbanks, Charles, ed. *Walking by Faith: The Diary of Angelina Grimké, 1828–1835.* Columbia: University of South Carolina Press, 2003.

Wilentz, Sean. *The Rise of American Democracy: Jefferson to Lincoln.* New York: W. W. Norton, 2005.

Williams, Michael. *Shadow of the Pope.* New York: Kessinger Publishing Company, 1932.

Wilson, Howard McKnight. *Lexington Presbytery Heritage: The Presbytery of Lexington and its Churches in the Synod of Virginia, Presbyterian Church in the United States.* Verona, VA: McClure Press, 1971.

Wolin, Sheldon. *Democracy Inc.: Managed Democracy and the Specter of Inverted Totalitarianism.* Princeton, NJ: Princeton University Press, 2008.

Wood, Gordon. *Empire of Liberty: A History of the Early Republic, 1789–1815.* New York: Oxford University Press, 2011.

———. *The Radicalism of the American Revolution.* New York: Vintage Books, 1991.

Wyatt-Brown, Bertram. *Lewis Tappan and the Evangelical War against Slavery.* Cleveland: Press of Case Western Reserve University, 1969.

Yacovazzi, Cassandra L. *Escaped Nuns: True Womanhood and the Campaign against Convents in Antebellum America.* New York: Oxford University Press, 2018.

Yellin, Jean Fagan, and John C. Van Horne, eds. *The Abolitionist Sisterhood: Women's Political Culture in Antebellum America.* Ithaca, NY: Cornell University Press, 1994.

York, Robert M. *George B. Cheever: Religious and Social Reformer, 1807–1890.* Orono: University of Maine Press, 1955.

Zanca, Kenneth J., ed. *American Catholics and Slavery, 1789–1866: An Anthology of Primary Documents.* Lanham, MD: University Press of America, 1994.

Zeigler, Stephen. "Niles, Hezekiah." *American National Biography Online.* February 2000, http://www.anb.org/articles/16/16-01202.html.

Ziesche, Philipp. *Cosmopolitan Patriots: Americans in Paris in the Age of Revolution.* Charlottesville: University of Virginia Press, 2010.

Journal Articles

Billington, Ray. "Anti-Catholic Propaganda and the Home Missionary Movement, 1800–1860." *Mississippi Valley Historical Review* 22, no. 3 (December 1935): 361–84.

Bourne, Theodore. "George Bourne, the Pioneer of American Antislavery." *Methodist Quarterly Review* LXIV (January 1882): 71–92.

Bruce, Dickson Jr. "National Identity and African-American Colonization, 1773–1817." *Historian* 58, no. 1 (Autumn 1995): 15–28.

Butler, O. R. "'The Uncle Tom's Cabin of Nativism': Anti-Catholic Novels, Politics and Violence in the Antebellum United States." *Working With English: Medieval and Modern Language, Literature and Drama* 2, no. 1 (2006): 12–19.

Clark-Beattie, Rosemary. "Fables of Rebellion: Anti-Catholicism and the Structure of Villette." *ELH* 53, no. 4 (Winter 1986): 821–47.

Cohen, Daniel. "The Respectability of Rebecca Reed: Genteel Womanhood and Sectarian Conflict in Antebellum America." *Journal of the Early Republic* 16, no. 3 (Autumn 1996): 419–61.

Cole, Charles Jr. "Horace Bushnell and the Slavery Question." *New England Quarterly* 23, no. 1 (March 1950): 19–30.

Davis, David Brion. "The Emergence of Immediatism in British and American Antislavery Thought." *Mississippi Valley Historical Review* 49, no. 2 (September 1962): 209–30.

———. "Some Ideological Functions of Prejudice in Ante-Bellum America." *American Quarterly* 15, no. 2, part I (Summer 1963): 115–25.

———. "Some Themes of Counter-Subversion: An Analysis of Anti-Masonic, Anti-Catholic, and Anti-Mormon Literature." *Mississippi Valley Historical Review* 47, no. 2 (September 1960): 205–24.

Dillon, Merton. "Gilbert H. Barnes and Dwight L. Dumond: An Appraisal." *Reviews in American History* 21, no. 3 (September 1993): 539–52.

Egerton, Douglas. "'Its Origin Is Not a Little Curious': A New Look at the American Colonization Society." *Journal of the Early Republic* 5, no. 4 (Winter 1985): 463–80.

Fatovic, Clement. "The Anti-Catholic Roots of Liberal and Republican Conception of Freedom in English Political Thought." *Journal of the History of Ideas* 66, no. 1 (January 2005): 37–58.

Fenton, Elizabeth. "Religious Liberties: Anti-Catholicism and Liberal Democracy in U.S. Literature and Culture, 1774–1789." PhD dissertation, Rice University, 2006.

Fessenden, Tracy. "The Convent, the Brothel, and the Protestant Woman's Sphere." *Signs* 25, no. 2 (Winter 2000): 451–78.

Forbes, Ella. "African-American Resistance to Colonization." *Journal of Black Studies,* "Afrocentricity" 21, no. 2 (December 1990): 210–23.

Friedman, Lawrence. "Confidence and Pertinacity in Evangelical Abolitionism: Lewis Tappan's Circle." *American Quarterly* 31, no. 1 (Spring 1979): 81–106.

Gelpi, Albert. "The Catholic Presence in American Culture." *American Literary History* 11, no. 1 (March 1999): 196–212.

Gjerde, Jon. "'Here in America There Is Neither King nor Tyrant': European Encounters with Race, 'Freedom,' and Their European Pasts." *Journal of the Early Republic* 19, no. 4 (Winter 1999): 673–90.

Griffin, Susan. "Awful Disclosures: Women's Evidence in the Escaped Nun's Tale." *Publications of the Modern Language Association of America* 111, no. 1 (January 1996): 93–107.

Hackett, David. "Gender and Religion in American Culture, 1870–1930." *Religion and American Culture* 5, no. 2 (Summer 1995): 127–57.

Harrill, J. Albert. "The Use of the New Testament in the American Slave Controversy: A Case of History in the Hermeneutical Tension between Biblical Criticism and Christian Moral Debate." *Religion and American Culture* 10, no. 2 (Summer 2000): 149–86.

Haynes, Stephen. "Race, National Destiny, and the Sons of Noah in the Thought of Benjamin Palmer." *Journal of Presbyterian History* 78 (Summer 2000): 125–44.

Heloise, Anne, and Frank Klingberg. "The Tappan Papers." *Journal of Negro History* 12, no. 2 (April 1927): 128–78.

Hoganson, Kristen. "Garrisonian Abolitionists and the Rhetoric of Gender, 1850–1860." *American Quarterly* 45, no. 4 (December 1993): 558–95.

Howe, Daniel Walker. "The Evangelical Movement and Political Culture in the North During the Second Party System." *Journal of American History* 77, no. 4 (March 1991): 1216–39.

Kelley, Mary. "Beyond the Boundaries." *Journal of the Early Republic* 12, no. 1 (Spring 2001).

Lambert, Frank. "The Great Awakening as Artifact: George Whitefield and the Construction of Intercolonial Revival, 1739–1745." *Church History* 60, no. 2 (June 1991): 223–46.

Loveland, Anne. "Evangelicalism and 'Immediate Abolitionism' in American Antislavery Thought." *Journal of Southern History* 32, no. 2 (May 1966): 172–88.

Mullin, Robert Bruce. "Biblical Critics and the Battle Over Slavery." *Journal of Presbyterian History* 61 (Summer 1983): 210–26.

Osofsky, Gilbert. "Abolitionists, Irish Immigrants, and the Dilemmas of Romantic Nationalism." *American Historical Review* 80, no. 4 (October 1975): 889–912.

Pagliarini, Marie Anne. "The Pure American Women and the Wicked Catholic Priest: An Analysis of Anti-Catholic Literature in Antebellum America." *Religion and American Culture: A Journal of Interpretation* 9, no. 1 (Winter 1999): 97–128.

Pierson, Michael. "'Slavery Cannot Be Covered Up with Broadcloth or a Bandanna': The Evolution of White Abolitionist Attacks on the 'Patriarchal Institution.'" *Journal of the Early Republic* 25, no. 3 (Fall 2005): 383–415.

Quinn, John. "'Three Cheers for the Abolitionist Pope': American Reaction to Gregory XVI's Condemnation of the Slave Trade." *Catholic Historical Review* 90, no. 1 (January 2004): 67–93.

Reynolds, David S. "The Feminization Controversy: Sexual Stereotypes and the Paradoxes of Piety in Nineteenth-Century America." *New England Quarterly* 53, no. 1 (March 1980): 96–106.

———. "From Doctrine to Narrative: The Rise of Pulpit Storytelling in America." *American Quarterly* 32, no. 5 (December 1981).

Rubin, Jay. "Black Nativism: The European Immigrant in Negro Thought, 1830–1860." *Phylon (1960–)* 39, no. 3 (Third Quarter 1978): 193–202.

Shalhope, Robert. "Toward a Republican Synthesis." *William and Mary Quarterly* 29 (January 1972): 49–80.

Streifford, David M. "The American Colonization Society: An Application of Republican Ideology to Early Antebellum Reform." *Journal of Southern History* 45, no. 2 (May 1979): 201–20.

Tentler, Leslie. "On the Margins: The State of American Catholic History." *American Quarterly* 45 (March 1993): 104–27.

Wallace, William Jason. "The Medieval Specter: Catholics, Evangelicals, and the Limits of Political Protestantism." PhD dissertation, University of Virginia, 2005.

Walter, Herbert. "The Erotics of Purity: *The Marble Faun* and the Victorian Construction of Sexuality." *Representations* 36 (1991): 114–32.

Walters, Ronald G. "The Erotic South: Civilization and Sexuality in American Abolitionism." *American Quarterly* 25, no. 2 (May 1973).

Welter, Barbara. "The Cult of True Womanhood, 1820–1860," *American Quarterly* 18 (1966): 151–74.

White, Ed. "The Value of Conspiracy Theory." *American Literary History* 14, no. 1 (Spring 2002): 1–31.

Yacovone, Donald. "Bourne, George." *American National Biography Online,* Feb. 2000. http://www.anb.org/articles/08/08-00158.html.

INDEX

www.ingramcontent.com/pod-product-compliance
Lightning Source LLC
Chambersburg PA
CBHW030300100426
42812CB00002B/519